Project Editor: Agnès Saint-Laurent
Art Direction & Design: Josée Amyotte
Graphic Design: Chantal Landry
Translation: Matthew Brown, Louisa Sage
Revision: Robert Ronald
Proofreading: Jesse Corbeil

EXCLUSIVE DISTRIBUTOR:

For Canada and the United States:
Simon & Schuster Canada
166 King Street East, Suite 300
Toronto, ON M5A 1J3
phone: (647) 427-8882
      1-800-387-0446
Fax: (647) 430-9446
simonandschuster.ca

Catalogue data available from Bibliothèque
et Archives nationales du Québec

WARNING

As a city thirsty for new trends, New York is constantly changing, which means that the lifespan of bars, restaurants and hotels varies greatly. Right up until this book went to print, I walked through the city's neighborhoods time and time again to ensure that the information was up to date. However, as nothing is safe from the passing of time, know that some establishments might have moved or shut down when you'll be visiting New York. Menus, prices, fees and business hours are provided as a guideline and are also subject to change. Enjoy your stay!

Follow Marie-Joëlle Parent on Instagram:
@mariejoelleparent

01-17

© 2017 Juniper Publishing,
division of the Sogides Group Inc.,
a subsidiary of Québecor Média Inc.
(Montreal, Quebec)

Printed in Canada
Legal deposit: 2017
National Library of Québec
National Library of Canada

ISBN 978-1-988002-50-7

Conseil des Arts   Canada Council
du Canada   for the Arts

We gratefully acknowledge the support of the Canada Council for the Arts for its publishing program.

We acknowledge the financial support of the Government of Canada through the Canada Book Fund for our publishing activities.

MARIE-JOËLLE PARENT

300

REASONS TO LOVE
SAN FRANCISCO

Table of Contents

Introduction

I've always felt that there were two cities in the United States where I could easily live: New York City and, on the other side of the continent, San Francisco. I have a deep love for both cities, and feel no need to choose a favorite. As American author Gene Fowler said, "Every person should be allowed to love two cities, their own and San Francisco"—a maxim I adopted from the moment I first read it.

While I have lived in New York for nearly eight years now, I have visited my west coast favorite a great many times, and for many different reasons (at least 300!). One of those reasons, which is not listed in this book, is especially dear to my heart: San Francisco is where I met the love of my life. For me, the City by the Bay was love at first sight, times two!

When I think of San Francisco, I think of its pleasant pace of life, the sound of fog horns guiding boats through the thick blanket of fog, the crazy wind that starts to blow around two in the afternoon in the Mission, the layer of fog rolling down the hills west of Divisadero Street, the city's proximity to nature, the eucalyptus forests in the middle of the city, the staircases covered in flowers that you discover out of the blue while out for a stroll, the art-deco buildings and Victorian homes, the creative energy of the people and their obsession with dressing up—and organic products... San Franciscans are the vanguard of the green movement, digital technology, and just about everything else. They are progressive, passionate, supportive, dreamers, pioneers and artisans... They are engaged in their communities. Their city is truly a part of them. In San Francisco, the locavore movement has reached religious status.

In this book, you will find 300 reasons to love this truly unique city, including good restaurants, cafés, bars, museums, bookstores, beautiful staircases, buildings, hills, beaches, streets and endearing characters. Many restaurants are included in this guide; this was deliberate, because food is at the heart of life for San Franciscans. The people who live here are foodies: passionate about food and willing to wait in line for hours to try the latest restaurant, bite into the perfect loaf of bread, or enjoy the finest cup of espresso.

This guide is like a long walk, with the path leading you from one area to the next. While the city is only 46 square miles (119 square kilometers) in size, it encompasses over 40 districts, each with a distinct identity and, in many cases, an unofficial mayor. Listed by "megadistricts," the many reasons to fall in love with the city of fog will take you beyond its official city limits to Oakland, to Berkeley, in the Napa region, to Sonoma and Russian River, in Marin County, to Tomales Bay and Bodega Bay, to Half Moon Bay and Silicon Valley.

San Francisco has inspired a number of famous quotes, but none captures the love people feel for the city like this one, by the famous *San Francisco Chronicle* columnist Herb Caen: "One day if I do go to heaven...I'll look around and say, 'It ain't bad, but it ain't San Francisco.'"

My Top Picks

THE BEST RESTAURANTS

1 State Bird Provisions, 1529 Fillmore St. [REASON #57]
2 Liholiho Yacht Club, 871 Sutter St. [REASON #143]
3 Chez Panisse, 1517 Shattuck Ave. [REASON #265]
4 Cala, 149 Fell St. [REASON #156]
5 Tosca Cafe, 242 Columbus Ave. [REASON #80]
6 Kokkari Estiatorio, 200 Jackson St. [REASON #117]
7 Zuni Café, 1658 Market St. [REASON #154]
8 La Ciccia, 291 30th St. [REASON #217]
9 AL's Place, 1499 Valencia St. [REASON #185]
10 Swan Oyster Depot, 1517 Polk St. [REASON #103]

THE BEST BRUNCHS

1 Nopa, 560 Divisadero St. [REASON #66]
2 Outerlands, 4001 Judah St. [REASON #246]
3 Plow, 1299 18th St. [REASON #229]
4 Bar Tartine, 561 Valencia St. [REASON #185]
5 Mission Beach Cafe, 198 Guerrero St.
6 St. Francis Fountain, 2801 24th St. [REASON #182]
7 Rose's Café, 2298 Union St. [REASON #38]
8 Brenda's Meat & Three, 919 Divisadero St. [REASON #66]
9 Zazie, 941 Cole St. [REASON #210]
10 Pork Store Cafe, 1451 Haight St. [REASON #211]

THE BEST CAFÉS

1 Caffe Trieste, 601 Vallejo St. [REASON #77]
2 Sightglass Coffee, 270 7th St. and 3014 20th St. [REASONS #171 AND #201]
3 Saint Frank Coffee, 2340 Polk St. [REASON #95]
4 Four Barrel Coffee, 375 Valencia St. [REASON #201]
5 Stable Café, 2128 Folsom St. [REASON #190]

THE BEST PIZZAS

1. **Una Pizza Napoletana**, 210 11th St. [REASON #169]
2. **Del Popolo**, 855 Bush St. [REASON #105]
3. **A16**, 2355 Chestnut St. [REASON #40]
4. **Flour + Water**, 2401 Harrison St. [REASON #185]
5. **Boot & Shoe Service**, 3308 Grand Ave., Oakland [REASON #256]

THE BEST ICE CREAM PARLORS

1. **Mr. and Mrs. Miscellaneous**, 699 22nd St. [REASON #226]
2. **Mitchell's Ice Cream**, 688 San Jose Ave. [REASON #236]
3. **Three Twins Ice Cream**, 254 Fillmore St. [REASON #73]
4. **Lush Gelato**, 1817 Polk St. [REASON #110]
5. **Bi-Rite Creamery**, 3692 18th St. [REASON #176]

THE BEST BURRITOS

1. **El Castillito**, 136 Church St.
2. **La Taqueria**, 2889 Mission St. [REASON #181]
3. **Taqueria Cancún**, 2288 Mission St. [REASON #181]
4. **Pancho Villa Taqueria**, 3071 16th St. [REASON #181]
5. **Taqueria El Buen Sabor**, 699 Valencia St. [REASON #181]

THE BEST COCKTAIL BARS AND WINE BARS

1. **Trick Dog**, 3010 20th St. [REASON #196]
2. **The Treasury**, 115 Sansome St. [REASON #119]
3. **Benjamin Cooper**, 398 Geary St. [REASON #142]
4. **Comstock Saloon**, 155 Columbus Ave. [REASON #81]
5. **Smuggler's Cove**, 650 Gough St. [REASON #73]
6. **Bourbon & Branch**, 501 Jones St. [REASON #142]
7. **Trou Normand**, 140 New Montgomery St. [REASON #121]
8. **Union Larder**, 1945 Hyde St. [REASON #99]
9. **Lone Palm**, 3394 22nd St. [REASON #196]
10. **Amelie**, 1754 Polk St. [REASON #109]

THE MOST BEAUTIFUL VIEWS
1 Corona Heights Park [REASON #209]
2 Bernal Heights Park [REASON #235]
3 Eagle's Point at Lands End [REASON #12]
4 Twin Peaks [REASON #243]
5 De Young Museum Observation Tower [REASON #27]

THE MOST BEAUTIFUL STAIRCASES
1 16th Avenue Tiled Steps [REASON #242]
2 Lyon Street Steps [REASON #46]
3 Lincoln Park Steps [REASON #28]
4 Harry Street Steps [REASON #234]
5 Filbert Steps [REASON #90]

MUST-SEE EVENTS

1 **Bay to Breakers:** A 12K footrace, from San Francisco Bay to the Pacific Ocean, that has been going strong for over 100 years. Participants wear costumes, and alcohol flows freely. The race is held on the third Sunday in May. (baytobreakers.com)

2 **Outside Lands:** The summer event in San Francisco. This music festival takes place in Golden Gate Park over three days in August, and about 200,000 people attend. (sfoutsidelands.com)

3 **San Francisco Pride:** Held in June, this is the biggest gay pride parade in the country, and one of the biggest in the world—and it's definitely the most outrageous parade in San Francisco (barring a World Series championship for the Giants, or a Super Bowl victory for the 49ers). (sfpride.org)

4 **Stern Grove Festival:** This performing arts festival has been running since the 1930s. It's held in June at the Sigmund Stern Recreation Grove, an open-air amphitheater surrounded by eucalyptus trees, in the Lakeshore neighborhood. The programming is diverse (ballet, hip-hop, opera) and admission is free. (sterngrove.org)

5 **Dia de los Muertos (Day of the Dead):** On the first Sunday in November, people gather at the corner of 22nd Street and Bryant Street to celebrate the Dia de los Muertos. The Mexican tradition has been celebrated in the Mission, the Hispanic neighborhood, since the 1970s. Aztec dancers, women with bouquets of dead flowers and children wearing papier mâché skull masks walk together to Garfield Park, where they light candles in memory of the dead. (dayofthedeadsf.org)

WHERE TO STAY

1 **Airbnb.com:** Created in San Francisco in 2008, this app connects you with the best rooms and apartments for rent throughout the city. It's the best way to discover areas like a local instead of a tourist, and to get a feel for what daily life is like. The only area I would avoid is the Tenderloin (see **REASON #170**).

2 **Axiom Hotel:** A designer hotel in a 1908 building in the heart of downtown. There's a bookstore and a lovely café in front.

3 **Palace Hotel:** A historic hotel built in 1875 by an American banker who wanted to compete against the best hotels of Europe. The hotel's Pied Piper bar and Garden Court alone are worth seeing (see **REASON #130**).

4 **Inn at the Presidio:** A historic bed and breakfast with 22 rooms, in a former residence for army officers in the heart of the Presidio. Breakfast and aperitif are included (see **REASON #5**).

5 **Hotel G:** A mid-century modern designer hotel right near Union Square. There's a "secret" bar on the second floor, called Benjamin Cooper (see **REASON #142**).

6 **Hotel des Arts:** A funky boutique hotel in the Financial District. Each room has a different mural painted by a local artist. Breakfast is included.

7 **Hotel Vitale:** A hotel with minimalist decor in the Financial District, with a view of the Bay Bridge and the Ferry Building. There's a spa, and a terrace on the roof.

8 **Clift:** A hotel by designer Philippe Starck, just a stone's throw from Union Square. There's a superb art-deco bar called The Redwood Room on the ground floor (see **REASON #146**). Bike rentals are free.

9 **The Battery:** Located in the Financial District, this private club has 14 suites that are available to non-members. The rooms are luxurious and an overnight stay gives you access to members' services, like the restaurant, the four bars, the spa, the gym and the rooftop terrace.

10 **Cavallo Point Lodge:** A former army base at the foot of the Golden Gate Bridge in Sausalito that was transformed into a luxurious hotel with a renowned spa (see **REASON #267**).

The Presidio, Sea Cliff, Richmond District and Golden Gate Park

The northwest point of the city is my favorite part of San Francisco. Instead of shops, it has wild sections, sprawling green spaces, public beaches and breathtaking views of the Pacific Ocean. Often submerged in fog, the Richmond District has long been ignored by San Franciscans. In recent years however, cheaper rents have attracted newcomers who have transformed the neighborhood, bringing independent stores and delicious yet affordable restaurants.

The Presidio, Sea Cliff, Richmond District and Golden Gate Park

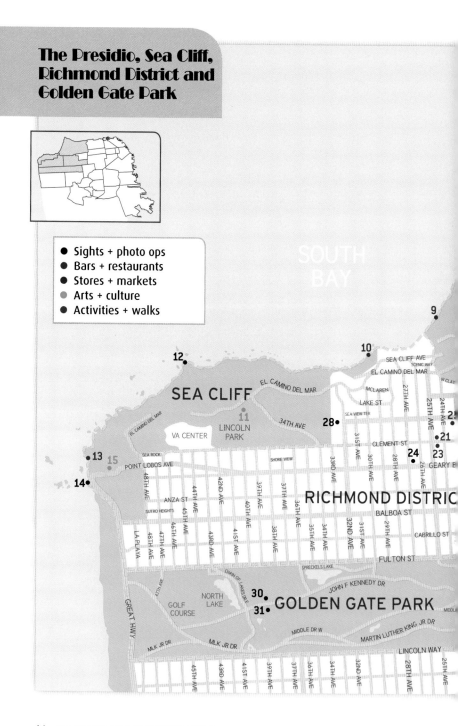

- ● Sights + photo ops
- ● Bars + restaurants
- ● Stores + markets
- ● Arts + culture
- ● Activities + walks

SOUTH BAY

9

10

12

SEA CLIFF AVE
SCENIC WAY
EL CAMINO DEL MAR

EL CAMINO DEL MAR

W CLAY

MCLAREN

LAKE ST

27TH AVE

25TH AVE

24TH AVE

SEA CLIFF

EL CAMINO DEL MAR

SEA VIEW TER

28

34TH AVE

2

11

VA CENTER

LINCOLN PARK

31ST AVE

CLEMENT ST

21

30TH AVE

28TH AVE

24

26TH AVE

23

13

SEA ROCK

SHORE VIEW

33RD AVE

GEARY B

15

POINT LOBOS AVE

14

48TH AVE

ANZA ST

44TH AVE

42ND AVE

39TH AVE

37TH AVE

36TH AVE

34TH AVE

32ND AVE

31ST AVE

29TH AVE

RICHMOND DISTRIC

SUTRO HEIGHTS

45TH AVE

40TH AVE

38TH AVE

35TH AVE

BALBOA ST

46TH AVE

43RD AVE

41ST AVE

CABRILLO ST

LA PLAYA

47TH AVE

48TH AVE

SPRECKELS LAKE

FULTON ST

47TH AVE

CHAIN OF LAKES DR

30

JOHN F KENNEDY DR

GOLF COURSE

NORTH LAKE

31

GOLDEN GATE PARK

MIDDL

GREAT HWY

MLK JR DR

MLK JR DR

MIDDLE DR W

MARTIN LUTHER KING JR DR

LINCOLN WAY

45TH AVE

43RD AVE

41ST AVE

39TH AVE

37TH AVE

36TH AVE

34TH AVE

32ND AVE

28TH AVE

25TH AVE

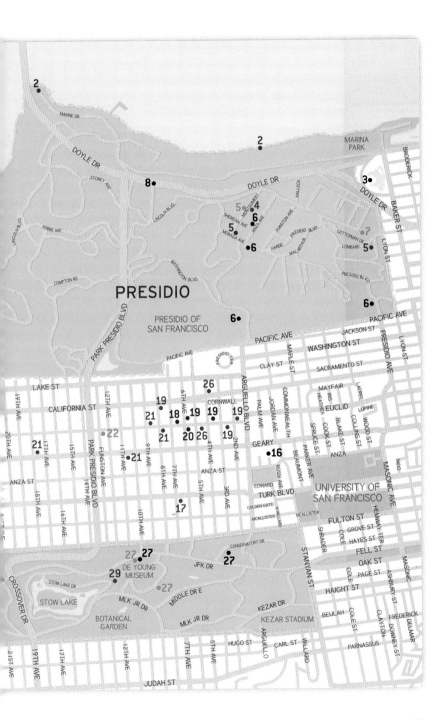

Karl

1 Everyone in San Francisco knows Karl—the name given to the city's famous fog by a Web surfer. Since 2010, a prolific San Franciscan (who remains anonymous) has assumed the identity of the weather phenomenon on social media.

Karl the Fog regularly posts from his Twitter account, with witty tweets such as "Stay in bed today, the city is mine," "Terrible day in San Francisco. Avoid at all costs," "I just ate San Francisco. It tastes like 860,000 people wondering how it went from Death Valley to winter tundra in 24hrs," and "Yesterday you got sunburned in the park. This morning you're back in your winter coat. Welcome to San Francisco."

Karl the Fog also has an Instagram account where he shares spectacular photos of the layer of fog that frequently surrounds the city. His muse, the Golden Gate Bridge, is a regular feature. Karl the Fog has become a local character and hashtag, which San Franciscans and tourists attach to photos or tweets when a picnic is ruined by fog.

In less than five years, he has become a social media star, with over 385,000 followers, including me. Karl's online humor makes him a bit more tolerable to locals. While many loathe the fog, it is one of the things I like most about San Francisco. It lends an air of mystery to the city.

The San Francisco climate has a lot of personality, running the full gamut of weather conditions in a given 24-hour period. The fog is especially prevalent at the start of summer, when the cold Pacific Ocean air meets the warm air from California's Central Valley, hence the expressions *May gray* and *June gloom*. In the early morning, the city is often steeped in a thick blanket of fog, which normally dissipates in the afternoon before returning again at the end of the day.

Karl is particularly fond of the west end neighborhoods and the hills, like Twin Peaks. His love of summer inspired Mark Twain's famous quote, "The coldest winter I ever spent was a summer in San Francisco." The fog disappears in spring, September and October, which are the best times to visit the city.

Fog rarely extends to the eastern part of the city, which makes neighborhoods like Mission District (also called the Mission), Noe Valley and SoMa more desirable. So the microclimate is another factor to consider when looking for a place to stay in San Francisco.

San Franciscans know the importance of layering to stay prepared for the different microclimates each day. The free application "Mr. Chilly" keeps you up to date on the weather in each neighborhood, making it easier to plan your day.

Ken Hopper High-Fives the World

2 My favorite ritual when I go to San Francisco is to go for a run or walk at **Crissy Field** (A). San Francisco Bay is a great companion during a workout: Alcatraz lingers in the distance and the Golden Gate Bridge stretches across the horizon like a majestic finish line.

A former airfield, Crissy Field is always bustling, especially on Sunday mornings. All of San Francisco seems to be out walking their dog—it's a canine paradise. The grassy field has picnic tables, and hosts all kinds of sports events and art installations.

Some of the former aircraft hangars have been converted into recreation areas. They include **House of Air**, a trampoline park [926 Old Mason St.] and **Planet Granite**, which has yoga and indoor climbing [924 Old Mason St.].

My route starts at the corner of Divisadero Street and Marina Boulevard. From there I go to Fort Point, two miles (three kilometers) to the east. Fort Point is a brick fortress built between 1853 and 1861. Tucked under an abutment of the Golden Gate Bridge, it's where Alfred Hitchcock shot the memorable scene in *Vertigo* where Scottie (James Stewart) saves Madeleine (Kim Novak) from drowning.

Be sure to visit the roof of **Fort Point** (B) (it's free). Brace yourself against the wind and look to the west. With the Pacific Ocean stretching as far as the eye can see, you'll really appreciate that San Francisco is truly at the edge of the continent. When the weather's good, you'll see plenty of surfers riding the waves beside Fort Point. The view is not to be missed.

San Francisco's joggers have a ritual: When they get to the fort at the end of Marine Drive, they touch a plaque decorated with two orange hands on the chain-link fence. The plaque, known as **Hoppers Hands** (C), was created by Ken Hopper, an ironworker who does maintenance work on the Golden Gate Bridge.

Hopper spent a long time observing joggers' particular habit of touching the fence before turning back. Eventually it gave him the idea of painting two life-sized hands that would return the high five. A smaller sign hangs a little lower down, with dogs' paws.

After my run, I stop at **The Warming Hut** for a hot drink [983 Marine Dr.]. The café also has different items for sale, including books about the city. When you're leaving, stop and see the crab and salmon fishermen on **Torpedo Wharf** (D). They sometimes reel in small sharks, which they're happy to display to curious onlookers.

2C

HOPPERS HANDS

2D

2A 2B

The Palace from Another Time

3 The most romantic spot in San Francisco, bar none, is the **Palace of Fine Arts**. One of the last traces of the 1915 Panama-Pacific International Exposition, the beaux-arts-style building has miraculously endured over the years. I appreciate its beauty, but I also love it because San Franciscans have worked so hard to preserve it. Before the exposition had even ended, a petition was circulating to prevent it from being destroyed along with the other buildings.

The Palace of Fine Arts was saved from demolition once again in the 1950s, thanks to generous donations, and was completely restored in the 1960s. It was designed by Californian architect Bernard Maybeck, who was inspired by classical Greek and Roman architecture. Located between the Marina District and the Presidio, the site is beloved by tourists and San Franciscans alike, and is a popular spot for weddings. The standard shot features the palace and its reflection in the pond that lies in front of it. Keep your eyes peeled for the pond's many swans, and its turtles, frogs and ducks [3301 Lyon St.].

The Food Truck Park

4 On Thursday evenings (5 p.m. to 9 p.m.) and Sundays (11 a.m. to 4 p.m.), April through November, the **Off the Grid** food truck collective organizes a huge picnic on the Main Post Lawn in the Presidio. About a dozen trucks and 20 stands run by local restaurants set up shop there. It's the perfect spot to taste the best of the city's mobile gastronomic offerings, with a spectacular view of the Golden Gate Bridge. Check the dates at offthegrid.com.

Wander the Presidio

5 The **Presidio** is an incredible 1,480-acre (six-square-kilometer) park on the site of a former military base established by the Spanish in 1776. It's so big—almost twice as big as Golden Gate Park—that you could easily get lost in it.

More than 3,000 people actually live in the park, surrounded by its natural beauty. Some are in the luxury apartments of the former Marine hospital, and others have homes in the majestic former officers' residences. The waiting list for these homes is very long. The park is also home to the **Presidio Social Club**, a restaurant located in a historic building from 1903 [563 Ruger St.]; the 12 bowling lanes of the century-old **Presidio Bowling Center** [93 Moraga Ave.]; the **Inn at the Presidio**, a charming 22-room bed and breakfast [42 Moraga Ave.]; and **The Walt Disney Family Museum**. Founded by Walt Disney's daughter, Diane, in 2009, the museum features the first sketches made by Mickey's creator, along with a 12-foot (3.6-meter) model of Disneyland as the artist himself imagined it. The 10 galleries in the museum span his entire career up to his death in 1966. All his awards are displayed in the hall, including an Honorary Oscar he won for *Snow White and the Seven Dwarfs*—a regular-sized Oscar statue along with seven miniature statuettes. With a wealth of information, the museum gives visitors the chance to really get to know Disney the man. There are some great stories, such as that of a hat he particularly loved. One day, his wife tried to get rid of the old thing, but Walt found it, fashioned the upper part into a heart and gave it to his wife on Valentine's Day. The museum offers a fun experience for adults and children alike [104 Montgomery St.].

6A

Works of Art as Big as Nature

6 Don't miss the oversized installations by British artist **Andy Goldsworthy** in the Presidio. There are four Goldsworthy sculptures to see: *Spire,* a wooden arrow rising more than 100 feet (30 meters) into the air (Arguello Gate, beside the golf club parking area); *Wood Line,* a long sinuous line stretching more than 1,200 feet (365 meters) along the ground (when you pass the Presidio Gate, the installation is on your right, at the edge of Lovers' Lane); *Tree Fall,* in a former munitions depot [95 Anza Ave.]; and *Earth Wall* (A), a clay wall with a spherical sculpture carved into it [50 Moraga Ave.].

Yoda

7 The Presidio's former military facilities house different businesses, the most famous of which is the **Letterman Digital Arts Center**. The Center is home to the headquarters of Lucasfilm Ltd., the company founded by George Lucas. Sci-fi fans will want to visit the hall with figurines, books and other memorabilia from the *Star Wars* saga, including a life-sized statue of Darth Vader (standing at an intimidating 6' 6" tall). An exact replica of **Yoda** (A) overlooks a fountain in front of the building. You can almost hear the strange creature greeting you with "May the force be with you." Open Monday to Friday, 9 a.m. to 5 p.m. [Building B Courtyard, 1 Letterman Dr.].

7A

Fido's Final Resting Place

The **National Cemetery** has an impressive 26,000 tombstones. But northwest of it, under the viaduct leading to the Golden Gate Bridge, there lies a different kind of cemetery. It's enclosed by a white wooden fence and has small hand-painted tombstones with names like Heidi, Willie and Mr. Iguana. It's a pet cemetery: a resting place for cats and dogs, not to mention snakes, parakeets, canaries, rabbits, hamsters, goldfish, rats and mice. The oldest tombstones date from 1950, but they say that military personnel buried guard dogs and horses there as long ago as the 1800s. That's probably why the tombstones resemble those you find in military cemeteries: They give the animal's date of birth, its family name and even its owner's rank. And just like in human cemeteries, some tombstones are marked as "unknown." The cemetery is now closed officially, but you can still take a look from the other side of the fence [McDowell Ave.].

The Birthplace of Burning Man

9 **Baker Beach** is the first spot I ever visited in San Francisco. In the golden light of the setting sun, with my toes in the sand, the Golden Gate Bridge and Sea Cliff's colorful houses as a backdrop, I fell in love. It was a picture-postcard view. The legendary Burning Man festival was invented at the northern section of this public beach in 1986. The festival's creators, Larry Harvey and Jerry James, decided to celebrate the summer solstice by building a man out of wood and setting it alight. The impromptu event attracted about 20 people. The experience was recreated each of the next three years. On the fourth year, the police showed up and shut down the celebration. The festival then moved to the desert in Nevada, growing from 20 people in 1986 to almost 66,000 people in 2014. The very first wooden man was eight feet (2.40 meters) high; in 2014, it measured over 100 feet (32 meters). Warning: Nudism is practiced at the northern section of the beach.

The Secret Beach

10 I'm partial to the tranquility of Baker Beach's little sister, **China Beach**. A ways off from the tourist circuit, it has few visitors. In fact, it feels like you've discovered a secret beach right in the middle of the city. You can get to the beach by going through the Sea Cliff neighborhood, which will give you a great view of the luxury houses on Sea Cliff Avenue. These homes, perched on cliffs, have the most coveted view in town. In the Gold Rush era (1848), China Beach was used as a campground by Chinese fishermen working in the Bay area.

Alma's Gift

11

The **Legion of Honor** museum (A), on top of a green hill overlooking the Pacific Ocean, is one of San Francisco's jewels. Built in 1924, its architecture is inspired by the Palais de la Légion d'Honneur in Paris. The fine arts museum has a range of treasures. It features dozens of sculptures by Rodin, the Salon Doré (an 18th-century room from Paris' Hôtel de La Trémoille) and works by Monet, Degas, Renoir, Cézanne, Gauguin, Picasso, Dalí, Matisse and more.

A scene from Alfred Hitchcock's film *Vertigo* was shot in the museum's Gallery 6. In it, the Madeleine character stares at length at a famous painting, *Portrait of Carlotta,* which depicts a young woman who resembles herself. But you won't see that painting there today: Made especially for the film, the canvas mysteriously disappeared after the shoot.

Philanthropist and socialite **Alma de Bretteville Spreckels** convinced her husband, Adolph, to donate the museum as a gift to the city of San Francisco. The white neo-classical building is dedicated to the memory of the 3,600 Californian soldiers who died on the battlefield in the north of France during World War I [100 34th Ave.].

Alma is a woman who fascinates me. Her generosity earned her the nickname "The Great Grandmother of San Francisco," and her height—she was 6 feet (1.83 meters) tall—earned her the nickname "Big Alma." The daughter of Danish immigrants, she was born in the city's Sunset District in 1881. Because her family was poor, Alma did nude modelling to earn money during her studies. She was also the model for the **Goddess of Victory statue** (B) that sits atop the Dewey Monument in the heart of Union Square. It was through that job that she met her future husband. Adolph Spreckels was chair of the selection committee for the monument; the wealthy heir courted Alma for five years. They were finally married in

1908, when Alma was 27 and Adolph was 51. Because her husband's family made its fortune in the sugar industry, Alma began to refer to him as her "sugar daddy"—a term that has entered common usage.

The beaux-arts-style mansion that Adolph had built for his wife in 1912 still stands today in the posh neighborhood of Pacific Heights. It remains the most lavish home in the city. Alma lived there until her death in 1968. The 55-room building was later bought by the best-selling author Danielle Steel, and has attracted hordes of tourists ever since. With its 30-foot (nine-meter) hedge—which is detested by the neighbors—at the corner of Washington and Octavia streets, it's impossible to miss.

A Labyrinth of Stones

12 Lands End is a spectacular and mystical park at the northwest tip of the city. It's my favorite spot in San Francisco by far—and the only area in the city that's still wild. The Native American Yelamu tribe, part of the Ohlone group, lived there before the Spanish arrived in 1776.

The coastal trails, lined with cypress trees, remind me of the Cinque Terre on the Italian Mediterranean coast—and they're perfect for long walks. It's hard to believe you're only 20 minutes from downtown. Old wrecks lie rotting at the foot of the cliffs, and if you're lucky, you can see dolphins on the horizon.

The name "Lands End" is apt: You really feel like you're at the edge of the continent. That's especially true at **Eagle's Point**, an overlook with an incredible view of the Golden Gate Bridge. Follow the signs for Eagle's Point by walking the Lands End Trail. Go down the stairs, but instead of turning left, keep going straight:

There you'll find a **labyrinth made of stones**. A local artist, Eduardo Aguilera, created the piece in 2004, intending it to be a kind of sanctuary. The arrangement of stones has become a pilgrimage site for hikers and explorers.

The installation was destroyed by vandals at least four times, but each time a number of San Franciscans got together to rebuild it. The volunteers created a human chain that stretched all the way to **Mile Rock Beach**, over 50 yards below, to collect the rocks. The site is especially popular during equinoxes and solstices, when people light lanterns during their visit. The red-and-white column visible on the horizon is **Mile Rocks Lighthouse**. It was built in the 20th century, after almost 300 vessels had sunk in the vicinity of the Golden Gate Bridge.

Sutro's Pools

13 Only a few walls, concrete stairs, a tunnel and a body of water remain; but it's easy to imagine how enchanting this place once was. The **Sutro Baths** were a complex of indoor pools designed by Adolph Sutro, a German immigrant and millionaire who made his fortune in the mining industry. Sutro was mayor of San Francisco from 1894 to 1896. He had the idea of building a huge recreational park in Lands End, one that would be affordable and accessible to all San Franciscans. He even funded the building of a steam train linking the complex with downtown San Francisco (the trip cost five cents at the time).

Sutro's venture was the largest indoor swimming pool complex in the world. At high tide, the ocean filled the indoor pools with two million gallons (7,600 cubic meters) of seawater. An immense glass dome sheltered swimmers from inclement weather, and there were seven pools to choose from (six saltwater and one freshwater), all with different temperatures. The pools measured about 500 feet by 250 feet (150 meters by 75 meters). The complex also included a skating rink, a natural history museum, a 2,700-seat theater and **Cliff House**, an eight-story Victorian chateau. Cliff House burned down in 1907, and was later rebuilt in a neo-classical style. The two restaurants it houses today are favorite destinations for tourists. The pool complex also burned down, in 1966, and the ruins remain at the site today. I like to go sit on one of the walls overlooking the ocean; it feels like discovering a lost paradise [680 Point Lobos Ave.].

A Unique Camera

14

Don't miss the **Camera Obscura** behind the Cliff House restaurants. Created in 1946 by the owner of the Cliff House, the tiny building resembles a 35 mm camera, with the lens pointed upward to the sky. It's dark inside the building, and a table sits in the middle of the room; the sharp, bright image from the lens is projected onto it. The lens rotates, making four stops every six minutes. You can see the sparkling ocean, the rocks on the shore, pelicans and Ocean Beach. It's the biggest camera obscura you're likely to find. In the 1970s and in 1999, there was talk of the camera being taken away due to lack of money for maintenance; but both times it was saved by a major public campaign. On May 23, 2001, the camera was added to the National Register of Historic Places so that it would be preserved for posterity. It's open every day from 11 a.m. to 5 p.m., except in rain or fog; entry price is $3 [1096 Point Lobos Ave.].

Breakfast with a View

15

"More coffee, honey?" is a phrase you'll hear a lot at **Louis' Restaurant**. Founded in 1937, the family-run institution has definitely remained authentic. It's also considered one of the best diners in the city. But it's the view that makes it truly unique. Situated above the ruins of the Sutro Baths, the restaurant is lined with windows on three sides. Diners sit at booths with the ocean as a stunning backdrop. Louis' is run by the grandchildren of Louis and Helen Hontalas (who emigrated from Greece in the early 20th century), along with some nieces, nephews and cousins. Family photos line the walls. Louis' is known for its omelets and eggs Benedict, as well as for its hamburgers and its fish-and-chips [902 Point Lobos Ave.].

Guardian of the Urns

16 Located at the end of a dead-end street, the **San Francisco Columbarium** is a mysterious place: both extremely beautiful and a little morbid. Its neo-classical architecture and huge copper dome stand in sharp contrast to the pastel-colored houses of the neighborhood.

Emmitt Watson has been caretaker of the premises for 30 years. A painter in his sixties, Watson knows the history of each person interred within. He supervised the long restoration process for the building, which had been abandoned for decades. He refers to the spaces where the urns are kept as "condos" or "apartments;" it's his way of keeping the inhabitants alive. The decorated niches display the history of the city since the 1890s, from the earthquake of 1906 to the assassination of Harvey Milk (the politician and gay rights activist has his own niche, which also houses some of his personal belongings) and the terrible ravages of the AIDS epidemic.

The thousands of San Franciscans interred there were lucky to have been able to remain within their city. Built in 1898 as a resting place for San Francisco's elite, the Columbarium survived a 1901 law prohibiting new burials within city limits. Since then, San Franciscans have been buried in Colma, a small city south of San Francisco, not far from the airport. Much of Colma is now occupied by cemeteries, earning it the nickname "city of the dead" [1 Loraine Ct.].

Sushi with Nobu and Yoshimi

17 A place of worship for sushi lovers, **Tekka** serves the freshest fish in the city. The small restaurant (only 11 seats) is run by an elderly Japanese couple, Nobu and his wife Yoshimi. Dining there is a true experience, and just getting a table is an achievement. They don't take reservations, and the restaurant is closed on weekends. Customers line up starting from 5:30 p.m. Yoshimi opens the doors at 7, counts the first 11 people and warns the rest that they'll have to come back at 9:30 for the second serving. Once inside, the fortunate few must follow a list of rules displayed on the wall: no forks, no soda, no teriyaki, no complaining, no rush service, no to-go—and cash only. Here, sushi is a serious business. Chef Nobu works in silence, as focused as a monk, while his wife takes care of the customers. The dish to get is the sashimi combo. The fish portions are generous—gigantic, in fact. Tekka's fish literally melts in your mouth. People say that Nobu's age and experience give him a great advantage when he's making his choices at the fish market [537 Balboa St.].

The Perfect Bookstore

18 **Green Apple Books**, a bookstore with more than 160,000 new and used books, is a destination unto itself. The 50-year-old store takes up several floors in a hundred-year-old building. The floors creak underfoot, and the smell of old books permeates the air. You'll find a wide range of books on art and cooking, children's books and collector's editions. There's also a large selection of stationery [506 Clement St.].

Hit the Stores on Clement Street

19 Before you get started, head to Eats, popular for its fresh and delicious—and hearty—brunches. I recommend the Huevos Rancheros plate, the blueberry crepes, and the Caprese Scramble [50 Clement St.]. With Japanese, Chinese, Californian, Mexican and Indian influences, the brunch menu at B* Star is one of the most eclectic around. It has something for everyone [127 Clement St.]. Also worth tasting is the egg sandwich on a brioche bun at Village Market general store [4555 California St.].

Once you've fueled up, it's time to discover the neighborhood's shops. Park Life (A), a design items store, has a large selection of art magazines, photography coffee-table books, household items, limited edition posters, jewelry and some clothes. It's a great place to find an unusual gift [220 Clement St.]. Right beside it, Seedstore is a clothing store that has a nice selection of coats and leather bags, blankets, hats and accessories for men and women. Take the opportunity to pick up the perfect San Francisco outfit [212 Clement St.]. Foggy Notion has a wide range of accessories, beauty products and decorative items made by local artisans [275 6th Ave.].

21A

The Tea Master

20 I always like stopping at **Aroma Tea**. Take a seat at the small counter and the friendly owner, Haymen Daluz, will give you free samples of all sorts of teas. He's a passionate tea-lover, and he loves to joke around. Each year he travels to China with his wife and kids to choose his teas. The large tea jars on the shelves have playful labels: the English Breakfast jar has a photo of Queen Elizabeth II; the Vanilla tea has a photo of Vanilla Ice [302 6th Ave].

20

Eating Well for a Few Dollars

21 The Richmond District has fantastic restaurants where you can fill up without breaking the bank. The small restaurant counter, **Good Luck Dim Sum**, doesn't look too impressive, but it serves excellent dumplings (three for $2) in cute pink boxes for takeout [736 Clement St.]. **My Tofu House** specializes in tofu soup, Bibimbap and seafood crepes. They don't serve alcohol [4627 Geary Blvd.]. For Vietnamese food, **PPQ Dungeness Island** is a neighborhood favorite. This spot is known for its garlic crab [2332 Clement St.]. For dim sum, the **Hong Kong Lounge** Chinese restaurant is *the* place to go. Try their Peking duck and their pork buns [5322 Geary Blvd]. Don't be fooled by **Halu**'s ordinary exterior. Inside, the small restaurant serves excellent ramen and yakitori—chicken pieces grilled on a skewer [312 8th Ave].

Preserving the Internet

22 On Funston Avenue in the Richmond District, not far from the Presidio, stands a large white neo-classical church with Corinthian columns. Behind the brass double doors of this building (a former Christian Science Church) is a very special library: the **Internet Archive**.

This nonprofit organization is dedicated to archiving the Web. The monumental task was started more than 20 years ago by computer scientist Brewster Kahle, an MIT graduate who made his fortune selling computer systems. Inspired by the greatest library of antiquity, Kahle wanted to create the Library of Alexandria, version 2.0.

The Internet Archive is the strangest spot I've visited in San Francisco. The church pews and altar on the second floor have been preserved; the pews are occupied by one hundred 35-inch (90-centimeter) statues of the organization's employees. Hard drives piled as high as the ceiling give off an audible hum. The constantly flashing servers contain data from more than 480 billion web pages. The system is known as the Wayback Machine, and it stores and indexes everything found on the Web (the average lifespan of a web page is 70 days before it's changed). You can consult older versions of websites dating back to the early days of the Internet. Two to three million users consult the site every day. To ensure that data is protected, copies of the servers are kept in Egypt, Amsterdam and outside of Oakland.

In the basement, a team of more than 50 engineers, programmers, archivists and volunteers are busy scanning and archiving an immense collection of books, films, songs and television and radio programs. Teams in eight other countries are at work on the same task. To date, more than three million books in 184 languages have been digitized. Brewster Kahle will be 60 years old in 2020. His goal is to have enough books archived to be able to educate a child until adulthood at no cost. You can visit the library on Fridays from 1 p.m. to 3 p.m. You may even be lucky enough to have Kahle himself as your guide [300 Funston Ave.].

22

Diner of Local Heros

23 **Bill's Place** opened in 1959, and the diner has become a neighborhood institution. Its hamburgers are named after local stars, like the famous *San Francisco Chronicle* journalist Herb Caen and Jefferson Airplane guitarist Paul Kantner, and are served with a generous portion of french fries. The kitsch decor hasn't changed since the 1950s [2315 Clement St.].

24A

The Gem of Little Russia

24 Stop for a peek inside the **Holy Virgin Cathedral** (A) [6210 Geary Blvd.], a magnificent Russian Orthodox church. With its 24-carat-gold-covered domes, you can't miss it. The interior walls are covered in mosaics and icons, lit up by a large chandelier. Its beauty is breathtaking. Entry is free, and photos are permitted. The church is located in the heart of **Little Russia**. To really feel like you've been transported to Russia, also visit some of the grocery stores on Geary Boulevard.

The Neighborhood Pizzeria

25 Located on a residential street in the Richmond District, **Pizzetta 211** is an adorable local restaurant. The artisanal pizzas are garnished with local products and the menu changes each week. Try the potato and sausage, or the margherita. There are only 20 seats, and the wait is shorter during the day, but the charm is at its peak in the evening. The wait has its perks: the tree in front of the restaurant is adorned with little lights, and the owner offers a glass of wine and a blanket to clients waiting for a table on foggy evenings [211 23rd Ave].

A Quick Trip to Burma

26 I fell in love with Burmese food...in San Francisco. The Bay area has the largest Burmese diaspora in the United States (according to the 2010 census). There are no fewer than 30 restaurants devoted to this cuisine, which offers a wonderful mix of Thai, Indian and Chinese flavors. My mouth still waters at the thought of the coconut-milk chicken soup or the fermented tea salad (Lap Pat Dok) at **Burma Superstar** [309 Clement St.]. Consisting of lettuce, tomatoes, peanuts, roasted lentils, sesame seeds and lemon juice, the dish is an explosion of flavors. Save room for their black rice pudding with coconut milk.

The owner of **Mandalay** (A), Sherry Dung, welcomes you like a member of the family. This Richmond District institution with a canary yellow facade opened its doors in 1984, and was the first Burmese restaurant on U.S. soil. Upon entering, you'll encounter a table of offerings and a replica of a Burmese golden temple. You're likely to see a few hipsters along with families and regulars. Try the samosa soup, mango chicken and their special curried noodle plate. Heavenly [4348 California St.].

26A

The Lungs of San Francisco

27

Golden Gate Park is the jewel of San Francisco. Before it was built, the 1,017-acre (4.5-square-kilometer) park (20 percent bigger than Central Park) was nothing more than sand dunes as far as the eye could see—inaccessible and uninhabitable. The area of was nicknamed "Outside Lands" (which is also the name of a popular music festival held in Golden Gate Park in August).

At the peak of the Gold Rush in 1850, San Francisco had scarcely 35,000 residents. Twenty years later, its population had grown to 149,000. Then the tenth largest city in the United States, San Francisco had earned the right to be given a proper green space. Landscape architect William Hammond Hall had to put his imagination to the test and find a way to conquer the dunes, lashed constantly by wind from the Pacific Ocean. After much trial and error, Hall discovered that barley would be a way to stabilize the soil. Almost one million trees now grow in Golden Gate Park. I like the park because much of it is wild, you can easily get lost in it and never ceases to amaze. It's like Central Park's older hippy brother.

I usually start my visit at the **Conservatory of Flowers** (A), the large white Victorian-style greenhouse at the northeast corner of the park. It's a replica of the palm greenhouse at the Kew Gardens in London. You'll find close to 1,700 species, including different orchids, and aquatic and tropical plants. Opened in 1879, the greenhouse was destroyed by fire three times, and by a historic winter storm in 1995. In 1998, a major funding campaign collected $25 million for its restoration [100 John F. Kennedy Dr.].

Next, I go to the **de Young**, my favorite museum in San Francisco. This fine arts museum shines a spotlight on 17th-to 20th-century American art, international contemporary art, textiles and costumes. Founded in 1895, it was damaged by the 1989 earthquake, and was entirely rebuilt in 2005. The current building, which looks a bit like an armored fortress, is a contentious subject among San Franciscans. Clad entirely in copper, it will oxidize and become green over time, like the Statue of Liberty. This should help it blend into the eucalyptus forest that surrounds it—at least, that's the effect the architects intended. After touring the galleries, head to the museum's **observation tower** (B). Standing 144 feet (44 meters) tall, the glass platform offers a 360-degree view of the city [50 Hagiwara Tea Garden Dr.].

Right across from the museum, on the other side of the **Music Concourse** plaza, you'll find another highlight: the **green roof** on the **California Academy of Sciences** natural history museum (C). Although its essential purpose is to protect the building, the hilly 2.5-acre (10,000-square-meter) garden is also a sanctuary for birds and butterflies. The plants were chosen because they require little water and can withstand wind and sea spray. The portholes in the hills might lead you to imagine that the Shire from *The Lord of the Rings* has been transplanted to the middle of the city. Architect Renzo Piano said he wanted to "lift" the park and slide the museum underneath. On Thursdays the roof is open for **NightLife** events. From 6 p.m. to 10 p.m. you can sip cocktails and beers while enjoying a lovely view of the park. The entrance price is $15; the musical program changes every week [55 Music Concourse Dr.].

27 A

27 B

27 C 27 D

Mosaic Masterpiece

28 San Francisco has a number of tiled staircases, but they tend to be busy and packed with tourists. The staircase leading to Lincoln Park in the Inner Richmond neighborhood has the advantage of being little-used. That makes it perfect for photo sessions. The Lincoln Park Steps, built in the early 1900s, were in a terrible state of disrepair until recently, when a community group raised money to restore them and cover them in small decorative tiles. To create the design, artist Aileen Barr took inspiration from archival photos of the old Sutro Baths and pavilions from the 1915 Panama-Pacific International Exhibition [32nd Ave and California St.].

Tea at a 19th-Century Japanese Tea Garden

29 Stop for tea at the **Japanese Tea Garden**, just a five-minute walk from the de Young Museum, and the most Zen spot in the city. It's the oldest Japanese public garden in the United States.

The best time of the year to visit the garden is between March and April, when the cherry trees are in bloom. The garden was designed in 1894 by landscape architect Makoto Hagiwara, who maintained the garden until his death in 1925. Hagiwara, a Japanese immigrant, was the first to serve fortune cookies in the United States. The tradition lives on in the teahouse overlooking the pond near the museum entrance. Order a green tea and mochi, a traditional cake made with glutinous rice [75 Hagiwara Tea Garden Dr.].

PLEASE DO NOT FEED THE BISON

SFRPD   PARK CODE 5.07

30

Park Bison

30 At the far west of Golden Gate Park, not far from the ocean, you can see **bison**—yes, actual bison. The park has been home to these animals since 1892; a first paddock was built in 1899. The species was threatened with extinction at the time, and the City of San Francisco wanted to do its part to help the bison reproduce in captivity. In 1984, Mayor Dianne Feinstein's husband, Richard Blum, bought her a new herd as a birthday gift. The six bison you see in the paddock are descendants of those animals [1237 John F. Kennedy Dr.].

Urban Fly Fishing

31 Head down the Golden Gate Equestrian Center road, just across the road from the bison paddock. When you reach the end of the road, take the path to the right. A few yards in, tucked away in the forest, are the **Casting Pools**, my favorite spot in the park. The three large blue ponds are spots for fishing enthusiasts to practice fly-fishing.

The Golden Gate Angling & Casting Club's wooden cabin was built in 1933. Some of the club members offer free lessons to visitors, but I prefer to sit on one of the benches surrounding the peaceful spot to read a book and enjoy the feeling of having discovered a secret society [1232 John F. Kennedy Dr.].

The Marina District and Pacific Heights

Lined with hundred-year-old trees, the streets in the hills of Pacific Heights intersect with dizzyingly steep stairways. Here, the city's most lavish homes are on show for lovers of architecture. With fantastic food and fresh ocean air, the Marina District near San Francisco Bay is a joy for shopping fanatics.

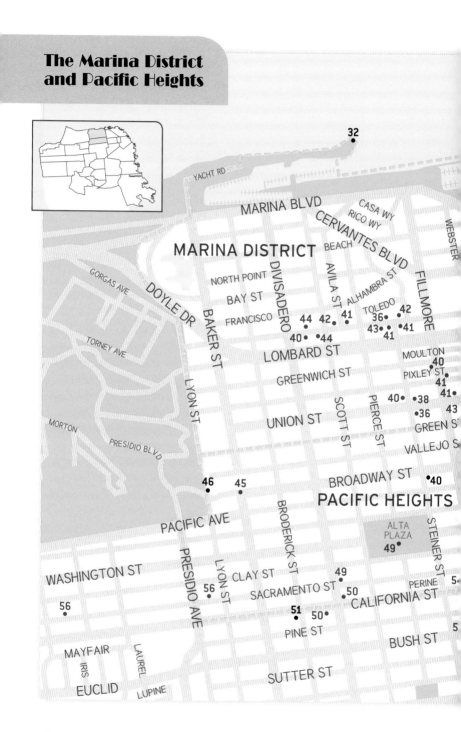

The Marina District and Pacific Heights

MARINA DISTRICT

PACIFIC HEIGHTS

Sights + photo ops
Bars + restaurants
Stores + markets
Arts + culture
Activities + walks

34
33

FORT MASON

BEACH ST

NORTH POINT ST

JONES ST

33

BAY ST

FRANCISCO ST

CHESTNUT

CHESTNUT ST

NOLIA

POLK ST

GOUGH ST

FILBERT ST

37

HYDE ST

LEAVENWORTH ST

ALLEN

41   40   42

LAGUNA ST

VAN NESS AVE

LARKIN ST

JONES ST

GLOVER ST

BERNARD ST

BUCHANAN ST

PACIFIC ST

FRANKLIN ST

JACKSON ST

47

48

CLAY ST

SHINGTON ST

LAFAYETTE
SQUARE

49

CLAY ST

PINE ST

GOUGH ST

AUSTIN

PINE ST

5

MOT ST

PINE ST

OCTAVIA

56

FERN ST

HEMLOCK

CEDAR

53

MYRTLE ST

52

POST ST

GEARY BLVD

O'FARRELL ST

OLIVE ST

The Music of the Bay

32

The Wave Organ is an acoustic sculpture located in the Marina District (also known as "The Marina"), at the very edge of Crissy Field. Go to the end of the little peninsula—passing the prestigious St. Francis Yacht Club, whose members have won just about every sailing race in the world—and you'll find something that looks like the ruins of a Roman temple. Get a little closer and you'll see a set of pipes emerging from large blocks of granite. Completed in 1986, the organ is the work of artists Peter Richards and George Gonzales. Its mysterious sounds are created by the movement of the waves entering and exiting the pipes. To hear more clearly, press your ear against the pipes, like a kid listening to the ocean sound in a seashell. The organ works best at high tide, and the best time to visit is at night during a full moon. Just walk to the end of the jetty that encloses the marina [1 Yacht Rd.].

Brunch on the Water

33

Fort Mason Center is a former military base located on the edge of the bay, between the Marina District and Russian Hill. The spot was used as a port by the U.S. army for more than 100 years. Today, the hangars have been converted into stores, research centers, artist studios and a theater. On Sundays, about 40 farmers set up stalls and sell organic products at the northwest corner of the fort, at the corner of Marina Boulevard and Laguna Street (9:30 a.m. to 1:30 p.m.). It's the perfect excuse to have a picnic and mingle with residents of the neighborhood. The roasted chicken stand is especially popular. On Fridays, from 5 p.m. to 10 p.m., food trucks take over the same space for Off the Grid nights (see Reason #4).

Greens Restaurant wins the prize for brunch with the best view. The spacious restaurant is walled with windows facing directly onto the marina and the Golden Gate Bridge. When weather permits, these paned windows are opened to let in the breeze from the bay. The haute-cuisine vegetarian restaurant, run by the San Francisco Zen Center, has been an institution at Fort Mason since 1979. All the ingredients come from the restaurant's farm in Marin County, north of the city. Chef Annie Somerville draws her ideas from world cuisines, creating dishes like Wild Mushroom Shepherd's Pie, Kashmiri Curry with root vegetables, spring rolls and quinoa chili. I recommend the Poached Eggs with Fall Vegetable Hash and the Banana Coconut Bread [2 Marina Blvd.].

Roger, the Sushi Master

35 Warning: If all you like is California rolls, this restaurant isn't for you. If you like to try exotic fish you've never even heard of, however, add **Zushi Puzzle** to your list of essential stops. This is the sushi restaurant I go to the most in San Francisco, and it's all because of Roger Chong, the friendly sushi chef behind the counter. Wearing a flowered shirt and ponytail, he looks like he should be exploring the beaches of Honolulu rather than running the kitchen in an acclaimed restaurant. Originally from China, Chong learned the art of sushi in Osaka, and opened his restaurant on Lombard Street in 2002. The decor is nothing special, but that's part of Zushi Puzzle's charm; you feel like you're part of a select group of insiders who know where to get the best fish in the city. Reserve one of the six seats at the bar to watch the chef in action. Ask for the omakase (chef's choice), and let Roger surprise you with whatever he's found at the market. He respects personal tastes, however; he'll ask you first whether there are any foods you aren't crazy about. It's a true omakase menu, since it's based on the preferences of each guest. However, Roger pushes me to be a little more adventurous each time I eat there. On my last visit, he served me marrow from a massive tuna bone. His enthusiasm is contagious, and he's proud of his work. Nor will he let you leave without trying one of the house sorbets [1910 Lombard St.].

Cocktail Scholars

34 Right next to Greens Restaurant, **The Interval** bar serves excellent cocktails. The bar's decor resembles a mad scientist's laboratory. The bar is also home to The Long Now Foundation, a nonprofit organization that works on long-term cultural projects—for instance, the building of a clock that will keep ticking for 10,000 years.

The Interval's cocktail specialist, Jennifer Colliau, uses high-quality ingredients and makes all the syrups herself. Her ideas are sparked by different countries and time periods; some recipes are even based on 19th-century drinks. The bar also houses a unique library. Feel free to peruse the 3,000 books that line the shelves; you'll find titles on mathematics, space travel, agronomy, metalworking, midwifery, construction and more. The collection is meant to be a "Manual for Civilization": a guide for how to rebuild the world in case of a disaster.

Q and Paul and Linda's Sandwiches

36

A family institution since 1929, **Lucca Delicatessen** (A) serves some of the best sandwiches in the entire Bay area. Paul Bosco and his sister Linda now run the small Italian shop, which was opened by their grandfather, Mike. They know their customers by name, as well as their favorite sandwich orders. There are 19 choices listed on the sign, but you can also create your own sandwich. The #1 Italian Combo is the most popular (salami, ham, mortadella, provolone, tomatoes and marinated peppers) but I have a weakness for the Caprese, a simple and delicious sandwich made from fresh mozzarella, tomatoes and olive oil. Sit on the bench in front of the deli to eat and watch the neighborhood's urban wildlife—it's one of my favorite pastimes [2120 Chestnut St.].

Four blocks to the south, on Union Street, **Marina Submarine** has been another neighborhood favorite since 1975. The reason is simple: the sandwiches are gigantic and delicious. Don't let the lineup deter you. The owner, Q, personally prepares each sandwich; watching him slice an avocado is a show in itself. The bread is toasted to perfection—and then there's the incredible secret sauce. I recommend ordering the meatball sub with homemade tomato sauce, or the turkey sub [2299 Union St.].

The Littlest Pub

37

In a space just seven feet wide and 19 feet long (12 square meters), **Black Horse London Pub** is the smallest bar in San Francisco. The colorful owner, James "Big Dawg" King, has a convenience store liquor license (hence the "The Black Horse London Deli" sign above the door). As a result, he can only serve bottles of beer that he keeps behind the bar in an ice-filled clawfoot bathtub. The beer selection depends on what he has picked up at the grocery store. If you want to hear stories from the neighborhood, this is the place to be. Cash only [1514 Union St.].

SERVING THE MARINA SINCE 1929

Breakfast Pizza

38 If you're in the mood to lounge on a terrace with a big bowl of café au lait, head to **Rose's Café**, a popular hangout for locals. The menu is Italian-inspired, and the terrace feels like a Parisian café. Their specialty is a thin-crust breakfast pizza with smoked salmon, crème fraiche and poached eggs ($18, but it's huge, so feel free to share). The pastries, breads, sorbets, jams and desserts are made in-house [2298 Union St.].

A Sacred House

39 In the midst of the Victorian homes in the Cow Hollow neighborhood is a strange lavender-colored house with red domes. The building really seems out of place. This exotic jewel is believed to be the first Hindu temple in the Western Hemisphere. The **Old Vedanta Temple**, built in 1905, is an architectural amalgam, combining British and Asian styles. The Vedanta Society of Northern California was founded by the spiritual leader Swami Vivekananda, who introduced Hinduism to North America in 1893. Vivekananda chose the location personally and raised money for the building of the temple, which was entirely restored in 2015. The towers are meant to symbolize harmony between religions [2963 Webster St.].

San Franciscans use the Uber app to go everywhere, and it's often more efficient than public transportation. With the Uber Pool option (where you share a ride with other passengers), you can get to the airport for about $15. It's also the best way to meet people. Uber is also used is also used as a verb, for example: "I'm ubering to the restaurant."

Fine Dining at the Marina

40 The owner of Rose's Café, Laurie Thomas, also owns the restaurant right across the street. **Terzo** is a friendly place with all-wood decor and large communal tables that are perfect for large groups. The Mediterranean menu consists of a wide selection of small dishes made with the freshest ingredients. Try the grilled calamari, the Mozzarella di Bufala, the meatballs with polenta, and the hummus and zaatar pitas. Truly exquisite [3011 Steiner St.]. The restaurant is located just three blocks from the beautiful **house from *Mrs. Doubtfire*** (A) [2640 Steiner St., at the corner of Broadway]. After Robin Williams' death in 2014, some of his fans created an improvised memorial, writing touching messages on the stones in front of the house.

My favorite Italian restaurant in the city is **Capannina**. The restaurant isn't on hipster or foodie radar, but it's the perfect spot for a romantic dinner. Quality control is strict, and the staff is very attentive. The pasta is homemade and the selection of wines and Italian cheeses is vast. Try the seafood risotto, the Veal Scaloppine with Lemon-Caper Sauce or the Pappardella with Mushroom and Wild Boar Ragu. From 5 p.m. to 6 p.m., the three-course dinner costs $25 [1809 Union St.].

Another excellent Italian restaurant, **A16** (B)—named after the highway that connects Naples to Canosa di Puglia—is famous for its Napolitano pizza, its antipasti and its many wines from the south of Italy. The owner and sommelier, Shelley Lindgren, has a reputation for finding unknown wines. The wood-fired pizzas are impeccable (I recommend the Romana), but if you prefer something different, the Maccaronara pasta is a popular favorite. To enjoy the restaurant on a budget, opt for the three-course tasting menu for lunch at $20 [2355 Chestnut St.].

If you're not on a tight budget, reserve a table at **Atelier Crenn**, the temple of molecular gastronomy in San Francisco. French chef Dominique Crenn (who has an impressive arm tattoo) is the first woman in North America to receive two Michelin stars. Describing her cuisine as "poetic culinarian," she makes every plate a work of art. The tasting menu is $200 per person, plus $150 for wine, sake or beer pairing [3127 Fillmore St.].

41A

Organic, Local, Vegan, Gluten-Free...

41 All the locals you see in Cow Hollow and the Marina seem to be in great shape; it's enough to give you a complex. On Saturday mornings, Union Street is filled with women in yoga pants, green juice in hand. They're either fresh out of a Pilates, Bar Method or SoulCycle class, or they've just finished jogging or cycling at Crissy Field. These are the health-and-exercise neighborhoods. It's no surprise, then, that the two main arteries (Union Street and Chestnut Street) have plenty of health food restaurants and juice bars. The **Rapha Cycle Club** (A) is a popular place for cycling enthusiasts to meet up for coffee. An ancient Citroën H-Van just in front of the store has been converted into a parklet—a miniature public space, with tables and benches, plants and bike parking [2198 Filbert St.].

My love affair with **Seed + Salt** is still going strong. I never lose my passion for the salads, sandwiches, soups and treats at this small organic, vegan and gluten-free restaurant. Try their breakfast sandwich or quinoa falafel (instead of pita bread, they use a large green cabbage leaf) and their "Nutella" brownie, which uses a dairy-free homemade version of the spread [2240 Chestnut St.]. **The Plant** is another spot I return to often, for the quinoa and vegetable bowl, nourishing salads and fresh smoothies. All the ingredients are organic and come from local farms [3352 Steiner St.]. For fresh-squeezed juices, my heart is pulled in two directions: **Urban Remedy** [1957 Union St.] and **Pressed Juicery** [2162 A Union St.], which has more reasonable prices. **Blue Barn**, a fast-food concept, sources all its food from local farms. It offers panini, grilled cheese and soups, but it's their choice of 11 hearty salads that really draws crowds [2105 Chestnut St.].

Great Food on the Go

42 Roam Artisan Burgers

describes itself as an environmentally responsible restaurant and uses only organic ingredients. The hamburgers are utterly delicious. Order at the counter and eat at one of the shared tables. When ordering, choose your burger (beef, turkey, bison or vegetarian) and the type of bun and toppings. The Sunny Side is a must (egg, aged cheddar, caramelized onions, tomatoes), as is the French and Fries (Parmesan fries with truffles, Gruyère, avocado, caramelized onions, watercress and Dijon). Top it off with one of their milkshakes: the salted caramel is a revelation [1785 Union St.].

Tacolicious also uses only organic ingredients. Choose from their many Californian and Mexican appetizers, then move on to the tacos: carnitas, mole chicken or cod. If you're looking for a vegetarian option, the kale, quinoa and grapefruit salad is as surprising as it is delicious. For dessert, achieve bliss by ordering their churros with chocolate dipping sauce [2031 Chestnut St.]. For a typically French experience, the **Le Marais** bistro (A) serves excellent croque monsieur, quiche, smoked salmon on a slice of bread and some of the best croissants in town [2066 Chestnut St.].

Neighborhood Wine Bars

43 A perfect place to start the

evening, the unpretentious local bar **West Coast Wine • Cheese** is a great spot to discover good wines from the western United States (California, Oregon and Washington). The menu offers 24 wines by the glass and 720 bottles, which are stacked in an impressive array against the wall. Take a seat at the counter and ask for their charcuterie and cheese platter. Their whipped burrata alone is worth the trip [2165 Union St.].

Greg O'Flynn, the owner of the **California Wine Merchant**, loves to share his passion for California wines. Opened in 1974, the shop combines a wine store and a bar with a relaxed atmosphere. Specializing in small producers, O'Flynn offers as many as 50 wines by the glass. Prices range from $3.50 to more than $25 a glass [2113 Chestnut St.].

Hora Feliz

44 If you're looking for a lively

happy hour, visit the excellent Mexican restaurant **Mamacita**. On weekdays from 5:30 p.m. to 6:30 p.m., tacos are two for $6 (try the duck confit tacos), a glass of sangria is $4, a beer $3, while bottles of wine are at half price [2317 Chestnut St.].

Causwells is an American bistro with an industrial decor, located within the superb art-deco-style Presidio Theatre. You can choose from 20 wines by the glass and 22 types of beer, which go great with a plate of deviled eggs or their homemade ricotta. It's also known for its burger with two well-charred beef patties and its donut bread pudding dessert [2346 Chestnut St.].

Paved with Gold

45 Pacific Heights is the most affluent neighborhood in San Francisco. The neighborhood is sometimes called The Gold Coast, and a section of Broadway Street has been nicknamed **Billionaire's Row**. To see how the other half lives, take a walk on Broadway and Pacific Avenue between Broderick and Lyon streets.

Perched on the highest point above the bay and looking out on the Presidio and the Golden Gate Bridge, Pacific Heights is coveted for its view of the city. Homes in Pacific Heights (in some cases, "castles" would be more accurate) were designed by preeminent 20th-century architects like William Wurster and Willis Polk. Polk was responsible for the Tudor-style home that was bought by Jonathan Ive, head of the team responsible for Apple's product designs [Broadway at Broderick St., northwest corner of the street].

Gordon Getty, heir to the Getty oil fortune, and his wife, Ann, combined their three adjacent homes in this neighborhood in order to create one enormous mansion [Broadway, between Broderick and Baker St.]. They even built a nursery school on the property for their grandchildren and other children of the neighborhood's elite.

Pacific Heights is an enclave for San Francisco's aristocracy. The children of prominent families all go to the same private schools: Stuart Hall, Cathedral, and Town for boys, and Convent of the Sacred Heart, Hamlin, and Burke's for girls.

Unlike many other major U.S. cities, high society is alive and well in Pacific Heights. Two illustrious families in particular—the Gettys and the Trainas—set the gold standard for the upper crust. The technological elite has also found its place in the sun here: several billionaires (including Mark Pincus of Zynga and Larry Ellison, co-founder of Oracle) have bought homes in recent years.

A Stairway Garden

46 California senator and former San Francisco mayor Dianne Feinstein owns one the most impressive homes in the area. It was built right on part of the **Lyon Street Steps** (A), a magnificent staircase that connects Pacific Heights and the Marina. The 244-step stairway is popular among fitness enthusiasts, who run up and down the staircase for exercise, especially on weekends. Elegant gardens and manicured hedges border the staircase; you can descend it all the way to the Palace of Fine Arts (see Reason #3). Be sure to get a view of the ***Migrant Heart*** (B), a sculpture of a golden heart, in front of Feinstein's residence. It's one of the 130 heart-shaped sculptures made by various artists scattered throughout the city. These works, about as tall as a person, are sold in annual "Hearts in San Francisco" auctions, with proceeds going to the San Francisco General Hospital Foundation.

46B

46A

Return to the Victorian Era

47

The **Haas-Lilienthal House** is the only Victorian-era home in San Francisco that's open to the public. It offers a rare glimpse inside a luxury home from that period, and gives visitors the chance to see how the wealthy of the neighborhood lived back then. Never having been renovated, the home remains a true time capsule from that era. The furniture is original and much of the decor dates from the 19th century. The rooms are stunning, but their true splendor lies in the fine details of the moldings, fireplaces, railings and door handles. Built in 1886 by Jewish immigrants, this Queen-Anne-style marvel miraculously survived the earthquakes of 1906 and 1989.

After the death of her husband, Samuel Lilienthal, in 1957, Alice Haas Lilienthal continued to live in the house until she passed away in 1972. Her heirs donated the residence to San Francisco Heritage, an organization dedicated to preserving the city's architecture. The doors of the Haas-Lilienthal House are open to the public on Wednesdays and Saturdays from noon to 3 p.m. and Sundays from 11 a.m. to 4 p.m. Entry price is $8. On Sundays at 12:30, the museum also offers fascinating two-hour guided tours ($8) of the architecture of Pacific Heights. There's no need to book ahead [2007 Franklin St.].

Always be careful when you open a car door, and make sure to look in all directions: 99 percent of the time, a cyclist will be riding by...

The Vintage-Car Collection

48 The Academy of Art University, founded in 1929 by Richard A. Stephens, houses a very special gallery available to its design students. The gallery features a collection of antique cars valued at more than $70 million. A serious car aficionado, Stephens started to build his collection in the 1920s. His granddaughter, Elisa Stephens, is now the president of the university, and is carrying the torch. About 50 cars dating from 1920 to 1965, all in perfect condition, are on display. There is something for everyone, from Buick to Cadillac through Ford, Packard, Mercedes Benz, Rolls Royce and many others. The family's collection includes almost 250 automobiles, which are on rotation in the gallery. The **Academy of Art University Automobile Museum** is open to the public on Tuesdays from 11 a.m. to 1 p.m. and on Thursdays from 2 p.m. to 4 p.m. To reserve a spot, go to academyautomuseum.org. Admission is $10, and proceeds go to charity [1849 Washington St.; entrance on Van Ness Ave.].

Panoramic Parks

49 Pacific Heights has the good fortune of having two of the best-maintained public parks in the city. With its large playground, green and hilly **Lafayette Park** (A) [Gough St. and Washington St.] is a favorite for families. Along with **Alta Plaza Park** [Jackson St. and Steiner St.], Lafayette Park was used as a camp for locals made homeless after the earthquake of 1906. It's divided into four terraces, and a stairway cuts across the southern slope of the park. From the top, you get a panoramic view of downtown San Francisco; you can even see Alcatraz. Dogs aren't required to have a leash, and on the first Sunday of each month, pug owners assemble for a picnic in the afternoon. The odd tradition has become quite popular: On some Sundays there are as many as 75 dogs.

If you are in the mood for a drink when near the park, you'll feel right at home at **Lion Pub**. You won't see a sign, and it may be hard to believe that a bar is hiding behind the vine-covered façade. Venture inside and you'll find a fireplace warming the room, large welcoming armchairs and green plants that brighten the atmosphere. Customers have fun climbing onto the lion sculpture for a photo-op. What keeps them coming back, apart from the decor, are the cocktails made from freshly squeezed juice [2062 Divisadero St.].

Croissants Worthy of Paris

50

When you're ready for a snack, **b. patisserie** offers pastries and tartines (try the one with wild mushrooms), just three blocks from Alta Plaza Park. Their croissants and macaroons are legendary; the aroma in the store is beyond description [2821 California St.]. Across the street, **b. on the go** serves top-notch sandwiches, with meat and roasted vegetables on homemade bread. Try the Greek chicken or the grilled cheese with the soup of the day [2794 California St.].

Plant Mosaic

51

Drew School, a private high school, has a façade on the Broderick Street side that's definitely worth seeing. It's a 1,800-square-foot (167-square-meter) living wall, created by French botanist Patrick Blanc. Almost 5,000 plants—with more than 100 species indigenous to California—cling to the three-story wall. Forming a vast quilt of various shades of green, the sight is most spectacular in the summer. It'll be a guaranteed hit on Instagram [2901 California St.].

Divine Dining on Fillmore Street

52 **SPQR** is *the* neighborhood spot for an original plate of pasta. The pasta is made by hand, and the flavors are inventive: for instance, the cocoa spaghetti, wild duck, butternut squash and Piave cheese. They use quality ingredients, and all the wines are from small producers in Italy. A tasting menu is offered on Thursdays ($59 per person); and the three-course lunch costs $35 [1911 Fillmore St.].

For pizza, I'm a loyal customer at **Delfina**, a Neapolitan pizzeria that's extremely popular. Get there early; if you don't, you'll have to enter your name on the large blackboard at the entrance and then wait on the sidewalk. I recommend the prosciutto pizza, the broccoli raab pizza, the clam pizza or the four cheese. And don't attempt to resist the antipasti or the grilled vegetables [2406 California St.].

Out the Door (A) serves contemporary Vietnamese cuisine in a clean, modern space. The open kitchen lets you see the chefs at work. I like to take a seat at the counter and order the spring rolls, green papaya salad and crab noodles. The chocolate peanut-butter cream pie is extremely addictive [2232 Bush St.].

DOSA serves reinvented South Indian cuisine. It's a popular spot for dosas, as the name suggests: large paper-thin crepes made of rice and lentils, filled with various curries and chutneys. The cocktails are infused with Indian spices [1700 Fillmore St.].

52A

Snapshot of the Past

53 I walked right by the narrow passageway called **Cottage Row** a number of times without even noticing it. That's typical for San Francisco. You're always discovering a new street, stairway or house—that's why I love the city so much. On Bush Street between Fillmore and Webster streets, you'll see a brick walkway lined with Victorian homes. This mini-neighborhood seems frozen in time. Most of the 22 houses on the lane are listed on the National Register of Historic Places. Still beautifully preserved, they were built by the architect William Hollis in the 1860s and '70s. Cottage Row offers a glimpse into pre-earthquake-era San Francisco. At the end of the lane you'll find a small park with several benches—a perfect spot for a picnic.

Ice Cream for Geeks

54 **Smitten Ice Cream** (A) stands out from the pack; the ice cream shop is like a laboratory more than anything else. The ice cream is made to order right before your eyes. To achieve this, the owner, Robyn Sue Fisher, invented a machine (known as "Brrr") that makes individual ice cream servings using liquid nitrogen. The whole process takes about 90 seconds. The texture is creamier and denser than traditional ice cream, and the flavors are more intense. Smitten uses only local and seasonal products [2404 California St.]. If you prefer something less rich, **Fraiche**, a restaurant nearby on Fillmore Street, serves organic and sugar-free frozen yogurt with homemade compotes, fresh fruit, chocolate and nuts [1910 Fillmore St.].

A Café Beloved by Laptoppers

55 The café **Jane** is the darling of the neighborhood. From 7 a.m. on it's filled with customers hooked on their Stumptown coffee, chocolate croissants with orange zest, breakfast panini, avocado toast, chia pudding, green smoothies and free Wi-Fi. I have an intense addiction to their unbelievable banana bread. It's also a popular lunch spot. Everything on the menu is delicious, and there are a number of gluten-free and vegan options. There always seems to be a cute dog tied up outside, ready to entertain the people in line [2123 Fillmore St.]. Across the street, **Grove** (A) is another popular spot for lunch or brunch, or for basking in the sun on the terrace. The decor is rustic, with large leather armchairs, a fireplace and well-cushioned wooden benches. The menu is a mix of comfort food and health food; it has something for everyone, and the prices are reasonable. Try the chicken pot pie, the macaroni and cheese, the breakfast tacos, the smoked salmon and goat cheese sandwich, the chili or the grilled cheese [2016 Fillmore St.].

The Crown Jewel of San Francisco's Restaurants

56 Offering gourmet food in an unpretentious setting, the bistro **Nico** (A) offers "carte blanche"-style dining. Don't worry about what to choose: put your trust in French chef Nicolas Delaroque. He improvises a new menu each evening based on the seasonal products available. With the quality of the food and the Michelin star (not to mention the attentive staff), the five-course meal ($65) is definitely a bargain in this neighborhood. You can also order from the evening menu at the bar [3228 Sacramento St.]. After filling your belly, why not see a movie at the theater just down the street? The **Vogue** (B), one of the city's oldest cinemas, opened its doors in 1910 and has maintained its now-retro look [3290 Sacramento St.].

Octavia was a revelation for me. I'm in awe of chef Melissa Perello's California cuisine, which is somehow both refined and rustic—and accessible. Octavia can raise a mere salad to an entirely new level. The menu at this Michelin-star-winning restaurant, which seats 55, changes based on what's available at the market. However, some dishes are always on offer; customers have insisted they can't live without them. These include the "deviled" egg: an egg served on a bed of Fresno chili relish and topped with spices. It's a simple dish that's perfectly executed. And don't pass on the Chilled Squid Ink Pasta with creamy vinaigrette dressing, lemon oil and pureed fennel, and the pasta with salt cod [1701 Octavia St.].

The elegant and sophisticated **Spruce** is the perfect setting for special occasions. Located in the chic Presidio Heights neighborhood, just west of Pacific Heights, the restaurant attracts wealthy retirees and businesspeople during the day, and couples and groups of friends in the evenings. Chef Mark Sullivan's cuisine is Californian and modern, and 80 percent of the products are sourced from a local farm. Their hamburger is one of the best. If you want to eat at Spruce without breaking the bank, brunch is a good option: Dishes are around $15. The bar is very pleasant during happy hour, and a small café at the front offers cookies, panini and salads for takeout [3640 Sacramento St.].

Western Addition

Japantown, Alamo Square and Hayes Valley

Prepare to be delighted by the pastel-colored Victorian architecture of Alamo Square; the concert halls, boutiques and independent restaurants of Hayes Valley; and the lost in translation-feeling you'll get in San Francisco's exotic Japantown.

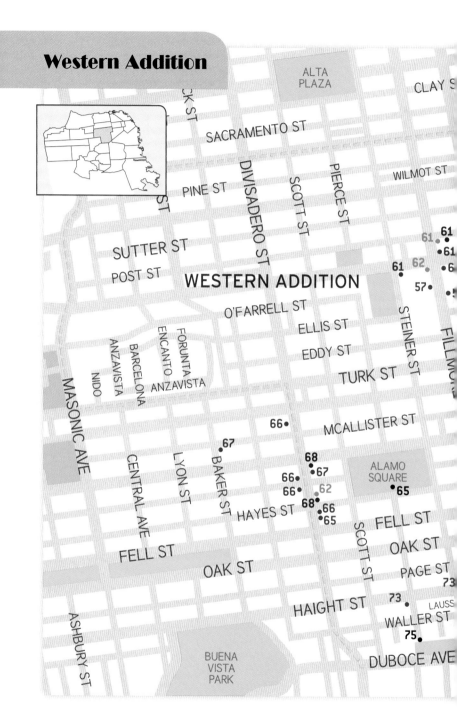

Western Addition

ALTA PLAZA

CLAY S

SACRAMENTO ST

WILMOT ST

PINE ST

DIVISADERO ST

SCOTT ST

PIERCE ST

SUTTER ST

POST ST

WESTERN ADDITION

61 •61
•61
61 62 •6
57•

O'FARRELL ST

ELLIS ST

EDDY ST

TURK ST

STEINER ST

FILLM

MASONIC AVE

ANZAVISTA

NIDO

BARCELONA

ENCANTO

FORUNTA

ANZAVISTA

66•

MCALLISTER ST

•67

68•
•67

66•
66•

68•

62

•66
•65

ALAMO SQUARE

•65

CENTRAL AVE

LYON ST

BAKER ST

HAYES ST

SCOTT ST

FELL ST

OAK ST

FELL ST

OAK ST

PAGE ST

73

ASHBURY ST

HAIGHT ST

73•

LAUSS

WALLER ST

75•

BUENA VISTA PARK

DUBOCE AVE

LAFAYETTE SQUARE

● Sights + photo ops
● Bars + restaurants
● Stores + markets
● Arts + culture
● Activities + walks

CALIFORNIA ST

PINE ST

OCTAVIA

59 ●

FERN ST

HEMLOCK

POLK ST

CEDAR

SH ST

● 60

● 61

61

POST ST

GEARY BLVD

MYRTLE ST

O'FARRELL ST

OLIVE ST

LAGUNA ST

CLEARY

ELLIS ST

WILLOW

LLIS

WILLOW

GOUGH ST

EDDY ST

ELLIS

EDDY ST

POLK ST

ELM

GOLDEN GATE AVE

FRANKLIN ST

● 73

FULTON ST

71
●

GROVE ST

IVY

IVY ST

71

69

OCTAVIA

69

72
●

HAYES ST

WEBSTER

70 ●

69

● 69

LINDEN ST

73 73

74

● 73

FELL ST

HICKORY

ST

HICKORY

OAK ST

4

HICKORY

LILY ST

71

MARKET ST

11TH ST

BUCHANAN

ROSE ST

HAIGHT ST

● 73
● 75

● 75

MANIA

HERMAN ST

DUBOCE

CLINTON PARK

PLUM

HOWARD ST

KISSLING

WOODWARD

A Custom-Made Culinary Adventure

57

If you try only one restaurant in San Francisco, it should be **State Bird Provisions**. It offers an updated version of dim sum, prepared with local California ingredients. Servers circulate among the diners with platters or carts, each one as delicious as the last, and diners take their pick. The married chef-owners Stuart Brioza and Nicole Krasinski make customers feel like they're joining the couple for a meal at their home. Their passion for food is contagious.

During my visit, I savored oysters garnished with kohlrabi kraut and sesame, grilled octopus with tomato and Kampot pepper, Hawaiian heart of palm salad with tahini-chili oil, garlic bread with burrata served in a mini cast-iron pan, and trout with toasted hazelnut-mandarin-garum vinaigrette. Need I say more?

Their signature dish is the quail. It's fried like chicken and topped with Parmesan shavings. Their tiny pancakes are another specialty. At State Bird Provisions, however, you pretty much never eat the same thing twice.

Half of the 60 seats are "reserved" for customers without a reservation; these impulsive types start to line up at the restaurant at 5:30 p.m. Get there early to make the first seating; if you miss that, you'll have to wait until 7 p.m. for the second. The wait is part of the experience, however; hot chocolate is served to people in line outside {1529 Fillmore St.}.

Stuart and Nicole also own the excellent restaurant, **The Progress**, right next door. Its industrial decor and large bar can accommodate those waiting for a table. It offers a similar type of inventive Californian cuisine, but with a different formula. The table decides collectively on the six dishes they want to order from the 13-dish menu, which changes each evening—so they design their own custom meal. The dishes are meant to be shared, family style. A six-course meal is $62 per person [1525 Fillmore St.].

Tom's Ice Cream

58 A paradise of childhood pleasures, **Miyako Old Fashion Ice Cream Shop** is an old-school ice cream parlor and candy store, located on a less than impressive stretch of Fillmore Street. Inside, you'll be greeted by Tom, an elderly man with sky-blue eyes. He's gentle and amiable—a rare jewel. He's owned the store for more than 20 years, and he loves introducing his customers to new flavors. He does not skimp on portions. His shop serves a hundred ice creams from local artisans. You'll find traditional flavors, but Tom also offers unusual ones, like avocado, ube (purple yam), Mexican chocolate and young coconut. It's the kind of business I love to support: authentic, affordable and packed with charm [1470 Fillmore St.].

The Temple of Sound

59 **The Audium** immerses you in darkness and bombards you with sound for an hour. It's the only theater of its kind in the United States. Audience members are led through a sound labyrinth until they reach the main performance space. This circular room has 25 seats arranged in concentric circles. More than 170 speakers are built into the walls, the floor, the ceiling and all the seats of the enclosed space. The end result: complete darkness. With their senses limited only to hearing, the audience is disarmed: They're ready to be transported. The composer, Stan Shaff, opened the theater in 1975, and performs his compositions live. He describes his pieces as "sound sculptures;" the sounds are modulated to direction, speed, intensity and the space around them. Here, sound becomes three-dimensional. The experience is both bizarre and meditative. In today's world, it's rare to do only one thing at a time; this show forces you to listen without being distracted by other stimuli. The result is a bit like seeing with your ears. Performances are Fridays and Saturdays at 8:30 p.m., and tickets are $20 [1616 Bush St.].

Sweets, Japan-Style

60 A historic district of mainly six blocks (Geary Boulevard to the south, Sutter Street to the north, Fillmore Street to the west and Laguna Street to the east), **Japantown** isn't quite what was in the 1940s. Back then, nearly 5,000 Japanese-Americans lived in the neighborhood, and it housed almost 200 Japanese businesses. The first Japanese immigrants arrived in San Francisco in 1869, and created the first truly Japanese neighborhood in the United States. After the Empire of Japan attacked Pearl Harbor in 1941, most of the Japanese nationals were dispossessed and forced to leave the city. They were sent to an internment camp in Utah, and freed only when the war was over. Only half returned to Japantown in 1946. It's a sad chapter in the city's history.

60 B

Today, you can still find a few authentic stores, like the Japanese bakery **Benkyodo Company** (A). Suyeichi Okamura opened the sweets shop, one of the first in Japantown, in 1906. During World War II, he was forced to close it. His son, Hirofumi, took over the bakery in 1951, and moved it to its current location a few weeks later. Today, Hirofumi's own sons, Ricky and Bobby, run the business, greeting each customer with a smile. The decor is as retro as it gets; it looks like nothing has been touched since the shop's beginnings. You feel like you're in a typical 1950s American diner. They sell an array of manju and mochi (about $1 each)—sticky little steamed rice cakes stuffed with bean paste. You can eat them at the counter. I love the texture of these desserts. Try the peanut butter mochi [1747 Buchanan St.].

On the other side of the street, you'll find another dessert destination. Inside the Japanese grocery store Super Mira is **Yasukochi's Sweet Shop** (B). It's basically nothing more than a counter with cakes and other pastries for sale. The octogenarian owner opened the pastry shop more than 40 years ago with his wife, Hatsy. Today his grandchildren work by his side, and are getting ready to take over. Each day, Thomas Yasukochi makes his famous "Coffee Crunch," considered by some to be the best cake in town. He makes 20 of them, and they fly off the shelves. On Thanksgiving Day, he sells hundreds. The secret to this cake is the contrast of textures. The three layers of light-as-air sponge cake are interspersed with whipped cream and coffee syrup. The whole package is covered in a thick layer of coffee-infused toffee. Most people buy a whole cake, but you can also get just a slice [1790 Sutter St.].

A Day in Japantown

61

Start your day with a moment of relaxation at **Kabuki Springs & Spa**. A favorite among San Franciscans, this urban oasis recreates the experience of *onsen:* an outdoor Japanese hot springs. It has hot and cold baths, a dry sauna, a steam room and showers. Sundays, Wednesdays and Fridays are women-only, Mondays, Thursdays and Saturdays are for men, and only Tuesdays are mixed. Swim caps are required. Tea, bath products, sea salt and cold facecloths are available. Entry price for the communal baths is $25, and you can stay as long as you like. Baths cost $15 when you book a body treatment with herbs, a facial or a massage (their shiatsu massage is incredible). Cell phones must remain off at all times, so bring a book or magazine, and just luxuriate in one of the lounge areas. You don't have to book ahead for the baths [1750 Geary Blvd.].

If Kabuki is full, **Imperial Day Spa**, a Korean establishment across the street, offers good treatments for a lower price. An acupressure session costs $60 for 50 minutes—the perfect option if you're planning to walk all day [1875 Geary Blvd.]. After a great massage, I usually stop at **YakiniQ Café** for their sweet potato latte [1640 Post St.]. For a big comforting bowl of ramen, I go to **Ramen Yamadaya** for the delicious Tonkotsu broth [1728 Buchanan St.], or to **Suzu Noodle House,** which serves Japanese ramen, udon or soba noodles with various toppings and very good tempura. The small restaurant is located in **Japan Center** (A). For an exotic adventure, check out the different floors of the center [1825 Post St.]. On the second floor is my favorite karaoke bar, the **Festa Wine & Cocktail Lounge**—it's surpasses Tokyo! Also in the Japan Center, I like to stop at **Kinokuniya** (B), an impressive bookstore that opened in 1969. The Japanese chain now has six stores in the United States. Along with a large collection of books in Japanese and other Asian languages, it has a number of books in English. I go there to flip through books on design, travel, history and cooking, and their fashion, architecture and design magazines. The place is a foutain of inspiration, as well as an explosion of colors [1581 Webster St.].

I end the day at my favorite theater, **Sundance Kabuki**. You can reserve a spot online or at the ticket booth, so there's no need to get there early. The cinema serves alcohol, and you can bring your glass or bottle into the theatre during screenings for 21-and-over audiences (there are a few each day). No plastic cups here: they use real glass. When you order food, you receive a pager that lets you know when it's ready. Sundance Kabuki is miles beyond what you find in the major theater chains, and the prices are ridiculously low. You can also choose from myriad appetizers and dishes, like the Mediterranean platter, gourmet pizzas, turkey club sandwiches and vegetarian hamburgers. They also serve local ice cream from Humphry Slocombe (see Reason #183) [1881 Post St.].

61A

61B

62

A Legendary Concert Hall

62 Seeing a show at The Fillmore is an experience that's intricately tied to the city's history. When the building opened in 1912, the venue was a ballroom. In the '60s, concert promoter Bill Graham took the reins, and the 1200-seat room became the epicenter of the psychedelic music scene and the hippie movement. Artists like Pink Floyd, Janis Joplin with Big Brother & the Holding Company, and the Grateful Dead all made their start there. In December 2011, the hard rock group Metallica celebrated its 30th year as a band by playing a weeklong series of concerts there. Expect a warm welcome when you enter The Fillmore. And when you leave you'll be given an apple (a tradition started by Bill Graham, originally intended to help those who have consumed illicit substances get back on their feet). If the event was sold out three weeks in advance, you'll also receive a free poster for the night's show. Don't miss the collection of artist photos and psychedelic posters on the mezzanine. Hanging in chronological order, they illustrate the rich history of this establishment, which has hosted so many of the greatest legends of music. Check the website for the schedule: thefillmore.com/calendar [1805 Geary Blvd.]. **The Independent** is another popular concert hall in the area. It usually hosts up-and-coming bands of different musical styles, and gives them the chance to play in a more intimate environment (the venue has a capacity of 500). The sound at The Independent is amazing. Get there early to stake out one of the benches along the walls in the upper section. You can find the program at theindependentsf.com [628 Divisadero St.].

The Li-bar-ary

63 For a bite to eat and a drink before the show, I recommend **The Social Study**, just next to The Fillmore. The bar has a long list of snacks like cheese or charcuterie platters, salads and sandwiches. My favorite is the Veggie Dream. Apart from the wine and beer list, it has eclectic cocktails. The Wojito (sauvignon blanc, lime, mint and sparkling water), the Spicy Coke (port, espresso and Coca-Cola) and the Chocolate Factory (Guinness, homemade chocolate syrup, espresso and milk chocolate chips) will thrill the more adventurous. In the evenings, a DJ sets up on the mezzanine, and during the day the bar transforms into a café. There are a number of books available for customers [1795 Geary Blvd.].

Disco Night at the Church

64 Three nights a week, the Sacred Heart Church on Fillmore Street transforms into a roller-disco rink. About a hundred skaters, many in sequined outfits, pour into the sacred space and skate laps under the glow of the colorful stained glass windows. Built in 1897, the Roman-style church survived the earthquakes of 1906 and 1989. In 2004, when the church needed repairs that would cost more than $8 million, the archdiocese of San Francisco decided to shut it down. That's when David Miles Jr., the godfather of San Francisco roller-skating, stepped in. His idea: to use the church as a spot where lovers of his favorite sport could congregate. Miles has toured the city on his skates each Saturday since 1989; the rest of the time, he skates in Golden Gate Park. After redoing the floor and hanging a disco ball from the ceiling, he renamed the building The Church of 8 Wheels. Miles chooses the music, playing funk hits from behind the DJ booth. Open Fridays from 7 p.m. to 11 p.m., and on Saturdays from 3 p.m. to 5 p.m., for kids, and 7 p.m. to 11 p.m for adults. Admission is $10 and skate rental is $5. It's an unforgettable night, guaranteed [554 Fillmore St.].

65 A

Picnic with a View

65 San Francisco has the original and most famous example of **Painted Ladies** (A): a row of iconic Victorian homes in pastel colors. The houses line the eastern edge of Alamo Square [Steiner St.]; they've become the park's best-known feature. If you feel like a picnic, the view from the park is sublime. Pick up supplies at **Bi-Rite Market** (B), a family-owned grocery store just a block from the park: It's a little slice of heaven for Epicureans. The sandwich-and-salad counter is most enticing. The shop has a wide selection of cheese, breads, chocolates, and organic fruits and vegetables [550 Divisadero St.].

65 B

66 A

Eating at the Fog Line

66 Divisadero Street marks the city's fog line. It isn't an exact science, but it's a generally accepted fact: West of Divisadero, San Francisco is often blanketed in fog, while the neighborhoods to the east soak up the sun. "Divis," as San Franciscans call it, is packed with good restaurants and cafés. For a great brunch, **Nopa** is your destination. It's a good idea to get there early or book ahead, but I've never had a problem getting a seat at the bar. The food here is organic and rustic, with a focus on wood-fired oven cooking. Served on beautiful ceramic plates, the dishes are prepared with seasonal ingredients from local producers. It's spacious inside, with a mezzanine and an open kitchen—you feel like you're eating in a huge loft. Try the custard French toast with grapes and caramelized thyme; the toasted bagel with smoked trout, garlic cheese, pickled onions and cucumbers; or the scrambled eggs with leeks, mushrooms, cream, bacon and herbed croutons. The artisanal cocktails are also popular. My favorite is The Grapefruit Cocktail. The restaurant doesn't close until one in the morning—a rarity in San Francisco [560 Divisadero St.].

Bar Crudo, one of the top raw-food bars in the city, serves only fish and other seafood, and most dishes are raw. The highlight is the bar that serves oysters, shellfish, crab and lobster. I particularly love their Crudo Sampler—"crudo" is basically ceviche. You can choose four kinds of fish for $14. I still daydream about their lobster beet salad with burrata, arugula and pistachios, and their grilled octopus. A tip to make your bill more manageable: Go between 5 p.m. and 6:30 p.m., when oysters are $1 and beers are $4 [655 Divisadero St.].

For comfort food, there are three main spots on my radar. **Brenda's Meat & Three** (A) is owned by the city's queen of soul food, Brenda Buenviajé. "Meat & Three" means a meat dish plus the choice of three side dishes. The restaurant is faithful to the culinary tradition the Southern states have fostered since the 1930s. My favorite meals at the restaurant are breakfast and brunch, for sandwiches, eggs, French toast and biscuits and gravy. Their specialties are the fried bologna sandwich and the peanut butter icebox pie. There are a few healthier options as well, like the kale & chicory salad with grapes, toasted almonds and feta, and a few vegan side dishes [919 Divisadero St.].

4505 Burgers & BBQ (B) has the best smoked meat in the city. Butcher Ryan Farr, who runs the restaurant, buys only meat produced by farmers who have good and sustainable rearing practices. After you order inside the shed, your food tray is brought to your picnic table on the sunny patio. On the menu: smoked meat dishes (fried chicken, beef brisket, ribs, pork shoulder), sandwiches (barbecue, hot dogs and one of the best cheeseburgers in town). Yes, there are a few vegetarian options, but you're really coming here for the meat [705 Divisadero St.].

The Perfect Toast

67

At **The Mill** (A), the smell of toast blends with the aroma of coffee. Run by star baker Josey Baker (who makes his own flour), it serves the best toast in town. At $4 a slice, some refer to it as hipster toast; The Mill raises the simple dish to a whole new level. The menu changes daily. Choose between four types of bread: country bread; rye; "everything," with whole wheat and sesame; and the bread of the week, which changes according to the season. The slices are thick, dense and toasted to perfection. The toppings I usually pick are almond butter and homemade jam. The butter and "Nutella" are also made in-house. Flooded with natural light, the space has a very Scandinavian feel. I love starting the day reading a newspaper at the big common table; I always end up meeting interesting people [736 Divisadero St.].

Not far from there, the neighborhood café **Matching Half Café** sells delicious homemade "Pop-Tarts." The flavors change based on what's available at the market (apricot, plum, orange, etc.) These treats go great with a delicious cappuccino. With the building's large windows, golden light pours in during the afternoon [1799 McAllister St.].

67A

Discover Rare Objects

68

Rare Device has unusual items for the home. The shop has a vast selection of stationery, candles, jewelry, handbags, cups, calendars, bath products, artisanal chocolates, children's clothes, magazines and more. Each object has its own story and was carefully chosen by the owner, Giselle. I love the fantastical feeling of this colorful shop; it's an integral part of the neighborhood. The store also organizes a children's party every month [600 Divisadero St.].

The Perish Trust (A) has modernized the concept of the general store. The shelves are a hodgepodge of gifts, antiques, vintage clothes, photo books, old typewriters, beauty products, pottery and Pendleton wool blankets. You'll feel like you're in the eclectic house from Wes Anderson's *The Royal Tenenbaums* [728 Divisadero St.].

67A 68A

Razzia Shopping

69 Hayes Street, between Franklin and Laguna streets, has a number of independent clothing and accessories stores. **Reliquary** will transport you to the U.S. Southwest. The owner, Leah Bershad, is definitely influenced by that region of the country in selecting the store's items. It has blankets from Santa Fe, biker jewelry, bohemian necklaces, Native American jewelry, hippie scarves, colorful baskets with tassels, embroidered Mexican tunics and jean jackets. Bershad focuses on brands from independent creators and vintage items to create her unique collection [544 Hayes St.].

Rand + Statler, a clothing store for men and women, specializes in ready-to-wear by luxury brands like Acne Studios, A.P.C., Phillip Lim, Opening Ceremony and Comme des Garçons. You'll also find jewelry, beauty products and a number of vintage Chanel accessories from the 1980s [425 Hayes St.]. **Azalea** offers slightly more affordable clothing for men and women. I love their selection of hats, leather bags and Illesteva sunglasses [411 Hayes St.]. For clothes from minimalist designers like Rachel Comey, Rick Owens and Public School, **Acrinomy** is a good bet [333 Hayes St.]. And for nice stationary and decorations, **Lavish** doesn't disappoint [508 Hayes St.].

Don't miss the boutique **Seldom Seen** on Octavia at Hayes. The charming owner, Natasha, has a great selection of jewelry and clothing from European designers, as well as a number of local creators. It's one of my essential stops [522 Octavia St.].

Greek Delights

70 **Souvla**, a small restaurant decorated with black-and-white portraits, is one of my favorite spots for lunch. The menu is as simple as can be: Pick your protein (lamb, pork, chicken or vegetarian) and the pita bread sandwich or salad option. Not trying their Greek fries (large strips of potato drizzled with olive oil, lemon, parsley and mizithra cheese) would be a colossal mistake. The Greek wine comes in big copper mugs, and their famous frozen yogurt is served in the iconic Anthora cup. You've probably seen the cup in movies: It has the colors of the Greek flag and reads "We are happy to serve you." Their special yogurt recipe is prepared in a machine at the front of the restaurant. You can get the plain yogurt garnished with olive oil and sea salt, honey, pieces of baklava or sour cherry syrup. You won't regret lining up to try this heavenly dessert [517 Hayes St.].

Three Modern Bistros

71

A fox-shaped neon sign hangs over the door outside **Monsieur Benjamin** (A)—a nod to *Le Petit Prince,* the famous story by Saint-Exupéry. Inside, the French bistro has an open, industrial feel. Chefs Corey Lee and Jason Berthold, formerly of renowned restaurant The French Laundry, opened Monsieur Benjamin in 2014. Their contemporary take on classic French cuisine has been drawing crowds since it opened. The menu features a seafood platter, escargots (snails), Foie Gras Torchon, Steak Tartare, roast chicken, a famous steak with french fries and even frog legs. For dessert, indulge in the crepe cake or the Gâteau Marjolaine. Warning: The prices are steep. To limit the damage to your wallet, order appetizers and small plates. A bonus here is that the kitchen closes at 1 a.m. [451 Gough St.].

Smaller and more modest but just as delicious, **Rich Table** focuses on local ingredients for their daily-changing menu. The married owners, Evan and Sarah Rich, believe that eating in a restaurant should be exciting and fun—an escape. You can order à la carte, but I strongly suggest you try the tasting menu ($89 per person)—some dishes are only available that way. Don't forget to order their sourdough bread, baked on-site [199 Gough St.].

The French bistro **Petit Crenn** will transport you to another dimension. Large cushions are scattered on the benches, inviting diners to get comfortable and making the all-white decor more homey. The chef, Dominique Crenn (see Reason #40), offers modern Breton-inspired cuisine, with seafood and vegetables taking the spotlight. The menu changes each day based on what's available at the market. A five-course meal is $79 per person (including service but not alcohol). You can also order à la carte at the bar without a reservation [609 Hayes St.].

Wi-Fi in the Garden

72

The main attraction at the lovely **Arlequin Cafe & Food-To-Go** is the sizeable flower garden in the back. It's beloved by laptoppers who want to do some work in a magical setting—an oasis in the heart of the city. Their specialties are the grilled sandwiches (the grilled cheese is delicious), salads and desserts. The food goes great with one of the many wines offered by the glass—all affordable. The condiments, chutneys, cookies, biscotti and granola are all made in-house. Try the breakfast burrito with pork confit and the chai-brioche donut. Yum [384 Hayes St.].

Raise a Glass

73

Hayes Valley is one of the neighborhoods with the most bars in San Francisco. I love **Two Sisters Bar & Books**, a bar with European charm. It has old-fashioned cocktails, charcuterie platters and shelves packed with books [579 Hayes St.].

The authentic Bavarian restaurant **Suppenküche** specializes in import beers: German, Austrian and Belgian. The menu features pork dishes of all kinds, pretzels, schnitzel and small potato pancakes with apple sauce [525 Laguna St.]. The owners also run the popular outdoor Biergarten at the corner of Octavia and Fell. Take a seat at one of the large communal tables and order a German beer or a bottle of cider, and enhance the experience with a sausage served on a pretzel. Open Wednesday to Sunday [424 Octavia St.].

Black Sands Brewery is another establishment that specializes in beers. At this microbrewery and bar, you can taste beers fresh out of the fermentation tanks. In fact, you even can go a step further by leaving with the recipe and buying the equipment to make it at home [701 Haight St.].

At bar-restaurant **Maven**, each dish is served with a cocktail that perfectly matches its flavors. Sample the 5 spot (rum, ginger, lime, maple, Thai basil and five spice), that comes with an order of Chinatown duck sliders. The cocktails are prepared with great care—even the ice cubes are perfect spheres [598 Haight St.].

For decor and above all for rum, you can't beat **Smuggler's Cove**. It's the perfect kitsch bar: a Polynesian paradise in the heart of the city, and the best tiki bar in San Francisco. Barrels, lanterns, ropes and nets hang from the ceiling, like the hold of a pirate ship. The cocktails are big enough to swim in. They're served in a miniature barrel, a Polynesian statue or a flaming skull (watch your hair!). There are more than 70 cocktails on the menu, and the bar offers more than 500 kinds of rum from around the world. Try the Banana Daquiri: The banana liqueur is homemade [650 Gough St.].

A pub with no pretension, **Toronado** has been a hangout for locals since 1987. You can choose from some 50 artisanal beers on tap and a hundred more in bottles. The servers have personality to spare, and it only adds to the charm of the place. Warning: It is prohibited to play the Grateful Dead on the jukebox. Warning #2: Cash only. To make sure you don't go to bed after multiple beers on an empty stomach (a guaranteed recipe for hangover), stop at **Iza Ramen** [237 Fillmore St.]. Top the night off with a cone at **Three Twins Ice Cream** across the street. The ice cream is 100-percent organic [254 Fillmore St.].

Never refer to the city as "Frisco" or "San Fran," which may annoy some locals; "San Francisco" or the abbreviation "S.F." are the only acceptable options.

Lunch on a Terrace Near Duboce Park

75 The tables and rattan chairs in front of **Café du Soleil** (A) give this pleasant and reasonably priced restaurant the air of a Parisian bistro. Their specialty is sandwiches (ham and Gruyère, chicken, goat cheese, smoked salmon and crème fraîche, tomato, tapenade and feta or humus and vegetable), served with a generous helping of salad. All can be had for $8. They also have a variety of meal salads at $8, and an excellent almond croissant [200 Fillmore St.]. From there it's only a few steps to **Revolver**, which sells clothes, accessories and a variety of items for the home [136 Fillmore St.]. **Duboce Park Cafe** is also popular for its terrace at the edge of the park. It serves grilled sandwiches (try the tuna), salads, pizzas, smoothies and freshly squeezed juices. Everything is organic, you can eat for $12, and the WiFi is free [2 Sanchez St.]. Don't miss the pretty colored houses on Pierce Street, north of the park and south of Waller Street.

Candy Heaven

74 **Miette** is the most charming boutique in Hayes Valley. This confectionary and pastry shop is decorated with an explosion of pastels. Floral wallpaper covers the walls, which are lined with rows of glass jars filled with colored candies. The assortment of old-fashioned candies and licorice (more than 20 varieties) is impressive. The sweets come from all over the world, but Miette also makes its own specialties, like Ballpark Brittle, (toffee with Spanish peanuts), Turkish Delight, macaroons and sumptuous cupcakes. The cute-looking shop is hard to miss: The front is painted candy-pink. Miette also has a shop in the Ferry Building in the Embarcadero neighborhood [449 Octavia St.].

Russian Hill and North Beach

North Beach is a treasure; the neighborhood has resisted the passage of time. Aging beatnicks can still be spotted in its bars and cafés. With cable cars and leafy fig trees, Hyde Street in Russian Hill epitomizes San Francisco's charm.

FISHERMAN'S WHARF

JEFFERSON ST

BEACH ST

COLUMBUS AVE

BAY ST

RUSSIAN HILL

FRANCISCO

96

96

BAY ST

CHESTNUT

JONES ST

LOMBARD

GREENWICH

FILBERT ST

94

TAYLOR ST

VAN NESS AVE

POLK ST

HYDE ST

ALLEN

99

97

99

99

UNION ST

94

98

98

95

99

99

99

GOUGH ST

GREEN ST

98

LARKIN ST

VALLEJO ST

GLOVER

9

98

BROADWAY ST

BERNARD ST

98

PACIFIC ST

LEAVENWORTH ST

FRANKLIN ST

POLK ST

JACKSON ST

WASHINGTON

CLAY ST

SACRAMENTO

93

98

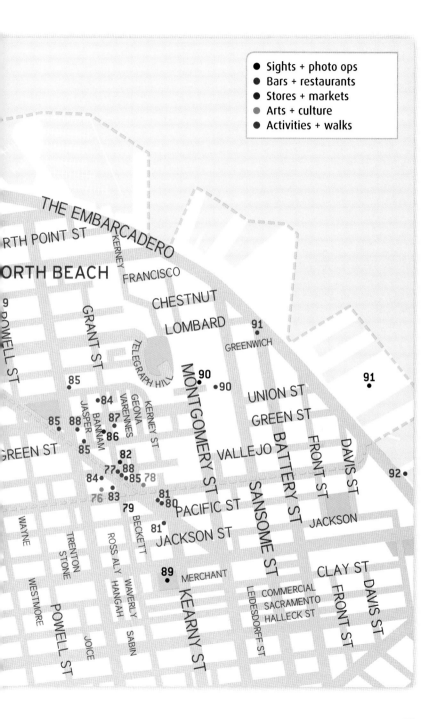

- ● Sights + photo ops
- ● Bars + restaurants
- ● Stores + markets
- ● Arts + culture
- ● Activities + walks

THE EMBARCADERO

RTH POINT ST

NORTH BEACH

FRANCISCO

KERNEY

9

POWELL ST

GRANT ST

CHESTNUT

LOMBARD

91

GREENWICH

TELEGRAPH HILL

MONTGOMERY ST

90

•90

UNION ST

GREEN ST

91

85

84

GEONA

VARENNES

KERNEY ST

85 88

JASPER

BANNAM

87

86

VALLEJO

BATTERY ST

FRONT ST

DAVIS ST

GREEN ST

85

82

77 •88

84 •85 78

76 83

79

81

•80

PACIFIC ST

SANSOME ST

92 •

JACKSON

WAYNE

TRENTON

STONE

ROSS ALY

BECKETT

HANGAH

81

WAVERLY

JACKSON ST

KEARNY ST

89

MERCHANT

LEIDESDORFF ST

CLAY ST

COMMERCIAL

SACRAMENTO

HALLECK ST

FRONT ST

DAVIS ST

WESTMORE

POWELL ST

JOICE

SABIN

A Trip to the 1920s

76 In the basement of a former dim sum restaurant, at the border between North Beach and Chinatown, is a unique theater-bar. Recreating the atmosphere of illegal nightclubs from the days of Prohibition, **The Speakeasy** offers a one-of-a-kind interactive theatrical experience. The typical characters are all there: showgirls, barflies, war veterans and mafia bosses. It's a bit like the hit New York show *Sleep No More*: Guests are free to move from room to room and interact with the 35 cabaret actors. You can even find a few secret passageways. The story you experience is nonlinear, and if you are there long enough, some scenes may repeat themselves.

Spectators are encouraged to come in 1920s costumes, and I recommend you follow the suggestion. When you blur the line between viewer and participant, the experience is that much more memorable. At certain points in the evening, you won't even be able to tell who's actually part of the show. Performances take place Thursday through Saturday at 7:30 p.m., and every other Sunday at 5 p.m. Alcohol is served. Tickets can be purchased at thespeakeasysf.com [644 Broadway].

The Artists' Café

77 Populated by eccentric characters who sip coffee all day, **Caffe Trieste** is one of San Francisco's last bohemian enclaves. It's also the oldest café in the city, and the oldest espresso bar on the entire West Coast. Founded by an Italian immigrant in 1956, it has long served as an unofficial social club for poets, writers and artists. The walls are covered in fading photos of families and famous customers, including Luciano Pavarotti and Lawrence Ferlinghetti. Francis Ford Coppola wrote part of the script for *The Godfather* in this very spot. His portrait hangs above the mosaic table where he always sat. An old jukebox in the back of the café plays classical music, and on some Saturdays, the piano is used for performances of opera and Italian folk songs. Order an iced coffee and mingle with the crowd of fedoras and berets; some of them may have created some life-changing art [601 Vallejo St.].

The Keeper of the Beat

78

He is known as "The Mayor of North Beach." In this traditionally Italian neighborhood, where the Beat Generation flourished in the 1950s, everyone knows **Jerry Cimino**, the sixty-something expert on the famous literary and artistic movement. "They changed the world!" he exclaims. "Back in the day, this area was the center of the universe!"

In the streets of North Beach, people greet him at every corner. A walking encyclopedia of the Beat Generation, he has stories to tell about every building, every bar, every park. His hat and bag, both emblazoned with "Kerouac," attest to his passion.

As we pass Washington Square Park, he explains, "Carolyn Cassady and Jack Kerouac would come to read on the bench here." On Broadway, he points out the many strip clubs, like the famous Condor and the Hungry. "At the time, they were all jazz clubs. Charlie Parker played here. Kerouac loved going to listen to jazz. It was the hip-hop music of the time. He realized he could learn a lot from jazz musicians. He changed his prose to the fluid and spontaneous style that he's known for, and which made *On the Road* such a success."

Born in Baltimore, Maryland, Jerry Cimino arrived in California in 1988 with his wife, Estelle. He was working at IBM at the time; however, his true passion has always been literature and poetry, in particular the work of Jack Kerouac and Lawrence Ferlinghetti. "I fell for their poetry after a breakup," he laughed.

Three years later, in Monterey, the couple opened a bookstore that specialized in the literature of the Beat Generation. To promote the bookstore, Cimino managed to get the toll free number 1-800-KEROUAC, and later, the domain name "kerouac.com." A stroke of genius.

During a trip to Amsterdam, he stumbled upon the small hemp museum in the middle of the city's red-light district. "I had a revelation. Why couldn't San Francisco have its own Beat Generation museum?"

So he transformed the bookstore into a "Beat Museum," and people spontaneously started bringing him items from that era. "The day we opened, a man handed me a red vinyl record, a first edition of a poetry reading by Lawrence Ferlinghetti and Kenneth Rexroth. I told the guy "this is worth three hundred dollars," but I didn't have any money. He said "I don't want money, I want you to hang this on your wall." Since then, the museum has continued to grow. While there is no budget for acquisitions, many objects have been donated by people who knew some of the beatniks.

In 2003, Jerry Cimino found a bigger space in San Francisco's North Beach neighborhood, just steps from the legendary City Lights Bookstore, the then-epicenter of the movement. He mortgaged his house.

Thus, the **Beat Museum** was born [540 Broadway]. Spanning two floors, the

collection now includes over 1,000 photos, rare books, paintings, posters, and an array of objects, including a plaid jacket that belonged to Kerouac, Allen Ginsberg's typewriter and organ, and a striped shirt that belonged to Neal Cassady. There is even a 1949 brown Hudson (similar to the car Jack Kerouac and Neal Cassady drove across the United States), which was donated by director Walter Salles after the filming of *On the Road* (2012).

Visitors learn about the context in which the Beat Generation emerged: the Cold War, the influence of jazz on their literary style, their rejection of the status quo and their influence on the 1960s counter culture.

The artistic movement of the Beat Generation began in Manhattan's Upper West Side, and moved to San Francisco toward the end of the 1940s. "What actually happened," Cimino explained, "is that Neal Cassady followed a girl named Carolyn, who later became his wife. She wanted to make her mark as a Hollywood costume designer, but ended up in San Francisco. Jack Kerouac followed his friend Neal, and Allen Ginsberg followed his friend Jack. They fell in love with the culture. They wanted to be part of the scene. North Beach was hip at the time—an enclave of thinkers, poets, drinkers, jazz musicians and pot smokers. Everything that we consider normal today, the beatniks were talking about way back then, like concern for the environment. They were all white writers who mixed with African-Americans, Hispanics and Asians in the 1940s. They treated them as their intellectual equals, as they did women. Gays and lesbians were the leaders of the group. They were nonconformists, irresponsible, unemployed, but they changed the world."

The Headquarters of the Beat Generation

79

If you can only make it to one bookstore in San Francisco, this should be the one. Founded by poet Lawrence Ferlinghetti, **City Lights Bookstore** remains a mecca for fans of the San Francisco literary scene.

Ferlinghetti is one of the fathers of the Beat Generation. The New Yorker arrived in San Francisco in 1951 and opened the small bookstore and publishing house two years later. It sits at the corner of Columbus and Broadway, right in the heart of North Beach—the city's artistic hub at the time.

Jack Kerouac, William Burroughs and Allen Ginsberg, the leading poets of the time, made the bookstore their adopted home. It was Ferlinghetti who first published Ginsberg's poem *Howl* in 1957. The piece caused a major scandal: The first 520 copies were seized by U.S. Customs, and Ferlinghetti was charged with publishing obscene material. The lengthy court battle thrust the bookstore into the spotlight for the entire world to see. Suddenly, everyone wanted to read the infamous dirty poem.

The bookstore covers three floors. In the basement you'll find essays and general interest books, many focused on counterculture. Literature is on the main floor, and a poetry room lies upstairs. There are lots of chairs inviting customers to take their time and peruse. American authors take up a lot of the space, but there are some foreign books as well. Different literary events are held at the bookstore each week [261 Columbus Ave.].

Ferlinghetti was born in 1919—as I write this, he's 97 years old. He still lives in the neighborhood, walks its streets and spends time at the bookstore. You might run into him at **Cafe Francisco**, a nice café that's out of North Beach's tourist zone. An ideal lunch spot, they serve delicious salads, sandwiches, and bagels with smoked salmon [2161 Powell St.].

An Italian Classic

80 **Tosca Cafe** is a true institution that opened in 1919. Many prominent people have passed through its doors over the years: author Hunter S. Thompson, rock band Metallica, journalist Herb Caen, Mikhail Baryshnikov, Bono and Lauren Hutton, to name a few. It's an authentic dive bar, the kind they just don't make anymore. The owner, Jeannette Etheredge, treats every customer like a member of the family. In 2012, the bar faced bankruptcy and was considering shutting its doors. That's when Sean Penn, a regular, urged New York chefs April Bloomfield and Ken Friedman (the team behind the popular restaurant The Spotted Pig) to take over the business. Aside from creating an open kitchen, they kept the bohemian spirit of the place. The red leather benches, chandeliers, murals depicting Rome and Venice, checkered floors, the old jukebox that plays opera, and the intimate lighting were left pretty much untouched.

The menu is fairly pricey, but the food is succulent. Highlights include grilled polenta with mushrooms, lumaconi with prosciutto, Gemelli (essentially mac and cheese for adults, with pepper and pecorino) and crispy duck-fat potatoes. You won't find the homemade meatball focaccia on the menu, but it's definitely worth ordering. The star, however, is the roast chicken with ricotta, pine nuts and Marsala sauce. The dish, which is meant to be shared ($42), takes an hour to make, but the wait is so worth it. Order a Negroni in the meantime—they make it better than anyone else. And don't leave without trying their House "Cappuccino" 1919. There's no coffee in this cocktail, but rather Armagnac, bourbon, chocolate ganache and milk. It's a good idea to make a reservation, or go very late in the evening. You can also eat at the bar, and the kitchen closes at 1 a.m. [242 Columbus Ave.].

Concept Bars

81 Right next to Tosca Cafe is **The Devil's Acre**. It's a concept bar that will take you back to the Gold Rush: a time when pharmacists served elixirs and remedies to their customers during the day, and transformed their premises into saloons at night. The Devil's Acre aims at recreating that experience. It looks like a cross between an old pharmacy and a saloon, with a vast wooden bar and an upright piano for live music on certain nights. The walls are adorned with rows of antique medicine bottles, and menus come in the form of a 22-page almanac. Barmen are dressed like pharmacists from the era. To mix the cocktails, they use a device on wheels (which almost looks like some kind of torture instrument). Some cocktails have medicinal and aphrodisiac qualities (the menu shows a love potion); there's even a drink topped with gold dust. For a more intimate atmosphere, try the **Remedie Room**, another bar in the basement [256 Columbus Ave.].

Up until the start of Prohibition in 1920, San Francisco had a red light district known as the Barbary Coast. In the Gold Rush era, it was a place of brothels, jazz clubs, dance halls and concerts. **Comstock Saloon** (A), by far one of the most beautiful bars in San Francisco, is housed in a historic 1907 building, which also once housed the last of the Barbary Coast saloons. Enter the doors of the saloon and you immediately go back in time. The ceiling fan and the magnificent mahogany bar date from the early 20th century. On the mezzanine, a piano player or jazz band will be playing. The bartenders sport carefully-styled mustaches and ties or bow ties, with suspenders over their immaculate white shirts. They're also historians: Each cocktail comes with a story from the bartender. Try the Pisco Punch or the White Lily [155 Columbus Ave.].

The Greasy Spoon

83

After hitting the bars of North Beach, San Franciscans are likely to end up at **Sam's**. The tiny diner (closet-sized, really) closes around 2 a.m. For a greasy burger after a boozy night, this is your best bet. Take a seat at the counter (the television is usually playing old episodes of *Seinfeld*) and order the double cheeseburger with fries. I love the retro decor; nothing has changed since the place opened 50 years ago, not even the old orange cash register [618 Broadway].

The Tailor of Artists

82

Al Ribaya is an iconoclast—the kind that makes North Beach so authentic. His shop, **Al's Attire**, is the Ali Baba's cave of vintage clothing, fabrics, badges, shoes and tailor-made items. Ribaya was born in the Mission District, and opened his first shoemaker's shop when he was 18 years old. He specializes in leather boots, but he can make just about anything, from the fur coat of your dreams to an embroidered sports jacket to a special wedding dress. He even makes police hats for the local station. His clients include Carlos Santana, Win Butler from Arcade Fire and Herbie Hancock. Stop by the shop and say hello to his adorable dog, Vegas [1300 Grant Ave.].

San Franciscans love Fermet-Branca, an Italian liqueur which is consumed more here than anywhere else in the United States. Having a glass of this bitter liqueur is a rite of passage.

The Oldest Deli

84 No visit to San Francisco is complete without a submarine at **Molinari Delicatessen** (A), one of the oldest delis in the United States. P. G. Molinari, emigrated from the Piedmont region of Italy in 1896. His descendents run the shop today, and the place still basks in its Italian heritage. Yankees star Joe DiMaggio liked the place so much that he asked in his will that Molinari cater his funeral (which took place in 1999). "Hi, howareya? What can I getcha?" is what you'll hear, more or less, from one of the employees behind the counter. Take a number, choose your bread from the bin, then pick a sandwich from the list on the blackboard above the counter. There are 36 different sandwiches, and the price ranges from $6.75 for the Molinari Special Italian Combo to $10 for the Luciano Special, made from Parma ham, coppa, mozzarella, sundried tomatoes, onions and lettuce on toasted focaccia. Wash it down with a sparkling Italian lemonade while you sit at one of the tables outside [373 Columbus Ave.].

The sandwiches at **Little Vine** (B), a small specialty grocery store, are true delicacies. There are always two options: vegetarian, or meat. You'll also find everything you need for a fantastic picnic [1541 Grant Ave.].

Good Restaurants Around Washington Square Park

85

Right across from the park, **Mario's Bohemian Cigar Store Cafe** serves oven-baked focaccia sandwiches (my favorite is the meatball), panini and a few salads. Don't be misled by the name: They haven't sold cigars since the 1970s. It's the kind of place that's steeped in North Beach history, where local residents get together to chat over an espresso or a glass of Chianti. I like to sit outside to watch the stream of passersby. You're almost in the shadow of the magnificent spires of Saints Peter and Paul Church, on the other side of Washington Square Park [566 Columbus Ave.].

For brunch or lunch at any time of day, you can't beat **Mama's** (A). Everything is prepared at the restaurant, from the preserves to the pastries. If you go early or on weekdays, you won't have to wait in line to try their legendary omelets, French toast or eggs Benedict. The business has belonged to the Sanchez family for more than 50 years. Copies of the menu from different eras are hung on the walls [1701 Stockton St.].

Da Flora offers the perfect ambiance for a romantic evening. Rococo paintings, a handwritten menu, bright red walls, heavy curtains and a Murano glass chandelier complete the scene at this charismatic trattoria. The cozy restaurant serves creative interpretations of Venetian cuisine, but people mainly come for the sweet potato gnocchi—and the focaccia, which is served when you arrive, but gone in seconds. Everything is handmade [701 Columbus Ave.].

For the best seafood in the neighborhood, go to **Sotto Mare** and order the Cioppino, a huge bowl of crab legs, mussels, shrimp, white fish and clams in a savory broth with tomatoes, garlic and wine. Bibs are provided, and the staff suggests you share the dish between two people—personally, I'd say it's substantial enough to feed four. The dish originated in the area in the 19th century: Local Italian fishermen would fill a pot with whatever was leftover from the days fishing haul. Say hello to the owner, Rich Azzolino, who's a very sweet guy [552 Green St.].

Offering the perfect combination of Asian and American cuisine, **The House** has been a North Beach favorite since the 1990s. From the BLT sandwich and the grilled tuna with wasabi mayo to the signature dish, grilled sea bass with ginger soy sauce, the inventive cuisine of Larry and Angela Tse always delights [1230 Grant Ave.].

Travel Back in Time

86 Jim Schein is San Francisco's map master. His shop, **Schein & Schein**, specializes in old maps, engravings, atlases and other historical trinkets. The shelves are stacked from floor to ceiling with precious documents that must be handled with care. Jim, a veteran of the music industry (he toured for years with artists like Metallica and The Rolling Stones) has been fascinated by maps since he was a child. He's been collecting for decades and unearthed many of the store's items during his numerous trips. A few years ago, he decided to share his passion with the world. His collection includes specimens from the 19th and 20th century: There are maps from across the globe, although the focus is on San Francisco and California. A good place to find an original gift, the store's selection accomodates every budget, with prices ranging from $5 to $5,000 [1435 Grant Ave.].

Jacqueline's Soufflés

87 Across the street from Schein & Schein, **Cafe Jacqueline** will whisk you away to Paris. The little French bistrot with fresh roses on the tables is owned by local legend Jacqueline Margulis. She created one of the most unusual restaurants in the city, which specializes in soufflés, both sweet and savory. Since 1979, she's prepared each soufflé by hand, one at a time, as it is ordered. The menu also features salads and a delicious onion soup, along with about 20 soufflés. My favorite is the prosciutto and mushroom, and the lemon soufflé for dessert. Each soufflé is for two people [1454 Grant Ave.].

Perfect Pizza

88 The wait can be long, but the pizza made by Tony Gemignani, owner of **Tony's Pizza Napoletana**, is worth it. Tony is the first American to have won the prize for Best Margherita Pizza at the World Pizza Cup in Naples in 2007. He perfected his craft over the years, and his restaurant is a veritable museum of pizza styles from around the world. He offers 12 varieties, including New York, St. Louis, Sicilian, Napoletana and The Barcelona. The pizzas are cooked in seven different ovens (wood, coal, gas, electric, etc.) at different temperatures. If you'd like to try something unique, order the Romana, a large rectangular pizza with three different sections of toppings: one is for the appetizer (prosciutto, arugula and Parmigiano-Reggiano), one is a main course (meatballs with ricotta and garlic) and one is for dessert (dates, pecans, apple slices, Nutella, honey and gorgonzola). It's for sharing [1570 Stockton St.].

I'm also a fan of the pizza with homemade mozzarella at **Il Casaro**. Despite the modern decor, it somehow feels like you're in an Italian grandmother's kitchen [348 Columbus Ave.].

The Man Who's Seen it All

89 A few years ago, the author and journalist **Gary Kamiya** gave himself the somewhat outlandish goal of visiting every street in San Francisco as a way to deepen his understanding of the city he loves so much.

He called this exercise "Doing the Knowledge," inspired by the expression used by London taxi drivers, who have to know the streets by heart in order to pass their taxi-driver exams. Having himself been a taxi driver in San Francisco for seven years early in his career, he has enough stories to last a lifetime (a customer once held a gun to his head, for example).

"If you divide the city into 1,000 approximately quarter-mile-square grids, I can honestly say that I have set foot or bike tire on every them," said the editor of *San Francisco Magazine*.

Born in Oakland in 1953, Gary grew up in Berkeley and has spent his entire adult life in San Francisco. This pilgrimage through the city took over a year, and he now proudly bears the title of "Walking Encyclopedia". You can also let yourself be transported by Gary's soothing voice by downloading the **Detour** application (detour.com/detours/san-francisco/cool-gray-city), in which he narrates a fascinating tour of North Beach and Chinatown.

His research and findings led him to write *Cool Gray City of Love: 49 Views of San Francisco*, one of my favorite works about the city. In each chapter, he introduces readers to an area of San Francisco through personal and historical anecdotes. "Because of its unique topography, each neighborhood developed its own character." Through the lens of history, geology and topography, Gary helps you discover the city from new perspectives. The expression *cool gray city of love* comes from a poem by George Sterling.

Why 49 views? "The number 49 is symbolic in San Francisco. It refers to the Gold Rush (1849) and the gold-seekers, who were called "forty-niners." There is also the 49-Mile Scenic Drive, the scenic route through the city." And San Francisco's NFL team is called the 49ers.

Gary Kamiya agreed to meet me in a café in North Beach, close to where he lives. It's a neighborhood he describes as a happy valley surrounded by three beautiful hills: Telegraph Hill, Russian Hill and Nob Hill. "Historically, this was ground zero for San Francisco. During the Gold Rush, this area was the heart of the city, especially where **Portsmouth Square** borders Chinatown. This is where the first school was built."

He loves San Francisco, "a city borrowed from the sea," for its European feel, Mediterranean climate, and the fact that he can walk everywhere. He particularly likes the streets downtown, between Union Square and Nob Hill, because of the 1930s architecture. "This neighborhood exudes nostalgia."

I could listen to Gary talk for hours. His love for the city is contagious. "This is a city where you can show the side of you that's a bit crazy, a bit weird. It's a city of nonconformists—we don't follow New York's beat, we have our own pace."

"You can say you're San Franciscan if you come here open to new experiences. It's not how long you've been here that counts. Being San Franciscan is a state of mind," says Gary Kamiya.

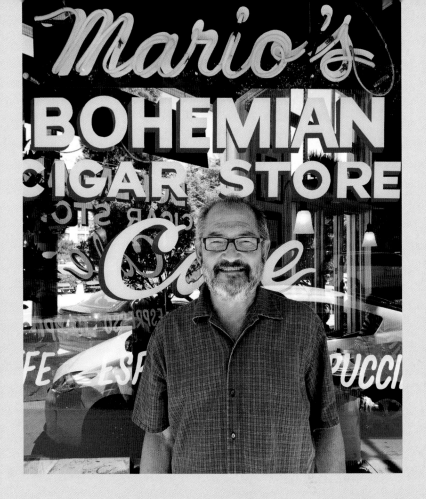

After all these years, the city continues to amaze him every day. "I have spent much of my life exploring San Francisco. But perhaps it is better not to see everything. To let a small mystery stand in for the great one. To know that somewhere far below, down there where the sea crashes endlessly into the land, is a rock that I will never climb," he wrote in conclusion to his work.

The Parakeets of Telegraph Hill

90

Because of its many hills, San Francisco is lined with staircases and secret passages—they form a kind of alternate grid in the city. Moving through them adds a sense of adventure and makes the everyday more interesting. Some streets transform into stairways; some stairways take up entire streets. There are almost 600 of these staircases, and each has a distinct personality—so moving around S.F. leads to constant amazement. For me, it's absolutely the best thing about the city. The **Filbert Steps** (A), a 400-step stairway, brings you from Sansome Street, at bay level, to Coit Tower, 275 feet (84 meters) higher. The stunning tower was erected in 1933 through a donation from the eccentric heiress Lillie Hitchcock Coit. The long staircase is lined with colorful houses and fuchsias, lemon trees, palms, cypresses and magnolias. Two wooden passageways connect perpendicularly with the staircase: Napier Lane and Darrell Place. You'll find the oldest homes in the city on these little streets.

Watch your surroundings carefully: Dozens of wild parakeets (red-masked, a South American breed) live in this enchanted site. No one knows how they got to Telegraph Hill. One hypothesis is that some birds escaped from a pet store owner sometime in the 1990s. As you climb the steps, look to the right when you get to Montgomery Street. You'll see the **Malloch Building** (B), an architectural marvel. The apartment building, built in 1937, is art deco in style—more specifically, it's streamline moderne: curved and resembling a ship. Its appartments offer an unsurpassed view of the bay [1360 Montgomery St.].

91A

The Fog Bridge

91

The **Exploratorium** museum has an original installation that honors San Francisco's famous fog. **Fog Bridge #72494** (A) is a 150-foot-long pedestrian bridge connecting Pier 15 and Pier 17. The bridge is bathed in thick fog, generated by 800 high-pressure nozzles—the effect as you walk across it is completely disorienting. The installation, by Japanese artist Fujiko Nakaya, is free to visit. While you're there, don't miss the exhibits inside the Exploratorium; most are interactive. The Exploratorium is one of the best 20th-century science museums [Pier 15 at Green St.].

After, stop at **Fog City** (B), a diner looking out on The Embarcadero. Most dishes are cooked in a wood oven. Oysters are $1.50 from 4 p.m. to 7 p.m., Monday to Friday. Kids get to feast on mac and cheese; the fries are also quite popular [1300 Battery St.].

Tapas on the Water

92

For quality tapas, Michael Chiarello's restaurant **Coqueta** offers a wide selection of the small Spanish dishes for sharing, including an excellent platter of cured meats and Iberian cheeses, and a paella which alone is worth the trip. The restaurant is right on the water, and there are a few outdoor tables. The view of the bay in the evening is sublime. Save room for churros, which you dip in chocolate, and their apple pie [Pier 5, The Embarcadero].

91B

Swimming in the Bay

93

Every day, rain or shine, some 200 people swim in the frigid waters of San Francisco Bay. Some venture as far as Alcatraz. Most of these swimmers are members of a very special group: The Dolphin Club, a bastion of authenticity in the most touristic part of the city, Fisherman's Wharf. Generally, the area is more or less the Times Square of San Francisco (and I don't mean that as a compliment).

I discovered the club by chance while walking near Aquatic Park, a small stretch of public beach in North Beach. Someone caught my attention: Seth Katzman, 69, wearing only a blue Speedo and an orange cap, preparing to dive into the bay. He looked like he was taken straight from the movie *The Life Aquatic*.

The water was just 62°F (17°C) that day. Katzman has been swimming with the club three to five times a week since he was 16 years old, without a wet suit!

The club's white-and-blue building was built in 1877 by German immigrants who wanted to have a sports club in their adopted city. When it opened, the swimming and rowboating club had 25 members; today there are more than 1,500. The club is private, but visitors can visit the premises if they're curious. Just ring the bell and someone will let you in. Ask to speak to the concierge, who will show you around the facilities.

It's a fascinating visit. Black-and-white photos of swimmers cover the mahogany walls. One is of Jack LaLanne. In 1974, LaLanne swam, towing a boat, all the way from Alcatraz to the club—and he did it while handcuffed and shackled. He managed the feat in less than 90 minutes.

Upstairs, swimmers read newspapers in the rest room, wedged into big captain's chairs, while one of the members prepares a huge meal in the kitchen.

In one of the workshops, you might see Julia, 25, building a wooden boat. She pretty much grew up at the club—her

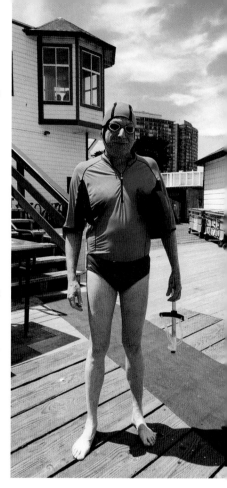

parents are honorary members—and today she builds its gleaming boats. She studied at the Northwest School of Wooden Boat Building, a prestigious school near Seattle. There she learned the craft of building the little nautical treasures—some of which are worth $200,000. The club takes them out in the bay on special occasions.

If you want to experience swimming in the bay and you're not afraid of turning a little blue, the club allows access to their facilities from Tuesday to Saturday (the cost is $10), from 10 a.m. to 6 p.m. It's an unforgettable experience [502 Jefferson St.].

95

Wooded Paradise

94 **Macondray Lane** is a magical place—the kind of place people dream of living in. The stone-paved pedestrian walkway, between Union and Green streets in the Russian Hill neighborhood, stretches for two blocks. Its houses—some dating from 1850—have been home to various artists, poets and writers over the years. The entrance to the lane is on Taylor Street. Climb the large wooden staircase: You'll find a miniature forest at the top. It's dense and lush, with eucalyptus, fern beds, a fountain and a statue of Buddha. The vegetation absorbs the city's noise. **Havens Street** is another flowery passageway right nearby. The entrance to the staircase is on Leavenworth, between Filbert and Union. Don't miss **Ina Coolbrith Park** (named after the famous American poet and grand dame of San Francisco) in the same neighborhood. The multi-level flower garden offers a view of the Bay Bridge and Coit Tower. You'll sometimes see wild parakeets there. The entrance is at the corner of Vallejo and Taylor streets.

The Saint of Coffee

95 There's no shortage of cafés in San Francisco, but I have a special fondness for **Saint Frank Coffee**. The name is an homage to Saint Francis of Assisi, San Francisco's namesake. With a minimalist Scandinavian design, the café is Kevin Bohlin's baby. Bohlin is a former high school teacher, and today the café is his career and his passion. During his travels, he has formed close relationships with coffee producers in Honduras, Guatemala, Bolivia, Kenya and India. He shares these growers' stories and speaks warmly about the origin of each beverage as he makes espressos. He decided to lower the height of the counters and hide the coffee machines underneath, to allow for more fluid conversation between baristas and clients. Be sure to sample the homemade almond-macadamia lattés, and the Kaffe Tonic, a surprising and refreshing blend of espresso and sparkling water, served on ice. Laptops are welcome on the main floor [2340 Polk St.].

Diego Rivera's Mural

96 The **San Francisco Art Institute** is one of the oldest and most prestigious modern art schools in the country. Founded in 1871, it occupied several different buildings before settling into its current location in 1925. This private university is open to the public, and the galleries, library and roof are worth a visit. The Spanish-style building has a large bell tower, built by Arthur Brown Jr.—the same architect who designed San Francisco City Hall, Coit Tower and the War Memorial Opera House. Visitors pass through an interior courtyard with a fountain in the middle and students' artworks displayed on the surrounding walls. The room to the left is a gallery space, where you can see a large mural by Diego Rivera—it reaches stories high. The Mexican artist painted "The Making of a Fresco Showing the Building of a City," in 1931.

Behind the main building, there's a concrete annex; visit the roof for a panoramic view of the city. The rooftop café is also open to the public. A number of masters of film and photography studied at the school, including Annie Leibovitz, who began taking photos for *Rolling Stone* magazine in 1968, while she was still a student. Ansel Adams founded the school's photography department in 1945 [800 Chestnut St.]. **Caffe Sapore**, right nearby, serves soups, salads and excellent sandwiches and bagels [790 Lombard St.].

Rare Jewels

97 For unique and refined jewelry, I like to visit **No. 3** boutique. The owner, Jenny Chung, has impeccable style and an obvious flair for finding pieces from emerging designers—just take a look at the many rings on her fingers. If you're looking for an original wedding ring, this is the place. During my last visit, the sign in front of the shop gave clear instructions: "Put a ring on it!" [1987 Hyde St.].

Gourmet Across the Globe

98 Polk Street isn't part of the normal tourist circuit. But it's a good place to find cafés, bars, independent boutiques and restaurants with cuisine from all over the world. Here are the places I like to eat in Russian Hill:

For a taste of the Alps, I go to **Leopold's**. The warm, kitchy, playful vibe of the restaurant will transport you directly to a Bavarian *gasthaus* (chalet). The yellow walls are adorned with family photos, old oil paintings, hunting trophies and stuffed deer heads with felt hats. The male servers even wear the traditional garb of Alpine farmers, while the female servers dress like the damsels on the label of St. Pauli Girl beer. Plates of schnitzel and sauerkraut are generously portioned, and the beer flows freely. Try the tagliatelle with butternut squash, the chicken soup, the pancetta-wrapped trout and the apple strudel [2400 Polk St.].

For a New York-style pizza, head to the family-run restaurant **Gioia Pizzeria**. Try the Rosa Bianca pizza (olives, red onions, mozzarella, marjoram and tomatoes) or the Julian (house-made sausage, kale, red onion, fresh garlic and chili flakes). They also serve great seasonal salads as appetizers [2240 Polk St.].

Aux Delices is one of the best Vietnamese restaurants in the city—the perfect place to get pho with chicken or beef. Most dishes cost less than $12 [2327 Polk St.].

Don't be fooled by the outdated decor of **Dim Sum Club**; the food is delicious and affordable. Order the Shanghai soup dumplings and the eggplant with black bean sauce. Truly a feast for just a couple of dollars [2550 Van Ness Ave.].

Another spot with dubious decor (bright red walls, crystal chandeliers, disco ball, SpongeBob piñata, etc.) is **Nick's Crispy Tacos**. With plenty of TV screens hanging from the ceiling, the spot is especially popular during sporting events. A taqueria during the day, it converts to a nightclub in the evening (hence the design choices). Try the fried fish tacos and the chips-and-guacamole appetizer. Tacos are about $4 each, and they take cash only [1500 Broadway, at the corner of Polk St.].

For excellent sandwiches, the gourmet corner market **Cheese Plus** has a takeout counter that's perfect for picking up picnic supplies. The sandwiches are named after famous San Francisco residents. Try the Willie Brown Bird (named in honor of the city's former mayor). It has smoked duck breast, provolone and fig chutney [2001 Polk St.].

A Romantic Evening on Hyde Street

99 Hyde Street is one of the most romantic streets in the city. It's lined with trees and quality restaurants with a few tables on the terraces. Cable cars climb and descend the hill, to the delight of smiling and waving tourists. It's picture-postcard San Francisco. Start your evening at **Union Larder** (A), a former garage that's been converted into a wine bar with large windows looking out on the street. Their specialties are cheese and charcuterie platters, but they also have small dishes to share, like raclette, fondue and oysters [1945 Hyde St.].

Don't forget to check out the surrounding area. The house right around the corner, at 29 Russell Street, is where Jack Kerouac stayed as a guest in 1951 and 1952; his friends Neal and Carolyn Cassady lived there and let him stay with them. It was in the attic of this small house that Kerouac wrote *Visions of Cody*, *Doctor Sax* and his greatest success, *On the Road.*

The hushed, intimate atmosphere of the local bistro **Frascati** makes it ideal for a romantic rendezvous. The Mediterranean-inspired menu changes regularly, but some dishes are staples, like the russet potato gnocchi, fresh pasta, risotto and black-and-white-chocolate bread pudding [1901 Hyde St.].

Across the street is another charming neighborhood bistro. **Stones Throw** specializes in New American cuisine, and its influences come from all over. Try the puffed potato and eggs, the squid ink pasta, the duck breast, the duck pâté, and the peanut butter and jelly donuts. Everything goes great with their Pimm's Cup cocktail. You'll want to return for brunch the very next day [1896 Hyde St.].

For a wonderfully relaxing evening, visit **Za Pizza**. The friendly and colorful owner, Buzzy Campisano, decided to place a few tables on the distinctly sloping sidewalk. Eating at them is a balancing act, but that's just part of the charm. The large pizzas are crunchy with a thin crust. I love the Popeye the Greek (spinach and feta) and the Vincent Van Dough (Italian tomatoes, basil and garlic). The walls of the restaurant are covered in drawings by neighborhood children; Buzzy has watched many of them grow up over the years [1919 Hyde St.].

Elephant Sushi is directly across from Za Pizza. The place is small and very popular, so unless you go early, you may have to wait a bit. Customers keep coming back because of chef Tom Tamir's originality, and because a meal at Elephant Sushi is an event in itself. The raw fish is served on a block of Himalayan sea salt. The sea bass roll, wrapped in aluminum foil, is flaming when it arrives at your table. One of their sushi dishes is called Beastie Boy: a sure sign that the place is rock 'n' roll. At the end of the meal, customers write their comments on a piece of white paper hanging in the entrance [1916 Hyde St.]. A few doors down, **Okoze Sushi** also has a loyal following. The menu is more traditional and the fish is always fresh [1207 Union St.].

Complete your evening with an ice cream at **Swensen's Ice Cream** (B), a neighborhood staple since 1948. The founder, Earle Swensen, learned how to make ice cream while he was in the army during World War II. He created more than 150 flavors. The ice cream is still made on the premises, using Earle's original recipes. Order the Sticky Chewy Chocolate, and eat your cone under the neon Ice Cream Sherbet in front of the shop. Closed on Mondays [1999 Hyde St.].

Nob Hill, Chinatown and the Financial District

Rising at a steep incline, Nob Hill is home to a neo-Gothic cathedral, big hotels, and magnificent homes clinging to its hillsides. Contrasting sharply with "Snob Hill," Chinatown, at the bottom of the hill, offers much more exotic scenery, and the big market on Stockton Street is bustling on Saturday afternoons. Go to the Financial District to experience its skyscrapers, beaux-arts-style buildings and rooftop gardens.

HOBART BUILDING

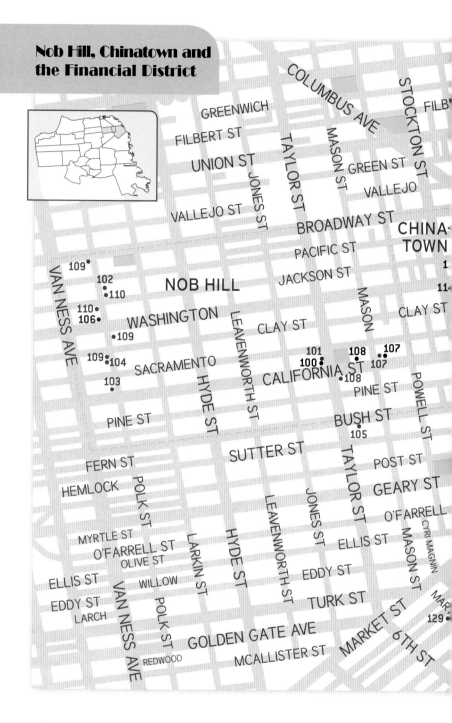

Nob Hill, Chinatown and the Financial District

COLUMBUS AVE
STOCKTON ST
FILB
GREENWICH
FILBERT ST
UNION ST
TAYLOR ST
MASON ST
GREEN ST
VALLEJO
JONES ST
VALLEJO ST
BROADWAY ST
CHINA-TOWN
PACIFIC ST
1
109
JACKSON ST
102
NOB HILL
110
11
110
MASON
CLAY ST
106
WASHINGTON
109
CLAY ST
LEAVENWORTH ST
109
104
101
108
107
100
108
107
SACRAMENTO
CALIFORNIA ST
103
108
PINE ST
HYDE ST
POWELL ST
PINE ST
BUSH ST
105
SUTTER ST
FERN ST
POST ST
HEMLOCK
GEARY ST
POLK ST
O'FARRELL
TAYLOR ST
JONES ST
CYRIL MAGNIN
MYRTLE ST
LEAVENWORTH ST
O'FARRELL ST
OLIVE ST
LARKIN ST
HYDE ST
ELLIS ST
MASON ST
ELLIS ST
WILLOW
EDDY ST
EDDY ST
VAN NESS AVE
TURK ST
MAR
LARCH
POLK ST
GOLDEN GATE AVE
MARKET ST
129
REDWOOD
MCALLISTER ST
6TH ST
VAN NESS AVE

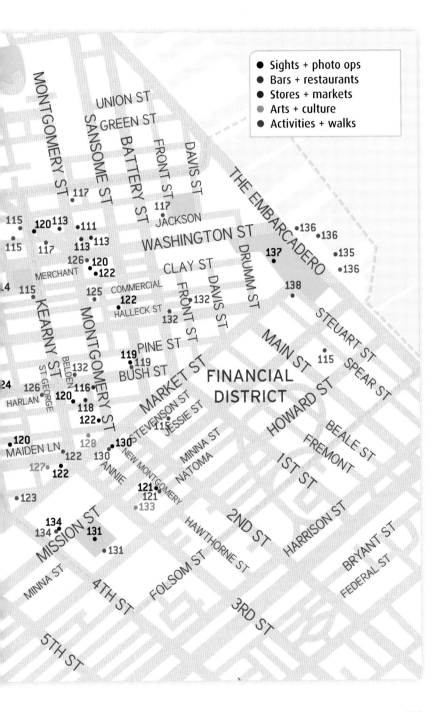

● Sights + photo ops
● Bars + restaurants
● Stores + markets
● Arts + culture
● Activities + walks

MONTGOMERY ST
UNION ST
GREEN ST
SANSOME ST
BATTERY ST
FRONT ST
DAVIS ST
THE EMBARCADERO

117
117
JACKSON
115 120 113 111
115 117 113 113
126 120
MERCHANT 122
115
125 COMMERCIAL
122
HALLECK ST
WASHINGTON ST
CLAY ST
DRUMM ST
136 136
137
135
136
138
STEUART ST

4
KEARNY ST
MONTGOMERY ST
132
132
FRONT ST
DAVIS ST
MAIN ST
115
SPEAR ST

119 PINE ST
119
BUSH ST
BELDEN
ST GEORGE
132
24 126 116
HARLAN 120
118
122
MARKET ST
STEVENSON ST
JESSIE ST
FINANCIAL
DISTRICT
HOWARD ST
BEALE ST
FREMONT
1ST ST

120
MAIDEN LN
128
122 130 130
127
122
ANNIE
NEW MONTGOMERY
115
MINNA ST
NATOMA

123
121
121
133
2ND ST
HARRISON ST

134
134 MISSION ST 131
131
HAWTHORNE ST
FOLSOM ST
3RD ST
BRYANT ST
FEDERAL ST

MINNA ST
4TH ST

5TH ST

The Sisters of Perpetual Indulgence

100 I saw her in the distance, climbing confidently up California Street, balancing on sky-high heels; she must have been at least two meters tall. Around her neck, a turquoise boa fluttered playfully in the wind; there was no doubting that this was **Sister Roma**.

I met her on the steps of Grace Cathedral in Nob Hill. Dressed in drag, wearing leather leggings and a sequined jacket, she looked out of place in the very exclusive neighborhood where we found ourselves, nicknamed "Snob Hill."

"Great! We need more queens in this neighborhood," said a resident, amazed to see Sister Roma in this part of town. "We were driven out by the families invading The Castro—now we're moving to Nob Hill!" Sister Roma joked in response.

A young gay man approached us. "Roma! I've been sober for six months." Roma replied with a tender "Congratulations."

A group of tourists got out of a bus. Gawking, they took out their cameras. "Hi everyone, we are an order of sisters that's been around for 35 years—we're coming to your city soon, watch out!" Roma quipped.

Sister Roma is a member of the Order of Perpetual Indulgence, an LGBT activist movement born in San Francisco in 1979, in the Castro District. The order now has "convents" in 20 U.S. and European cities. We were later joined by **Sister Madelyne**, who explained, "I'd been watching them since 1998, and I finally got it in 2013. At first I thought it was a secret organization."

The sisters use Catholic imagery and nuns' clothing in festive and theatrical ways. Some of their names are equally theatrical: Sister Grand Mother Vicious Power Hungry Bitch; Sister Tina Noodle Cocktail; Sister Angelina Holi; or Sister Mina J'Trois.

Born Michael Williams in a remote part of Michigan, Sister Roma found a job with the sisters on arriving in San Francisco in the late 1980s. "Their values helped me find myself," Roma explained. "I was 22 years old. The sisters saved my life. They lifted me out of drug hell."

The Sisters fight against homophobia, transphobia, racism, discrimination, sexism and homelessness. They have raised over one million dollars for a variety of social causes, and were at the forefront of the fight against AIDS in the 1980s. One of their founding members, Bobbi Campbell (Sister Florence Nightmare), became one of the faces of AIDS after being featured on the cover of *Newsweek* magazine in 1983.

"When I started, we were always being asked if it was Halloween," said Sister Roma. Their antics earned them a place in the list of papal heretics in 1987, after Pope John Paul II visited San Francisco. "I know some real sisters and they love us!" said Sister Roma, who dresses up at least twice a week to host charity events. It takes more than two hours to prepare. "There is no separation between who I am and my character." Sister Roma makes a living as an art director for a gay porn site.

San Franciscans are very respectful of the organization. "We worked very hard to earn that respect. San Francisco is the most progressive city in the United States, and the only place where an organization like ours could be born and become part of the cultural and political fabric of the city. It is a city where a man can dress up as a nun and wear makeup to raise money for his community, and people get it. San Francisco has always been a city where people want to change things, express themselves, and adopt new ideas and cultures."

The Grace Cathedral Labryrinth

101

Construction of **Grace Cathedral**, a neo-Gothic style Episcopal cathedral, was completed in 1964, after almost 115 years. The highlight is the limestone labyrinth near the entrance. It's an exact reproduction of the medieval labyrinth at the Chartres Cathedral, southwest of Paris. Take a meditative journey on its path: It's an experience to add to your scrapbook. You can also see a Keith Haring piece, dedicated to victims of AIDS, in the alcove to the right of the door at the entrance [1100 California St.].

Dinner at the Butcher's

102

Belcampo Meat Co. is a carnivore's heaven. An organic meat counter is set up near the entrance; a dining area is attached, with wooden walls and blue leather booths. The steak tartare is one of their specialties, as is the roast beef sandwich and the lamb burger (with feta, arugula and kalamata olives). All the meat comes from their ranch at the foot of Mount Shasta in Northern California [1998 Polk St.].

Lunch at the Fish Shop

103

Take a seat at **Swan Oyster Depot**, a small restaurant that seats 20, and order the oysters, shrimp salad, lobster, octopus, raw scallops, smoked salmon, clam chowder, sea urchin, and their specialty: Dungeness crab. Regulars know to order the crab back; your sourdough bread is perfect for dipping in its delectable fat. The seafood is served with four sauces (cocktail, mignonette, horseradish and garlic), a bottle of Tabasco sauce, wedges of lemon and crackers. Wash it all down with a glass of sauvignon blanc. Chat with the friendly, mustachioed servers and peruse the yellowed photos on the walls. The charm of the place is unbeatable; you won't find a more authentic spot. The business has been open for more than 100 years, and it's as popular as ever—so expect to wait in line. It's open from 10:30 a.m. to 5:30 p.m., six days a week (closed on Sundays). The lineup starts at 10:00, and some bring a bottle of wine to make the wait more enjoyable. Cash only [1517 Polk St.].

Legendary Donuts

104

"A balanced diet is a chocolate donut in each hand." That's the motto of **Bob's Donuts**, a family institution that opened its doors in 1960. The place hasn't changed; it still has the same melamine counter and brown leather stools. Open 24 hours a day, the donut shop really starts filling up after the bars close. I like going late. They make a new batch of donuts around midnight, and as the night goes on it starts to feel like the shop is a theater for an urban play, with a cast of tipsy, colorful guests. If you're brave of heart—and strong of stomach—order the Big Donut ($8). It's about the size of your head. The challenge is to eat the whole thing in less than three minutes. If you manage it, you'll win a T-shirt, and your name will be listed on the Hall of Fame. Definitely decadent [1621 Polk St.].

The People's Pizzeria

105

After your visit to Grace Cathedral, stop in at **Del Popolo**. The Neapolitan pizzas made by chef Jonathan Darsky have earned a cult following. I have a weakness for the Bianca pizza, with mozzarella, ricotta, basil and garlic. [855 Bush St.].

If there's a long wait, grab a drink at the bar a few doors down the street, **Stookey's Club Moderne**. The decor is styled after ocean liners from the 1930s [895 Bush St.].

Vintage Finds

106

To score the perfect leather jacket, jean jacket or nylon jacket (with the logo of your favorite sports team), rock T-shirts, a fantastic kimono, flowery dress or designer shoes, go to **Relove**. The clothing store's owner, Delila, has impeccable taste. She picks each item with care, and her collection skillfully combines vintage clothing with pieces by designers like Yves Saint Laurent, Isabel Marant and Jil Sander. Delila adds new items to the displays almost every day. The shop has an intimate feel; it's almost like you're looking through an elegant friend's wardrobe [1815 Polk St.].

Tempest in a Teacup

107

Having a drink at the **Tonga Room & Hurricane Bar** is a theatrical experience. The tiki bar is hidden in the basement of the luxurious Hotel Fairmont, at the top of Nob Hill. Formerly the hotel's pool (which was built in 1929), it was converted into a lagoon in 1945. On the lagoon is a barge carrying an orchestra that plays for guests. Every 20 minutes, an artificial storm breaks out, and it starts raining right in the middle of the restaurant. There's even thunder and lightning. The dance floor wood was originally from the S.S. *Forester*, one of the last wooden schooners that traveled between San Francisco and the South Sea Islands.

For cocktails, try the Mai Tai (first made in Oakland in the 1940s), the Lava Bowl or the Zombie: a blend of three rums and fruit juice, to share between two or four people, using two-foot-long straws. It's a paradise of little colored umbrellas, plastic leis and cocktails in pineapples and bowls. The Polynesian paradise also serves dishes inspired by South Pacific cuisine (tuna poke, Hawaiian dumplings, crab tacos, green papaya salad, BBQ pork chops and Tahitian mahimahi). Closed on Mondays and Tuesdays [950 Mason St.].

Don't miss the quiet, secluded gardens on the roof of the Fairmont Hotel, on the same floor as the hall, next to the Pavillion Room. Along with fountains and palm trees, you'll find a garden designed to attract bees. There are almost 300,000 bees in the beehive, collecting pollen from lavender, thyme, basil, chive and coriander flowers. The hotel manufactures its own honey and brews its own honey beer.

A Scotch in Old San Francisco

108

If you want to have a drink in an "old SF" atmosphere, I recommend **The Big 4**, the bar in The Scarlet Huntington Hotel. Music will be flowing from the grand piano at the entrance. Take a seat on one of the leather sofas and let yourself be transported to another time. The walls are covered in historic photos, vintage objects and memorabilia from California's fascinating history. The bar's name pays homage to a famous group of industrialists known as "The Big Four." Collis P. Huntington, Charles Crocker, Leland Stanford and Mark Hopkins were railway magnates who played a major role in San Francisco's development in the 19th century. They all lived in lavish residences in the neighborhood [1075 California St.].

There's an impressive mansion at 1000 California Street, just across the street from the bar. It belonged to the wealthy industrialist James C. Flood, who made his fortune in precious metals. The house is considered the very first brownstone (referring to the reddish-brown sandstone used) west of the Mississippi River. Along with the Fairmont Hotel across the street, it's the only structure in the neighborhood that survived the 1906 earthquake. The house is the headquarters of the **Pacific-Union Club** (A). The very select private club has been around for more than 125 years. Only men are admitted—wives still have to enter through a back door to dine with their husbands.

108 A

An Evening on Polk Street

109

Start your evening at the wine bar **Amelie**. The small candle-lit bar, with two French owners, has a wide selection of French wines, as well as bottles from South Africa, California, Chile, New Zealand and Australia. Jazz musicians play in the entrance. From 5:00 p.m. to 7 p.m., three glasses of wine are just $10. The decor is eclectic: Barrels serve as tables, and old theater seats are used as chairs. You can order from a range of cheeses, charcuterie and small dishes to share at the bar [1754 Polk St.].

Continue the fun at **Lord Stanley**, a restaurant that serves contemporary British-influenced cuisine. The menu ranges between dishes that are rustic but refined (such as butternut squash tarte Tatin, quince and curry), and other more complex ones, like a deconstructed bouillabaisse. The couple that owns the restaurant learned their craft in top New York restaurants and at Le Manoir aux Quat'Saisons in England. Note: like in Europe, all the prices include service. There's no need to tip [2065 Polk St.].

Finish things off at **Harper & Rye**, a two-floor bar with rustic and industrial decor. It has a pool table, a piano, delicious specialty cocktails and punch bowls [1695 Polk St.].

Ice Cream Like no Other

110

Vietnamese cinnamon, goat cheese, prosciutto and dates, brie and strawberry, eucalyptus, honey and wasabi, tequila and strawberry, buttermilk and cucumber, and jalapeno and peanut butter—the mix of flavors might not seem to have much in common. But they're all unusual flavors of Italian ice cream you can sample at **Lush Gelato**. The Argentinian owner, Federico Murtagh, is the genius behind these creations. The selection changes from day to day, so each visit to his little shop is always a surprise. Federico makes his own ice cream base, and he infuses all his flavors with ingredients from local farms. A big window lets you see what's happening in the kitchen. Give in to the temptation to try the famous ice cream sandwich, which has a donut in place of a cookie. Delectable. [1817 Polk St.].

For a lighter option, I like the smoothies and frozen acai bowls at **Basik Cafe**, a chain originally from Kona, Hawaii. Try the Banyan bowl (natural peanut butter, cashew milk and acai, topped with almonds, hemp seeds, granola and pollen). It's a little expensive, but fabulous [1958 Polk St.].

The Mecca of Art Books

111

I love shopping at **William Stout Architectural Books**; it's one of my favorite bookstores and a major source of inspiration. It has more than 20,000 books on architecture, art, urban planning, furniture, landscape architecture, and interior and industrial graphic design. The owner, William Stout, an architect by trade, started the shop more than 30 years ago. His friends and colleagues would always ask him to bring back books on design and architecture when he traveled to Europe. Over the years he has amassed an impressive collection, with a number of real rarities. The books are stacked to the ceiling [804 Montgomery St.].

Make Your Own Fortune Cookie

112

In the middle of the oldest alley in Chinatown, the aroma of vanilla will show you the way to the **Golden Gate Fortune Cookie Company**. Operating since 1962, the small factory still makes fortune cookies by hand for many Chinatown restaurants. Visitors can see the premises and buy cookies individually or by the bag. For $1, you can write a wish on a slip of paper and have it inserted into a cookie. They'll give it to you in a tiny box to take home—a sweet little souvenir.

The production line is run by just three employees. One is Nancy Tom, who has been making cookies for 39 years—and she has marks on her hands to prove it. Sitting in front of an old griddle press, she grabs each disk of dough while it's still hot. Then she inserts a little piece of paper bearing a fortune or a wise saying, and folds the dough by hand on a metal rod. Because the cookies harden instantly, Tom has to work fast, risking burnt fingers in the process. Scraps and broken cookies are placed in a box at the front so customers can snack on them [56 Ross Alley].

114A

Magic Potions

114

Great China Herb Co. (A), a Chinese pharmacy open since 1922, will seem truly exotic to anyone who's unfamiliar with Chinese medicine. The business has been in the same family for three generations, and they don't speak much English. Dr. Mary, an acupuncturist and herbalist, starts by taking your pulse. She then asks you a flurry of questions about your health, and writes a prescription, in Mandarin, that will cure all your ills. Take the slip of paper to the herb counter. There, the pharmacists will dig through dozens of jars and drawers filled with roots, ginseng, apricot kernel, goji berries, honeysuckle flowers, dried chrysanthemum and so on. For a few dollars, you'll leave with bags of herbs that have been meticulously weighed on ancient scales, and your bill is calculated on an old wooden abacus. Your instructions are to boil each mixture in water and drink the infusion. As for the taste—don't ask. The herbalist is in on Tuesdays, Thursdays and Saturdays [857 Washington St.].

Tea lovers will fall for the **Red Blossom Tea Company**. Siblings Peter and Alice Luong run the place, which was founded by their parents. They're true tea enthusiasts, and their passion is contagious. Each year during spring harvest, the duo travels the world in search of rare teas. You can try more than 100 imported teas in their little shop [831 Grant Ave.].

Designer Boutiques in the Historical District

113

Jackson Square is one of the oldest neighborhoods in San Francisco. The streets are lined with trees, and most of the buildings date back to the Gold Rush era. I like to stroll around and check out the treasures in the many designer and fashion boutiques. French designer **Isabel Marant** has a great store in the neighborhood [455 Jackson St.]. I also like to stop at **Filson**, a boutique founded in Seattle in 1897. The store has a range of travel bags, camera bags, leather accessories and outdoor goods. The company **Shinola** shares the same space; its products (watches, bikes, leather goods) are made in Detroit [722 Montgomery St.].

After that, I usually go to **Eden & Eden**. Rachel, the boutique owner, always has a unique selection of vintage clothes, accessories, jewelry, candles, bags, and designer items [560 Jackson St.].

A Chinese Feast

115

There's nothing more satisfying than a meal at **House of Nanking** (A), a Chinese restaurant owned by the Fang family. They serve specialities from Shanghai. The decor is casual, and you'll have to share the large tables with other customers. Try the House Noodles (fresh egg noodles drizzled with sesame sauce, peppers and spices, and garnished with grilled vegetables with garlic). It's a simple dish that you'll be thinking about for a very long time. Order it with the sesame chicken, the garlic scallops, the small dishes of green vegetables with ginger, a few bottles of Tsingtao beer and flower tea. The service has a bit of an authoritarian feel—somehow it just adds to the charm of the place. You may well encounter Francis Ford Coppola, one of the regulars [919 Kearny St.].

To replenish yourself after spending hours walking, **Hunan's Home Restaurant** is a good bet. The portions are gigantic. A family restaurant with pink and green decor, it specializes in cuisine from Hunan, a southern province of China. Try the hot and sour soup and the Broccoli Beef, sautéed in oyster sauce [622 Jackson St.].

On Sunday afternoons, in cold weather, I have only one desire: **Yank Sing**. The popular dim sum restaurant was founded by Alice Chan in 1958, and her grandchildren run it today. They make a hundred varieties of dim sum every day.

The servers in this lively restaurant push carts overflowing with dumplings between the tables. You'll be tempted to try them all. I recommend their specialty, the Shanghai Dumplings, or the chicken and mushroom, and the roasted duck. The restaurant closes at 4 p.m. on weekends and holidays and 3 p.m. on weekdays. There are two locations in the Financial District [49 Stevenson St., and 101 Spear St.].

If you're in the mood for a crab feast, **R & G Lounge** makes it their specialty. You choose your crab from an aquarium when you arrive; then it's fried and served just with salt and pepper. Expect an hour wait at the three-story restaurant, but don't be deterred: The shared platters are phenomenal. I also recommend the cod dish. It melts in your mouth [631 Kearny St.].

The etiquette to follow when taking the subway—or BART (Bay Area Rapid Transit) is to stand behind the patches of black lines on the platform. This is precisely where the doors of the train will open, so San Franciscans wisely line up behind these areas. If you plan to take public transport several times, buy a Clipper Card (a rechargeable pass), which is valid throughout the network.

116

Good Restaurants
in Jackson Square

117

Kokkari Estiatorio is the best Greek restaurant in town, and it also offers the best service. The staff make a point of giving you real Greek hospitality—don't be surprised if the owners, bartenders and servers remember your name on your second visit. With the restaurant's soft lighting and inviting decor, you feel almost like you're in a friend's house. The large wooden tables are set with big bouquets of flowers, the seats are cushioned, and copper pans hang from the ceiling. Large baskets of sourdough bread are placed on the bars, and chicken and lamb roast in the dining room. In the second dining room at the back, guests can see the chefs at work. The menu features traditional Aegean dishes, with a slight modern twist. Order the classic Greek feta salad (*Horiatiki*), the grilled octopus, the calamari stuffed with feta, fennel and orange, the divine lamb chops, the meatballs and the moussaka. You're in for an unbelievable feast [200 Jackson St.].

At **Cotogna**, one of the best Italian restaurants in the city, the decor is rustic, the atmosphere is friendly, and the large bay windows look out on the tree-lined streets of Jackson Square. Highlights include antipasti, grilled over high heat, wood-oven baked pizzas and fresh pasta (try the Strozzapreti cacio e pepe or the pappardelle with wild boar ragu). A special menu is offered every Sunday evening, and a set menu of three services ($30) will satisfy those wanting to sit at the bar [490 Pacific Ave.].

One block away, **Trestle** also serves a different set menu each night. The gourmet three-course meal only costs $35—a deal, in this neighborhood [531 Jackson St.].

A Bookstore
in Compartments

116

In 2012, inspired by the booksellers on the banks of the Seine River, in Paris, Rick Wilkinson decided to open a book stand in an alley right in the heart of the Financial District. He set his sights on three empty shop windows that previously belonged to a department store. They're just 14 feet long (4 meters), 2 feet deep (0.5 meter) and about 6 feet high (1.80 meter). **G.F. Wilkinson** sells only used books, many of which are about the history of San Francisco. Most customers come during their workday, taking advantage of a break to peruse the books. "I like the daily interaction with the people on the street" says the tall, bearded owner. Wilkinson owned a bookstore in the Tenderloin for more than 30 years, but had to close the shop because the neighborhood had become too dangerous. He sometimes sits in one of the windows to read a paper—passersby sometimes think it's a performance piece. His booth is open Monday to Friday, 11:00 a.m. to 4 p.m., in good weather [34 Trinity Pl.].

The 1930s Barber

118 A visit to **Nicky the Barber** is like traveling back in time 100 years, to the days when all men wore hats, and would ask the barber for a pompadour, or executive contour cut.

Nicky Calvenese specializes in typical haircuts from the 1890s to 1960s. "The golden age of barbers," he calls it, "before the Beatles came and ruined everything for us!"

He is particularly fond of the 1930s, and is himself immersed in a vintage aesthetic, at work and at home. His many tattoos are authentic designs from before World War II, and all his clothes are originals from that era.

His barbershop is filled with antiques, including the first hair dryer, marketed in 1923, and the first razors and lotions for men.

He even uses a book of mug shots from that time to help guide customers in their hairstyle choices. He particularly appreciates the style of Alvin "Creepy" Karpis, a gangster born in Montreal in 1907, who began his criminal career at the age of 10. It ended in Alcatraz, where he languished for 26 years. "His hair was impeccable."

So why the fascination with that era? "In the 1930s, a mechanic would show up to work in a suit and a hat. You could not distinguish between a businessman and a laborer. I like the decorum. I'm not a hipster barber, I love cutting hair for laborers, for the man in the street."

Some of his regular customers come from as far away as Virginia and even London. Among them are former Mayor Willie Brown, some of the 49ers football players, and members of the Rockefeller family. He created the vintage hairstyles for the series *Boardwalk Empire* and is the official barber of the Art Deco Society.

Nicky is in his early forties, but has more than 25 years of experience in the field. He's been cutting his friends' hair since he was 11. As a child, he would sneak into the Italian barbershops in his native Philadelphia, where he would get 50 cents to sweep the floor. "I always knew I wanted to be the guy behind the chair in a barber's jacket. I like the atmosphere of the shops—they are the last of the social clubs."

Nicky's salon is located inside **Cable Car Clothiers**, a menswear store. They have been selling almost exclusively British brands since the 1930s, including an impressive selection of hats. It is a place where the past lives on [110 Sutter St.].

119

Architectural Treasures

120

I've always liked San Francisco's Financial District. The elegant neighborhood has many beaux-arts-style buildings, most dating from the 1910s, and some are essential viewing.

Pause at Columbus Avenue and Kearny Street to snap a photo of the **Sentinel Building** (A), with the Transamerica Pyramid in the background. Green due to its oxidized copper, the Sentinel Building resembles the Flatiron Building in New York. You get 1907 and 1972, all in one photo. Unfortunately, the observation platform on the 27th floor of the tower has been closed since September 11, 2001.

The main attraction of the **Hallidie Building** (B) is its incredible glass curtain wall. The architect of the seven-story office building, Willis Polk, was the first in the country to use the construction technique in 1917. For a more complete view of the building, go up to the third floor of Crocker Galleria, on the other side of the street [130 Sutter St.].

In the middle of Maiden Lane, two blocks away, sits a large red building with no windows—the only opening is a door in the shape of a half-moon. Built in 1948, it's the only San Francisco building designed by the great American architect **Frank Lloyd Wright** (C). The spiral ramp inside is reminiscent of The Guggenheim in New York; some say the San Francisco building was actually a kind of prototype for the renowned art museum [140 Maiden Lane].

The Secret Mural

119

On the 10th floor of the **Stock Exchange Tower** (an art-deco masterpiece), you can see a colossal Diego Rivera mural from 1930—the first one he painted outside Mexico. Rivera was an artist with strong leftist political convictions, and his selection to paint the mural was met with some controversy at the time. The mural was to be located in the cathedral of capitalism, after all. Entitled "Allegory of California," the fresco depicts California's natural resources and industries [155 Sansome St.].

To continue with the 1930s theme, grab a drink at **The Treasury**, located right next door, in the historic building that once housed Standard Oil's headquarters. The ceiling alone is worth the visit [115 Sansome St.].

120 B 120 C 120 A

121

Haute Cuisine at PacBell

121

Another architectural marvel in the area is the **Pacific Telephone & Telegraph Building**. It has a magnificent, lumiscent art-deco-style hall—the ceiling is covered in unicorns. Built in 1925, the building was San Francisco's first skyscraper. It's where Winston Churchill made the first transatlantic phone call in 1929. Today, Yelp is the main tenant, and there are two excellent restaurants on the ground floor. One is **Mourad**, where I savored the city's best dish of chicken with lemon and olives. I also recommend the duck basteeya (a kind of Moroccan pie), the grilled octopus and the Blue Suede Shoes cocktail. There's also **Trou Normand**, which has excellent charcuterie platters (their specialty is salami) and a wide selection of cognacs. [140 New Montgomery St.].

The Rooftop Gardens

122

Having lunch on one of the city's terraces high above the city streets is always a pleasant way to spend the afternoon. First, stop by the **Transamerica Pyramid** (the highest skyscraper in San Francisco); in front, you'll find a miniature redwood forest. Some of the trees measure more than 330 feet (100 meters) tall. There's also a fountain honoring the great American writer Mark Twain. Note: The park is closed on weekends [600 Montgomery St.].

Another calming oasis can be found at **343 Sansome Street**. Take the elevator in the hall up to the 15th floor. There, you'll find a few tables and benches, and some olive trees that provide some shade. The view of the surrounding buildings is awesome. From the south side, try to spot the three 12-foot (3.5-meters) statues at the top of the building at 580 California Street. The strange faceless ghouls are known as the "Corporate Goddesses."

You can access a garden on another private building just a few blocks away. **One Kearny Rooftop** (A) is open from 10 a.m. to 5 p.m., Monday to Friday, and it offers a spectacular view of downtown. You'll need to show a piece of ID to the doorkeeper before taking the elevator to the 11th floor (the entrance is on 23 Geary St.). **Asha Tea House**, right around the corner, has delicious teas to go. My favorite is the matcha latte with almond milk [17 Kearny St.].

I also love the garden on the roof of the **Wells Fargo** bank (B) for its view of the many statues on Market Street [1 Montgomery St.].

Look out for the plaques identifying POPOS (Privately-Owned Public Open Spaces) on private buildings in the Financial District. This indicates that a park, atrium or garden is open to the public. There are dozens of them!

122A 122B

Sylvia's Organic Offerings

123

For a quick meal downtown, I love **Bio Cafe**, right across from Macy's department store. With healthy food and a great atmosphere, they serve excellent sandwiches, quiche, salads, chocolates and cake. Most dishes are gluten-free. The owner, Sylvia, originally from France, is super friendly [75 O'Farrell St.].

Little France

124

Some streets in the Financial District have names with a French feel, like "Claude Lane." When you start to notice them, you'll know you're in Little France. There are about 60,000 French immigrants living in the Bay area; one quarter of them work in high-tech. You can still find a number of French businesses on Bush Street and in the alleys adjacent to Belden Place (where they celebrate Bastille Day on July 14). The **Notre Dame des Victoires Church** [566 Bush St.] continues to offer mass in French on Sundays. The church was founded in 1856 to serve the needs of gold-seekers, and was rebuilt following the 1906 earthquake.

124

An Aperitif
à la Palm Beach

125

With its retro palm-tree wallpaper, rattan furniture, ferns, leather benches and large marble bar, **Leo's Oyster Bar** has the feel of New York or Palm Beach in the 1950s. The decor at this champagne-and-oyster bar is truly magnificent. Try the sea urchin toast, the baked oysters, the delicious lobster roll and the pineapple sundae. The bar opens at 3 p.m. on weekdays [568 Sacramento St.].

Omakase in the
Financial District

126

If you like omakase (chef's choice), there are two Japanese restaurants that are worth the trip. At **Kusakabe**, an 11-course meal is $95. Chef Nori, from Kyoto, starts by serving you a cup of tea at the long wooden counter, made from a single tree. Then comes a succession of morsels, each one tastier than the last: sashimi, miso soup with truffles, oysters, tempura, and finally a choice of fatty tuna (toro) or Wagyu beef, seared by blowtorch. With lots of natural light, the decor has a truly Zen feel [584 Washington St.].

The decor at **Akiko's** is completely different: brick walls and dark. You feel like you're eating in a grotto. The 15-course menu is between $80 and $100, and there's a focus on sustainable fishing. Here too, the meal ends with a piece of Wagyu beef—this one sprinkled with truffles. Finish it all with their signature dessert, a scoop of black sesame ice cream, encased in mochi, a sticky rice paste [431 Bush St.].

125

A Tower of Art Galleries

127

From the outside, the building at **49 Geary Street** looks like an ordinary office tower. But on the inside, you'll find more than 24 art galleries that are open to the public. I go often for the expositions at the **Fraenkel Gallery** [room no. 450]. It specializes in photography, and there's an impressive collection of works by Irving Penn, Eugène Atget, Diane Arbus, Lee Friedlander and other renowned photographers. On the first Thursday of each month, the galleries stay open until late at night. This tradition has been going strong since the early 1990s [49 Geary St.].

The Gold Rush Library

128 I was excited to visit the building at 57 Post Street after I saw a photo of its enormous spiral staircase; it looks like it's right out of a Hitchcock movie. To take an amazing pic, go up to the fourth floor and point your camera down. The historic beaux-arts-style building in the heart of the Financial District houses the **Mechanic's Institute Library and Chess Room**. The oldest library on the west coast of the United States, it was founded in 1854 for use by goldminers. Before the discovery of gold, San Francisco was a small town, with just 800 residents. After gold veins were discovered, the population exploded, rising to 35,000 in 1852 and more than 100,000 a year later. Most of the men in San Francisco left the city to go make their fortunes in the nearby gold mines. Many ended up disillusioned, discovering that the precious metal was more difficult to find than they had expected. They returned by the thousands to San Francisco, exhausted, dispirited and jobless. The institute was created to enable them to educate themselves and find skilled jobs. As the years went by, the collection of books expanded. Today the library has more than 175,000 volumes. Anyone can become a member; the space is open to all, but only members can consult the books. A guided tour of the site's architecture takes place on Wednesdays at noon. The fourth floor lodges the oldest chess club in the United States, founded in 1850. Photos of its members' victories over the decades line the walls. Repertory films are screened each Friday. The suggested price is $10; popcorn is included [57 Post St.].

The $20,000 Coffee

129 When I want a good coffee, **Blue Bottle Coffee** in Mint Plaza is one of my favorite spots. Housed in a 1912 building, the café is surrounded by large windows; amber light pours in at the end of the day. Their equipment is as sophisticated as it gets. One of their coffee machines, a siphon bar imported from Japan, is worth more than $20,000. They also have a small food menu, with sandwiches, chia bowls, salads and Belgian waffles. It's an ideal place to take a break [66 Mint St.].

Tea Ceremony at the Palace Hotel

130

I adore this hotel. To enjoy the premises without breaking the bank, go for tea at the Garden Court, the beaux-arts-style dining room. What better way to spend the afternoon than savoring the opulence of a bygone era? With a glass ceiling—made with 70,000 panels of glass—and 20 huge Austrian chandeliers, the hall is excquisite. It's the size of a train station, and it feels like you're in the *Titanic* ballroom. The place has been serving tea since the beginning of the 1900s. You can choose tidbits from the à la carte menu; otherwise, the tea ceremony costs $68 and includes tea, pastries, small sandwiches, homemade scones and rose petal jam. For $14 more, you can have a glass of Veuve Clicquot, making the ceremony that much richer. The **Palace Hotel** was built in 1875 by an American banker who wanted to compete with the top European hotels. Many stars have walked through its doors over the years, from Charlie Chaplin to Sophia Loren—even Oscar Wilde. The great banquet to inaugurate the United Nations was also held here in 1945 [2 New Montgomery St.].

Tea by the Garden

131

There's another spot where I love to have tea, not far from the Palace Hotel. The **Samovar Tea Lounge** is located high up in the **Yerba Buena Gardens**, with a wonderful view of the park and its many sculptures and fountains—outdoor symphonies are sometimes held there. Take a seat at one of the tables on the terrace outside. The Wi-Fi is free, and there are several outlets to plug into. Try the Masala Chai, or their California Rose blend, which has black tea, cardamom, orange peels, rose petals, bergamot and jasmine. The lunch menu is original (squash dumplings, tea-smoked chicken sandwich, chia pudding, quinoa waffle and more). Yerba Buena, which means "good herb" (it also refers to an indigenous plant) was the name for what is now San Francisco between 1835 and 1846, when it was merely a town [730 Howard St.].

Back to 1849

132 I fell in love with **Tadich Grill** (A) on my very first visit. It's the oldest restaurant in California, and the decor takes you back in time. A long bar has plenty of stools for diners in a rush. Wood panels line the walls, and floor tiles, art-deco lamps and large mirrors complete the scene. There's even a special menu on a blackboard for regulars. Their specialty is the Seafood Cioppino (a fish and seafood stew that you eat like a soup, great for dipping hunks of garlic bread into), the oysters Rockefeller and the Hangtown Fry, an unusual dish with scrambled eggs, oysters and bacon. They also have a special for each day of the week, including roast lamb on Monday, beef tongue on Tuesday, corned beef and cabbage on Thursday [240 California St.].

Afterward, you can go for a drink without leaving the 19th century. Walk left down Front Street; across the street is **Schroeder's** (B). The voluminous German beer hall opened its doors in 1893; women weren't admitted until the 1970s. The premises were entirely restored in 2014, bringing the original luster back to the wooden bars and to the superb murals by Hermann Richter. The traditional German menu was also brought up to date [240 Front St.].

Sam's Grill & Seafood Restaurant, another legendary canteen, has been around since 1867. With its all-wood decor, it's as old school as they come; the restaurant is actually one of the oldest in the United States. Sam's is open Monday to Friday (the clientele tends toward businesspeople and people in the financial sector), and serves fish and seafood. One area of the restaurant has special booths with curtains for privacy. Do yourself a favor: order a Bloody Mary, the crab cocktail and the fish of the day with creamed spinach [374 Bush St.].

San Franciscans love to dress up more than anyone else in the country. They'll take any occasion to delve into the special section of their closet where they keep their sequins and feather boas. The biggest event for dressing up is Bay to Breakers, a 12K race from San Francisco Bay to the Pacific Ocean that takes place on the third Sunday in May—and the outfits are legendary!

134

Warhol and the Roof Sculptures

133 Facing Yerba Buena Gardens is another San Francisco must-see. The **San Francisco Museum of Modern Art** (SFMOMA) is the largest contemporary art gallery in the United States. After three years of renovation work, which more than doubled its size, the museum finally re-opened in the spring of 2016. To see works by Matisse, Jasper Johns, de Kooning, Pollock, more than 50 by Andy Warhol, and more than 18,000 photographs, this is the place. Most of the artwork comes from the extensive modern and contemporary art collection of Donald and Doris Fisher, founders of the Gap. My favorite part of the museum is the outdoor sculpture garden on the fifth floor, with an enormous living wall made up of indigenous species. The museum is free for those 18 and younger [151 3rd St.].

Cocktails with a View

134 With its big domed starburst windows, the bar at the top of Marriott Marquis hotel offers a stunning view of downtown San Francisco. The best time to go is at the end of the day: The light that floods the room is simply magical (and your photos will be, too). The bar, very appropriately named **The View**, is open to all—there's no need to book a hotel room to relax on the 39th floor. Cocktails are $15 [780 Mission St.].

The Saturday Farmers' Market

135 Each Saturday from 8 a.m. to 2 p.m., a big farmers' market sets up behind the Ferry Building, by the ferry docks on the edge of the bay. Dozens of kiosks are set up, and some food trucks. The tables are loaded with fresh produce. Stroll through the aisles and sample the juicy peaches, almonds, cheese, bread, jams and pastries. Be prepared for crowds; if that's not your thing, it's better to go early in the morning. San Franciscans tend to prefer smaller local neighborhood farmers' markets, but the **Ferry Plaza Farmers Market** is something you have to experience at least once in your life—even if only to see it. A smaller version of the market is held in front of the building on Tuesdays and Thursdays [1 Ferry Building].

Ferry Building Feast

136

The **Ferry Building** was built in 1915. In the 1930s, as many as 50,000 passengers passed through its doors every day. But after the Golden Gate Bridge and the Bay Bridge were built, maritime transport started dropping off. Today, the massive nave of the beaux-arts-style building houses arcades, cafés, wine stores, an ice cream shop, a butcher shop and a number of restaurants. It's similar to the Chelsea Market in New York.

My favorite kiosks are: **Cowgirl Creamery Cheese Shop**, for its cheeses and grilled cheese (the best I've ever had); **Acme Bread Company**, for its olive bread; **Humphry Slocombe**, for its artisanal ice cream; and **Heath Ceramics**, for its pottery and cookbook collection. As for restaurants, **Boulettes Larder** has an excellent brunch menu on Sundays, available on the outdoor terrace with a view of the bay. The menu changes from season to season, but the dishes are always inventive. For example: their poached egg with Japanese, Korean or Sardinian flavors. Their homemade donuts have also made quite a name for themselves. The owners, Amaryll and Lori, do the cooking on a gas oven in the center of the dining room—it feels like you're eating in their kitchen at home.

The Slanted Door serves some of the best Vietnamese food in town. I always get the same thing: cellophane noodles with crab and sesame. The large restaurant has modern decor, and the expansive windows look out on the lights of Bay Bridge in the evenings. Magical.

For an oyster feast, go to **Hog Island Oysters Co.** (A), another restaurant with a view of the bay. The oysters come from the owners' aquaculture farm north of San Francisco, and they're served raw or grilled. The restaurant serves other seafood as well, including excellent mussels and french fries. It's a great place to unwind at the end of the day.

The menu at **Hard Water** (B) pays homage to New Orleans. More than 300 types of whiskey are on offer; the bottles fill the shelves to the ceiling. They also make some of the best fried chicken in town. It goes great with their mint julep. [At Pier 3, right beside the Ferry Building].

The Quebec Fountain

137

A large concrete sculpture that looks like an angular spider lurks in front of the Ferry Building, in the middle of Justin Herman Plaza. The piece was created by Quebec artist Armand Vaillancourt. During the unveiling ceremony in 1971, Vaillancourt painted the words "Québec libre" (free Quebec) in red letters at various spots on the sculpture. The graffiti was removed, but the slogan has lived on as a nickname for the sculpture. Sadly, as I write this, the **Vaillancourt Fountain** is dry, due to the historic drought of recent years.

On the last Friday of each month, hundreds of cyclists and activists gather at Justin Herman Plaza for an event known as **Critical Mass**. At 6 p.m., bikes storm the streets of San Francisco, accompanied by music. The event began in 1992. Warning: Some cyclists (mainly older men) show up for the ride nude. That's right—nude.

When traveling on the tram's F-Line, be aware that "Inbound" means you are heading toward Fisherman's Wharf, and "Outbound" is toward The Castro.

Time-Traveling Streetcars

138

The **F Line** is my favorite public transportation line in San Francisco. Inaugurated in 1995, its streetcars (the only vehicle on the F line) come from all over the world and from other parts of the United States: Philadelphia, Zurich, Milan, Los Angeles and Brussels, to name a few. With great retro colors and designs, each is named after its city of origin. Some were manufactured as long ago as the 1920s. The line runs six miles (10 kilometers), along Market Street and The Embarcardero. Unlike cable cars, which only tourists really use, the streetcars on the F Line are actually used by San Franciscans—it makes the experience that much more authentic. The cars go by about every 15 minutes, and a ride costs $2.25 (have exact change ready).

Downtown (Civic Center) and SoMa

SoMa is the world's epicenter for startups. The cafés are filled with young professionals wearing plaid shirts, all fired up to create the apps of tomorrow. On game days, Giants fans flood the streets. The gilded dome of City Hall dominates Civic Center, the heart of the city, where you'll find the main library, the opera, and more.

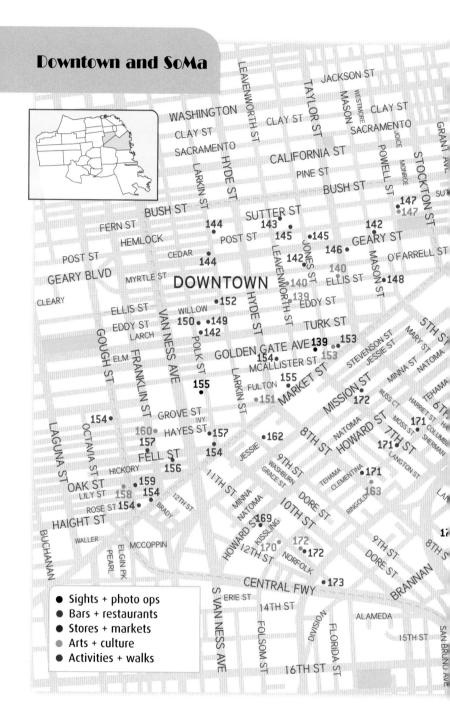

Downtown and SoMa

DOWNTOWN

- ● Sights + photo ops
- ● Bars + restaurants
- ● Stores + markets
- ● Arts + culture
- ● Activities + walks

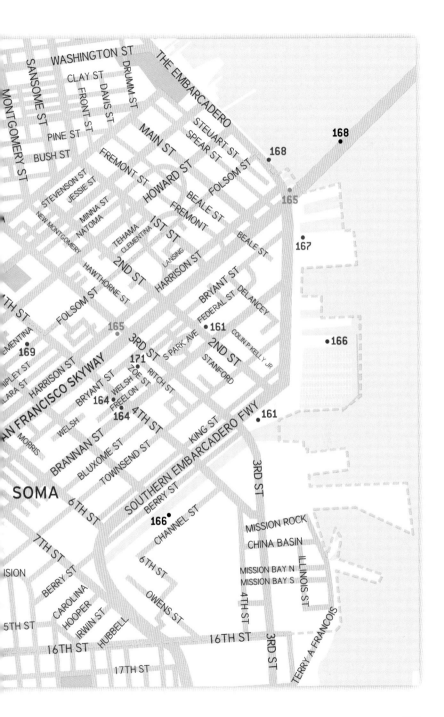

SOMA

The Mayor of the Tenderloin

139 I am completely bewildered by the Tenderloin, by far the most disturbing district in San Francisco. In the heart of one of the wealthiest cities in the world, this neighborhood is an island of poverty and despair, populated mainly by homeless people, drug addicts, drug dealers, people with mental illness, pimps and prostitutes. The crime rate is 35 times higher than anywhere else in the city. It is not uncommon to find syringes and human waste on the sidewalk or a homeless addict lying on the hood of your car. How is this possible in a city as wealthy as San Francisco? This is the question that everyone asks.

"Welcome to the flip side of wine country!" joked **Del Seymour**, a former resident of the neighborhood who now runs guided tours of its main "attractions."

Whereas in most big cities, the disenfranchised live on the margins of the city, in San Francisco, they live a block from the luxurious Union Square boutiques. If you turn the wrong way out of the Hilton Hotel, you'll find yourself surrounded by junkies. The people of the Tenderloin say they live "behind the Hilton" in the shadow of capitalism. In short, this is the kind of neighborhood that a traditional travel guide would say to avoid at all costs. On the contrary, I believe that the Tenderloin—an anomaly in this highly privileged city—is worth exploring, if only to learn more about its fascinating history.

Spanning about 40 blocks, the area is bordered by Van Ness Avenue to the west, Mason Street to the east, Geary Street to the north, and Market and McAllister streets to the south. The epicenter is at the corner of Turk and Taylor streets, where Compton's Cafeteria used to be, which was the site of the country's first gay and transgender protests in August of 1966.

"In the 1920s, the neighborhood was a mecca for entertainment, gambling and vice, with its many theaters, restaurants, hotels, brothels, speakeasies and nightclubs," Del explained, signaling me to hide my camera to avoid any trouble.

As an entry point for many immigrants arriving in San Francisco, the Tenderloin has a very high number of "SROs" (single-room occupancy), residential hotels subsidized by the government. The rooms cost from $500 to $1,000 a month for a little less than 65 square feet (six square meters). And it is precisely because of these SROs that the Tenderloin is still able to resist gentrification (unlike other neighborhoods, including the Mission). In the 1980s, the city enacted several laws that prevent any major changes.

Developers aren't allowed to convert SROs into tourist hotels without replacing the low-income housing units, and new buildings cannot be over 13 stories high. Also, several of the buildings in the neighborhood are owned by charities that help the homeless.

Nobody knows these streets better than Del Seymour, a Vietnam War veteran. After a personal bankruptcy, he ended up on the street, and was a taxi driver, addict, crack dealer and a pimp. "I was also married for 15 minutes," he said. "My Hollywood marriage!"

He has been sober for several years, and now leads tours and helps street youth find jobs in technology companies that are located near the neighborhood (Mid-Market), attracted by Mayor Ed Lee's tax credits. One example is Twitter, which has its headquarters at the corner of Market Street and 10th Street in a beautiful Art Deco building.

"I serve as a bridge between these companies that are reaching out to the community, and street youth," Del explained as we entered **St. Boniface Catholic Church**. Inside, a hundred or so

homeless people slept on the pews, surrounded by a symphony of snoring. During the day, the church turns into a dormitory for the homeless—a peaceful haven that smells of fragrant incense. "This is the only church in the world where you can do this," Del told me.

Homeless people are welcome from 6 a.m. to 3 p.m., Monday to Friday. "They have nine hours of sleeping in safety, which we call "sacred sleep." The Gubbio Project, the charity responsible for this endeavor, survives on private donations and pays rent to the church. It offers on-site massages, podiatry, and barber services, and the security guards are all volunteers. The church can accommodate up to 110 people [133 Golden Gate Ave.].

Just across the street, **St. Anthony's charity** serves up to 3,000 meals a day. "At the end of the month, the room is full," explained Del. "I used to eat here often."

At the back of the room, a man played the piano with a smile on his lips. The organization also has facilities with computers and printers, which homeless people can access to find a job or an apartment. They also have a free medical clinic.

Shelters in San Francisco, which provide about 1,200 beds, operate at full capacity, so if thousands of people are sleeping in the streets, it is because the shelters are full. In 2015, there were nearly 7,000 homeless in San Francisco.

With no grocery stores, but several alcohol vendors, this neighborhood is a veritable food desert. "After the 10th of the month, people are broke—that's why there are no grocery stores in the neighborhood. No one can survive on a 10-day cycle."

Next, Del took me to the **Cadillac Hotel**, the first SRO in the United States. It is also the first building rebuilt after the devastating earthquake in 1906. The first floor is now a history museum of the Tenderloin [398 Eddy St.], something that would have been unthinkable a few years ago.

The Avant-Garde Gospel

140

Every Sunday, **Glide Memorial** Methodist church, in the heart of the Tenderloin, fills with visitors. The congregation is mix of religions, sexual orientations, political beliefs and nationalities. The building also fills with powerful sounds. There are the sermons of the friendly pastor Cecil Williams and his wife, Janice Mirikitani, who speak passionately about social justice and addiction. Then there's the gospel choir, a varied assortment of transgender, gay, straight, white, black and Hispanic singers. The experience is guaranteed to move you. Diversity is at a maximum in this place of worship, and it's truly inspiring. Glide Memorial has been a pillar of the Tenderloin since the 1930s, and has played an active part in the struggle against AIDS, poverty and addiction. It also serves some 3,000 meals each week. A long lineup forms outside each day. Thursdays are the most popular; that's fried chicken day. The religious service takes place from 9 a.m. to 11 a.m. on Sunday mornings. Take a seat in the upper level to get the best view of the choir; however, the energy is more electric at the altar level [330 Ellis St.].

Showers for All

141

The spirit of helping your neighbor runs deep in San Francisco. The best example of this is probably **Lava Mae**, a nonprofit organization that gives homeless people the chance to take a shower in privacy, without leaving the street. The blue buses park in the Tenderloin, the Mission, the Castro, and in front of the library.

The founder, Doniece Sandoval, had the idea one evening when she encountered a young homeless person who told her they didn't have a way to clean up. "That upset me, so I went home and did some research." She later found out that there were only 16 showers for about 7,000 homeless people in the entire city. She also learned that the city had recently received a federal grant to replace its fleet of diesel buses with hybrids.

"I thought if we have food trucks, then why not shower trucks?" The city agreed to donate four old buses. Converting them was entirely paid for by private donations (including a generous amount from Google).

The buses each have two showers and two private toilets, and towels and soap are provided. Each person is given 20 minutes. For their water supply, the vehicles connect to fire hydrants. More than 2,000 homeless persons have been able to take more than 12,000 showers thanks to Lava Mae, since the service was launched in 2014.

"We are not trying to solve the problem of homelessness," says Sandoval, "but rather to restore some dignity to these people. And with dignity comes hope for the future."

From Speakeasy to Speakeasy

142

Having a drink at **Bourbon & Branch** is really an experience. The bar is housed in a former speakeasy that was set up in the 1920s, during Prohibition. Five tunnels were built out of the establishment—one for women only—to allow customers to make a quick escape when the police or government inspectors conducted a raid.

To find it, go to the corner of Jones and O'Farrell streets and look for the sign for the Anti-Saloon League. You'll need to make a reservation to get into the bar. They'll also give you a password that you're supposed to whisper to the hostess at the door.

When you enter, it's like you've leapt back in time to the days of Prohibition. The bar has five secret rooms that perfectly recreate the clandestine atmosphere of drinking establishments of the time. The lighting is dimmed, and you drink out of silver teapots. The bar has a number of rules to follow: Lower your voice when you order a cocktail; no using cell phones; no ordering cosmopolitans; smokers must use the rear door; no photos allowed; when you leave, be quiet and discreet. Basically, don't draw any attention from the authorities.

You don't need to make a reservation for a drink in the library room; just knock on the door and give the password "books." Sure enough, the space is filled to the ceiling with books.

My favorite room is **Wilson & Wilson**. It's designed to look like a detective's office. You can order cocktails à la carte, but I recommend the tasting menu (three cocktails for $30), which changes every night. For reservations, go to bourbonandbranch.com [501 Jones St.].

A five-minute walk away, the **Benjamin Cooper** bar is another place where finding the entrance is as much a part of the experience as enjoying your drink. The bar is on the second floor of Hotel G, and the door is on Mason Street. Look for the black-and-white sign with the face of a certain Benjamin Cooper (a fictional character). They serve cocktails and three varieties of oyster [398 Geary St.].

The **Whitechapel** is another bar that goes for the clandestine motif. The decor evokes an abandoned 1890 London subway station. With the vaulted barrel ceiling, the tiled subway walls and the archival photographs, they really pull it off. The bar-restaurant specializes in gins, offering the biggest selection in the United States [600 Polk St.].

Fusion Cuisine: Aloha!

143 When it comes to fusion cuisine, **Liholiho Yacht Club** is in a class of its own. Eating there is an absolute delight. The chef, Ravi Kapur, originally from Hawaii, is inspired by his homeland cuisine, but also incorporates Indian and Korean influences. It makes for inventive dishes with explosive flavors, like fried oyster with beef carpaccio and Thousand Island dressing on lettuce cups, or beef-tongue-filled poppy steam buns topped with kimchi; or the twice-cooked pork belly with pineapple, Thai basil and fennel. The desserts are colorful as well, like caramelized pineapple ice cream enclosed in meringue, and a five-spice apple pie with whipped sour cream and Madras curry.

But what really keeps customers returning is their signature dish: a bowl of fried rice, shrimp, abalone mushrooms and...SPAM. The last ingredient might have some shock value, but Liholiho actually uses a homemade version of the preserved ham beloved by Hawaiians). My favorite dish is the Manila clams, coconut curry and fresh turmeric, served with garlic naan bread to dip in the broth. Nectar of the gods!

The decor is modern, with large brick walls and wooden benches. Behind the bar hangs a giant photo of the chef's mother in the 1970s. Her long dark hair is blowing in the wind and there's a carefree smile of youth on her face. It encapsulates the *aloha* spirit [871 Sutter St.].

Hybrid Pastries

144 **Mr. Holmes Bakehouse** (A) is one of the most original bakeries in San Francisco. The small restaurant draws big crowds for their cruffins (a hybrid croissant and muffin). These amazing creations are put out for sale at 9 a.m, and they disappear in minutes. There's a new flavor each day (orange and cardamom, salted caramel, chai, peanut butter and pistachio, strawberry milkshake, and more). If you can't snatch up a cruffin, Mr. Holmes also makes excellent croissants and donuts. I have a weakness for the pear and blue cheese Danish, the artichoke Danish and the pastrami, sauerkraut and Thousand Island dressing Danish. Another hit is the California croissant with smoked salmon, wasabi, ginger and nori. It makes a sushi breakfast make sense. I also love the clean, simple decor with white subway tiles. The pink neon sign that reads "I got baked in San Francisco," is an Instagram favorite. The design of their to-go boxes with gold lettering was inspired by Mendl's, the bakery in *The Grand Budapest Hotel* [1042 Larkin St.].

Two street corners to the south, the café **Jane** serves excellent muffins, scones, brioche and banana bread. It's also a good place to have a healthy breakfast (poached egg sandwich, granola, muesli, chia pudding and avocado toast with poached egg) [925 Larkin St.].

Happy Hour on the Roof... and a Hangover Vaccine

145 The terrace at **Jones** (A) is the perfect spot to enjoy a sangria while watching the sunset or gazing at the night sky. Just a few minutes from Union Square, the restaurant is just above street level, offering a great view of the surrounding 1920s buildings. From 5 p.m. to 7 p.m., cocktails and glasses of wine are $5, and beers are $3 [620 Jones St.].

If you've had a few drinks and you're struck with a craving for burgers, **Pearl's Deluxe Burgers** is right nearby and makes one of the best burgers and fries in the city. They have types of burgers for everyone, including vegetarians. The sweet potato fries and the Bula Burger (bacon, Swiss cheese, grilled pineapple and teriyaki sauce) combo is particularly popular. Pair it with a chocolate peanut butter milkshake and you're all set [708 Post St.].

The Bar that Keeps an Eye on You

146 For a drink in the height of elegance, visit the bar in the Clift Hotel, just a couple of blocks southeast. **The Redwood Room** is aptly named. Its walls are made from slats of redwood (all coming from a single 2,000-year-old sequoia tree). The woodwork was installed in 1933. Digital artworks that change constantly are hanging on the walls; some of the portraits even follow you with their eyes [495 Geary St.].

Authentic Thai Food near Union Square

148 Good restaurants are rare in this extremely touristy part of the city, but **Kin Khao** is an exception. The owner of the restaurant, Pim Techamuanvivit, says she wants to "liberate Thai cuisine from the tyranny of peanut sauce." She prepares traditional Bangkok dishes such as Khao Soi, a wonderful chicken curry soup with tender egg noodles and condiments. The fish sauce, shrimp paste and other products come directly from Thailand. Save room for the black rice pudding for dessert. You get to add the toppings yourself: puffed rice, caramel and coconut cream [55 Cyril Magnin St., but the entrance is at the corner of Ellis St. and Mason St.].

Boas and Sequins for Brunch

147 For a totally unique brunch experience, get a table at **The Starlight Room** for the "Sunday's a Drag" event. The Starlight is a nightclub on the 21st floor of the Sir Francis Drake Hotel. The hotel puts on a Sunday morning brunch accompanied by a show with drag queens and transgender artists. With its red velvet banquettes and heavy curtains, the club is a lot like something out of the film *Moulin Rouge*. There are two shows, one at 11:30 a.m. and one at 2:00 p.m. The cost is $60 per person. Try to get there an hour early to enjoy the buffet before the show. Call ahead for reservations at 415-395-8595 [450 Powell St.].

A Pool for Rock Stars in the Tenderloin

149 One of the favorite destinations for a drink in the neighborhood is **Chambers Eat & Drink**, the resto-bar next to the pool at the **Phoenix Hotel**. Many different rock stars have stayed at the retro-style motel since it opened in the 1950s, including the members of Pearl Jam, Red Hot Chili Peppers and Nirvana, as well as Robert Plant and David Bowie. Touring bands like to stop there because parking is free; so are massages. It was a brilliant marketing move by the owners. The hotel became know as the "rock 'n' roll hotel." Courtney Love has been known to swim in the pool nude. Only two pools in the United States are designated historical monuments: those of the Roosevelt Hotel in Hollywood, and the Phoenix. The restaurant has 1970s decor and a massive collection of vinyl albums. It also serves a great hamburger, which goes great with a cocktail on the patio. It's a legendary spot [601 Eddy St.].

New Orleans-Style Breakfast

150 One of the most popular spots for brunch is **Brenda's French Soul Food**, just around the corner from the Phoenix Hotel. People line up for the comfort food prepared by the chef, Brenda Buenviaje, a Louisiana native. Highlights include Shrimp and Grits, buttermilk pancakes, and ham with molasses. I'm also crazy about the donuts (especially apple cinnamon). There are a few vegetarian items on the menu [652 Polk St.].

149

Delve into the Archives

151 If you're fascinated by San Francisco's history, the **San Francisco Historical Photograph Collection** is a must-see. The institution's vast collection includes some two million photographs of the city, from 1850 on. You'll find it on the sixth floor of the public library. The photos of the construction of the Golden Gate Bridge are particularly fascinating.

On the sixth floor, you'll find a very unusual office, belonging to Leah Esguerra, the library's social worker. San Francisco's library was the first in the country to provide social services, which started in 2009. The aim was to help homeless people to relax, sleep and clean up. They line up in front of the building every morning and wait for the doors to open. For many of them, the library is a last resort. Leah gives them the opportunity to shower and helps them find food, lodging and employment [100 Larkin St.].

Fantastic Pho

152 The best pho in all of San Francisco awaits you on a bustling street in the Tenderloin. I like to take refuge there when it's raining, and warm my bones with a steaming bowl of Phô Gà (chicken soup with noodles). **Turtle Tower** specializes in northern Vietnamese cuisine. The owner, Steven Nghia Pham, stands out from the pack through the quality of his broths and the freshness of his ingredients. He uses free-range chicken, and the rice noodles are made by hand each day. The soups are served without sprouts, basil, hoisin sauce—in other words, in the traditional Hanoi style. You can eat for just $7 or $8. Their excellent bánh mì sandwich, at $4.75, is one of the best deals in town [645 Larkin St.].

The Ultimate Drag Bar

153 **Aunt Charlie's Lounge** is the last remaining gay bar in the Tenderloin, and one of only places you can still see an underground show with some of the best drag queens in town. A caution: It's on one of the roughest blocks in the city. You may have to get past drug addicts hanging around the door, but it's worth it.

There's no stage, and that makes the experience even more intimate. The drag queens get up on the bar and crawl around on the floor. The best time to go is Friday or Saturday night, for The Hot Boxxx Girls Drag Show ($5).

Aunt Charlie's is the neighborhood's original dive bar, and it's filled with locals during the day. Some of the bartenders are close to 90 years old (so don't expect ultra-fast service). The decor hasn't changed since the 1980s; there are the same carpets and the same vinyl-covered barstools [133 Turk St.].

Great Restaurants Around City Hall

154

For a fast, healthy meal, **Little Gem** (A) serves fresh, nourishing meals from morning to night. A Californian restaurant with industrial decor, its dishes have no gluten, dairy products or refined sugars. I like the salmon on a bed of quinoa and spinach, the braised pork sandwich on naan bread and the curried cauliflower and sweet potato with rice [400 Grove St.].

I'm also a loyal patron at **Elmira Rosticceria**, an inexpensive neighborhood restaurant that serves delicious Italian food. Everything is homemade, from their succulent roast chicken and the chips that accompany the sandwiches, to the fresh pasta. To start your day on the right foot, try the frittata or the breakfast sandwich. For lunch, tuck into their heavenly chicken sandwich with pistachio pesto. Open Monday to Friday from 7:30 a.m. to 3 p.m. [154 McAllister St.].

Just a stone's throw from Twitter's headquarters on Market Street, **Alta CA** is the perfect spot to spend the evening mingling with people in the tech industry. Alta has a large selection of cocktails and small dishes (Castelvetrano olives with za'atar spice, deviled eggs, falafel and hummus, homemade pastrami, fried brussels sprouts and cheeseburgers). Sit at the huge triangle-shaped bar in the middle of the room. To get to the toilets, you have to go through the kitchen, which gives you a chance to see the frenzy of activity around the stoves. The bar-restaurant closes at 2 a.m., and the kitchen is open until 1 a.m. [1420 Market St.].

A bit farther south on Market Street, you'll find **Zuni Café** (B), a local institution. At lunch, customers sip sauvignon blanc and watch the parade of passersby. The little place reminds me of Paris. Opened in 1979, the café was a pioneer in the Slow Food movement in the United States. The roast chicken for two ($58), served with a Tuscan salad, is a must—I guarantee it'll be worth the visit [1658 Market St.].

After that, continue on to **Hotel Biron**, in the alley behind Zuni Café. It's a pleasant wine bar that also offers cheese and charcuterie platters [45 Rose St.].

Be Cinderella on the Steps of City Hall

155

San Francisco City Hall is by far the most majestic building in the city. Its dome is the fifth largest in the world—it's even bigger than that of the Capitol Building in Washington. Not bad for a city just 47 square miles (121 square kilometers) in size and with less than a million residents! Unlike cities like New York, where you have to make a reservation for a guided tour, City Hall opens its doors to visitors Monday to Friday from 8 a.m. to 6 p.m. Camera-wielding tourists and city employees are constantly intermingling here.

Fans of neoclassical architecture should make a point of visiting the 1915 building, which was entirely rebuilt after being destroyed in the 1906 earthquake. The 108-foot (33-meter) rotunda is particularly impressive; it's a masterpiece of the beaux-arts style. The monumental marble staircase is reminiscent of the Paris Opera. The rotunda is a popular spot for wedding ceremonies, especially on Fridays around 4 p.m. I love going there to see them; the applause and shouts of joy are always moving, and the energy is contagious.

Don't miss the expositions in the rooms on the ground floor. You can see photos of famous couples that were married here, including Marilyn Monroe and Joe DiMaggio in 1954.

City Hall also hosts artists in residence. They create artworks on-site, taking inspiration from the history of the place. One of these artists is Jeremy Fish, who spent 100 days drawing 100 pieces, to commemorate the 100th anniversary of the building. "They gave me an office in what was basically an old broom closet! I wanted to defend the honor and reputation of the city at a time when, for the first time since the Gold Rush, people were—and still are—moving here only in the hope of becoming rich. I felt it my job to educate all these newcomers," he said about his intentions with the project.

There's a large farmers' market in front of City Hall that has been taking place since the 1980s. Unlike other markets in the city, **Heart of the City Farmers Market** is not-for-profit. It's run by local farmers, and the prices are affordable. It's known as the people's market. The market is open on Wednesdays and Fridays from 7 a.m. to to 5 p.m., at the United Nations Plaza.

Gourmet Mexican Seafood

156

Cala is one of the best restaurants in the city. The chef, Gabriela Cámara, is a star in Mexico (her legion of fans includes Alice Waters and the Mexican-cooking legend, Diana Kennedy). She opened her first restaurant on U.S. soil in 2015, right in the heart of San Francisco. Gabriela lets you discover a specific side of Mexican cuisine: It's all about subtlety and simplicity, with a focus on fresh ingredients. She only serves fish and other seafood. Most of the dishes are for sharing, like the grilled rock cod. It's slathered with chili-infused salsa verde and served whole, with homemade tortillas.

Order the quesadillas with greens, the trout tostadas with avocado (the fish melts in your mouth), the Japanese clams in a chipotle broth (served with baguette from Tartine Bakery), or the signature item: sea urchin, in its shell, on a bed of masa (dough) with habanero leek relish. The dish begs to be photographed before you take a bite.

The entrance is separated from the dining room by a wall of vines, and fig trees decorate the interior of the restaurant. Dozens of black clay light fixtures glow overhead like a constellation of stars. The space is actually a former music studio. It's best to reserve a table, but you can also eat at the bar [149 Fell St.].

Jazzy Cocktails

157

To sip a cocktail as you listen to live jazz, visit **Mr. Tipple's Recording Studio**. They also serve food, and entry is free [39 Fell St.].

If you're looking for a more traditional jazz experience, the temple of jazz in San Francisco, the **SFJAZZ Center**, is just a couple of blocks away. Programming is quite varied. You can buy last-minute tickets at the venue, or reserve in advance at: sfjazz.org [201 Franklin St.].

The Family-Run Gallery

158

Across the street from the 20th Century Cafe is the art gallery run by Jules Maeght. Maeght is a Parisian who decided to pack his bags for San Francisco a few years ago. The expositions at the **Jules Maeght Gallery** are a mix of modern European artists and emerging artists from the Bay Area. Jules' grandfather, Aimé Maeght, was himself a famous gallery owner. He founded the Maeght Gallery in 1945 and exhibited drawings by Matisse during World War II. He was also the only person to exhibit works by major artists of the era such as Kandinsky, Giacometti, Chagall, Miró and Braque [149 Gough St.].

Viennese Treats

159

The 20th Century Cafe brings the spirit of famous European cafés to Californian soil. With flowered ceramics, green linoleum flooring, bouquets of flowers and 1920s music, the café is steeped in nostalgia (as its name suggests). The women who work there wear 1950s dresses and butterfly glasses. Working on a large marble counter, they create the pastries that make this place one of the top dessert destinations in the city. The chef, Michelle Polzine, is dressed in vintage items from head to toe. She's inspired by central European cuisine and the discoveries she has made during her travels. Her specialty is Russian honey cake: about a dozen layers of spongey cake separated by generous portions of honey-cream frosting. Michelle also makes her own bagels, fruit tarts, pastrami sandwiches, soups and pierogies [198 Gough St.].

Never ever leave anything in your car—not even a piece of paper! This is a cardinal rule. Some desperate San Franciscans leave their car doors unlocked at night to avoid having their windows smashed yet again.

Listen in the Box

160

The entrance to **SoundBox** is a door behind the San Francisco Opera that is normally reserved for artists. This door leads into an enormous warehouse with 50-foot (15-meter) ceilings. There, 500 audience members sit on ottomans, sipping cocktails and waiting with anticipation as a group of musicians prepares to play. Surrounding giant screens display underwater landscapes. It's the start of a singular experience.

In 2014, the San Francisco Opera decided it needed to attract a younger audience. It came up with the idea of holding evenings of musical exploration and creating a nightclub-type setting for them. It was a brilliant concept, and the public loved it.

Each show offers the audience a different musical program that draws on classical and contemporary repertoire. The San Francisco Symphony musicians overturn your expectations: a flute sings like a whale, a tuba impersonates an electric guitar, a pianist uses everyday objects to strike the piano strings.

Spectators are invited to move around during the performances, to drink and share their experiences on social media. It's a long way from the traditional stuffy concert hall. Thanks to the acoustic system (called Constellation, made by Meyer and consisting of 25 microphones and 85 speakers), it's an extraordinary experience. Get there early (doors open at 8 p.m.) if you want to get a seat. To reserve a ticket (about $35), go to sfsoundbox.com [300 Franklin St.].

Panoramic Baseball and Garlic Fries

161

If you're in town between April and October, you absolutely have to watch a Giants game at the **AT&T Park** stadium, especially on a Sunday afternoon. It's hard to find a lovelier panoramic view. San Francisco Bay and its many boats decorate the horizon. I also like the building itself, which is located right downtown (making it very accessible). It has great decor and a boisterous atmosphere, and best of all (no surprise in this city of foodies) the food is fantastic. Tacos, crab sandwiches, sushi, Chinese, gelato, vegetarian food and more; there's something for everyone. Don't leave without trying the garlic fries at **Gilroy Garlic Fries**.

If you can't get tickets, you can see part of the terrain for free from the south side of the stadium, on McCovey Cove. You'll find about 100 people taking advantage of the view during each game [24 Willie Mays Plaza].

Before each game, Giants fans congregate at the **21st Amendment Brewery**, a microbrewery. Get ready for a tide of orange jerseys, and be sure to try their watermelon beer [563 2nd St.].

The Greenest Restaurant in the U.S.

162

When you walk through the door of **The Perennial**, there's nothing to indicate that you're in the most environmentally friendly restaurant in the United States. The decor is sleek and modern. The tables, chairs and stools, industrial light fixtures and concrete walls are similar to restaurants in Stockholm. It's a far cry from the "granola" decor you would normally associate with environmentally friendly restaurants.

The fruit of two years' labor, The Perennial is the baby of Anthony Myint and Karen Leibowitz, partners in life and work. They've already created several hit restaurants, including Mission Chinese Food and Commonwealth. These restaurants all have a charitable component; Mission Chinese Food, for instance, donates part of its profits to local food banks.

After getting their hands on the 5,000-square-foot (465-square-meter) facility near Twitter headquarters, Anthony and Karen wanted to do something different: They decided to open the most environmentally sound restaurant possible. They didn't cut any corners.

All the pieces of kitchen equipment were chosen based on how much energy they used. The "smart" vent hood can detect particulate matter and only activates during cooking. The tiles on the walls are made from recycled clay. The furniture is recycled wood, and the plastic is recovered from the ocean. And that's only the beginning.

Anthony co-founded ZeroFoodprint, a nonprofit organization that advises restaurants on how to reduce their carbon emissions. Following a long study on greenhouse gas emissions from various restaurants around the world, he discovered that a restaurant's footprint depends mainly on the ingredients it uses.

Choosing the right ingredients is the crucial first step.

The two owners considered which breed of cow emits the least methane during its lifetime, and chose to buy from a supplier that raises livestock in a clean and humane way. Their bread is made with Kernza, a perennial wheat produced in Kansas. Its long roots (they reach up to 10 feet deep) capture a lot of carbon.

The farm-to-table movement is a household name by now. The goal at The Perennial, however, is table-to-farm. Karen and Anthony found a spot in Oakland to build an aquaponic greenhouse, a symbiotic system that uses fish farming to fertilize growing plants. Vegetable and meat scraps from the restaurant serve as food for worms and soldier fly larvae. When those creatures are dehydrated, they make excellent food for the fish in tanks. The nutrient-rich water from the tanks is used to water herbs and various types of lettuce. As for the solid waste from the fish, it's perfect for fertilizing the garden. "Our restaurant scraps help fertilize the earth at the farm, which is where the ingredients used in the

restaurant are grown," says Karen. "The cycle is complete."

And how about the menu itself? During my visit, I relished a pumpkin seed bisque, and grilled trout with sautéed parsnips, served in a mussel and bone-marrow broth. Lamb, pork, beef tartare and gnocchi are also on the menu, along with a number of vegetarian dishes created by the chef, Chris Kinuya, who studied at the now-defunct Copenhagen restaurant Noma.

Even the bar system has been overhauled. A number of cocktails are pre-prepared and served on tap to avoid the waste of ice and water. For some drinks, the ice is even frozen to the bottom of the glass (it creates a pretty cool effect). The fruit zests and peels from the kitchen are used to make hydrosols (floral waters) and essential oils, which are used in the cocktails.

"The goal is to ensure that guests feel like they are in a "real" restaurant. If diners want to learn more, the waiters can answer their questions. But, above all, it is the quality of the meal that counts. We are not critical," says Karen [59 9th St.].

San Franciscans have a slew of applications on their smartphones that the rest of the country probably hasn't even heard of yet. In the city of techies, there's an app for everything: washing clothes (Washio); fresh meal delivery (Munchery); renting your car to tourists when you're away on holiday (FlightCar); eating a gourmet meal at a stranger's house (EatWith); getting a meal delivered by bicycle from a restaurant that doesn't offer delivery services (Postmates); getting a valet to pick up your car when you can't find parking (Luxury); or having alcohol delivered to your home in less than an hour (Minibar).

The Prelingers' Book Collection

163 At the corner of 8th Street and Folsom, you'll find a beige and white building (there's a carpet dealer on the main floor). Press the buzzer and take the elevator to the second floor. Go past the different offices and a dance studio, and you'll get to door 215. Behind it lies the most original library in San Francisco. The pink neon sign above the door that says "Free Speech, Fear Free" sets the mood.

Rick and Megan Prelinger decided to open their private collection of almost 50,000 books to the public in 2004. **Prelinger Library** is an idiosyncratic library, to be sure. Overflowing with books, the six sections are a reflection of the owners' varied interests.

You'll find old copies of *TV Guide*, books on the destruction of a forgotten island, concert posters ripped from telephone poles, thousands of independent magazines, city archives, books on architecture, design, geography and natural history. Others on media, politics and cartography, and rare books about cities all over the world. The Prelingers have books and documents that you wouldn't normally find in public libraries. And the books aren't organized as they would be in a traditional library—they aren't even catalogued. Instead, Megan classifies them logically, by subject. The collection starts with San Francisco and ends with space. You don't come here to do specific research but to make discoveries. I spent a full afternoon losing myself in the section on California architecture. The library is open Wednesday from 1:00 p.m. to 8 p.m. It may open on other days as well; the schedule for the rest of the week is random. Take a look on prelingerlibrary.org/home. As a bonus, they also serve tea [301 8th St.].

Great Meals Near the Stadium

164

Marlowe (A) is a bistro that specializes in comfort food, reimagined. Their roasted tomato soup with smoked cheddar and sourdough is the perfect lunch. The regulars love the fried chicken sandwich and the boozy brunch. The modern decor is several shades of white and has some rustic touches; it feels a bit like a chic butcher shop [500 Brannan St.].

Right around the corner is **Cockscomb**. Run by celebrity chef Chris Cosentino, the restaurant offers a brand of California cuisine in which meat takes center stage. It's in almost every dish. In Chris' version of puttanesca, the pasta is replaced with pigs' ears, sliced like spaghetti; baked oysters are served with *nduja* (a sausage spread); and the sprout salad is garnished with pork rinds. The star of the menu is an entire pig's head, cooked in a wood-burning oven. Served with gold leaf on the snout, it's a sight worthy of *Game of Thrones*. The restaurant is situated in a two-story former shoe factory; there are stuffed animal heads on the walls [564 4th St.].

164A

Photo Exhibition Under the Bridge

165

In 2010, a onetime hangar under the Bay Bridge was converted into an exhibition hall named **Pier 24 Photography**. The project came about thanks to Andrew Pilara, a wealthy businessperson and photo collector who spent more than $12 million on the building. At 28,000 square feet (2,600 square meters), it's the largest photo gallery in the world. And yet, since only 20 people are admitted at one time, visiting it still feels like an intimate experience.

As you move through the vast space, you're likely to find yourself lingering in front of a single photo, getting lost in the image. It's open from Monday to Friday; make a reservation at pier24.org/visit. Entry is free. [Pier 24, The Embarcadero].

I also really like **RayKo Photo Center**, a large industrial space on the side of the highway in the same neighborhood. About 10 art shows are held there each year. Photographers can even rent the darkrooms in the back [428 3rd St.].

165

The Floating Homes of Mission Creek

166

Near AT&T Park, in the shadow of highway 280, lies a very special microneighborhood. It consists of about 20 homes floating on the Mission Creek Canal. When you arrive, you feel like you've walked into a tiny fishing village—and yet you're just a few minutes from downtown.

The **Mission Creek** houseboats community has been around since the 1960s. Most of the residents are artists, but some young professionals have started moving in the last few years. Each house has a distinct look. Some haven't been repaired in years; others look like they're fresh out of the pages of a design magazine. The residents live tranquil lives, lulled by the waves and with sea lions, rays and herring as neighbors. They even have a community garden.

The houses rise and fall with the tides, and water levels can change by more than six feet. For a long time, the community was completely isolated, but today new office towers loom overhead. That's just a part of life in San Francisco, where no one is safe from the ambitions of real estate developers. To get to the neighborhood, cross the 3rd Street bridge and walk down Channel Street till you get to Mission Creek Garden. From there you can kayak in the canal and around the baseball stadium. For information, go to citykayak.com.

The Diner on the Water

167

At Pier 30, you'll find **Red's Java House**, an old greasy spoon on the water. It's a great spot for the basics: bacon and eggs, fish-and-chips and hot dogs. The sign above the counter is unambiguous: "We don't serve lettuce or tomato." With a breathtaking view of the Bay Bridge, Red's is popular with old-timers as well as young employees who work at SoMa startups. Open since the 1930s, the restaurant used to serve longshoremen and sailors. Today, many cyclists and motorcyclists stop there during a ride. Red leather stools, yellow walls, windows that frame the Bay Bridge and archival photos complete the decor inside. Order the cheeseburger on sourdough with pickles and yellow mustard, and take a seat on the patio out back [Pier 30, The Embarcadero, at Bryant St.].

The Lights of Bay Bridge

168

Since 2013, the Bay Bridge has been illuminated with 25,000 LED lights hung on vertical suspension cables. It's the largest LED sculpture in the world. The work of artist Leo Villareal, originally from New Mexico, **The Bay Lights** glow from dusk to dawn. Each little light was individually programmed by the creator. Donations from patrons made the installation possible. Road safety was an obvious concern, but the lights aren't actually visible from the bridge itself. You can definitely admire them from The Embarcadero, however. I think the best view is from the Waterbar restaurant, where you can enjoy the experience while savoring oysters on the terrace. It's completely magical [399 The Embarcadero].

The Pizza Purist

169

The best pizza I've had in San Francisco was from **Una Pizza Napoletana** (A). The restaurant belongs to Anthony Mangieri, a pizza chef who's been perfecting his craft for more than 30 years. Mangieri, a mountain-biking fanatic whose arms are covered in punk and religious tattoos, specializes in Neopolitan pizza. It's a true obsession for him. Despite the popularity of the restaurant, he still makes every ball of dough, and garnishes and cooks every pizza, personally—in silence, by himself. In that respect, he's a bit like another pizza legend, Dom DeMarco from Brooklyn's Di Fara Pizza.

There's no hoopla at Anthony's restaurant. The oven sits in the middle of the room, surrounded by a few wooden tables. The austere decor leaves room for the pizza to take center stage. A maestro devoted to his work, Anthony prepares about 100 pizzas each night, while customers wait as patiently as they can for their meal to come out of the oven.

Born in New Jersey into an Italian-American family, Anthony fell in love with pizza at the age of 15. He spent more than 20 years mastering naturally leavened dough. His pizza crust comes close to perfection. The bare-bones menu has five kinds of pizzas: Marinara, Margherita, Bianca, Filetti and my favorite, Ilaria (smoked mozzarella, cherry tomatoes, arugula, olive oil and sea salt). On Saturday, Anthony adds the Apollonia (egg, salami, buffalo mozzarella, etc.) There are no appetizers or desserts. At $25 a pizza, it's not cheap, but pizza purists will be delighted. Open from Wednesday to Saturday, from 5 p.m. until the dough runs out. Try to get there early; they don't take reservatons [210 11th St.].

I also like the pizza at **Zero Zero**, a two-story restaurant in the same neighborhood. It requires less in the way of patience. They have a good selection of antipasti, and they serve soft ice cream for dessert, with a range of toppings [826 Folsom St.].

The Atrium of Airbnb

170 SoMa (South of Market) is San Francisco's tech company neighborhood. All the big names are there: Wired, Twitter, Dropbox and, of course, Airbnb, the famous community platform for renting out private residences that began in 2008. Airbnb's district has some of the nicest offices in the city. The company completely renovated a 1917 factory space. When you enter, you'll see an atrium with a 1,240-square-foot (115-square-meter) green wall. It's open to the public on Mondays and Fridays. Most of the employees come to work on their bikes; some even bring their dogs. Meeting rooms are decorated like Airbnb houses and apartments around the world. One looks like a Parisian flat; another imitates a house in Bali; another, a room in Milan. The cafeteria is an exact replica of CEO Brian Chesky's SoMa apartment—the very first Airbnb lodging [888 Brannan St.].

Twitter, Airbnb, Zinga, LinkedIn and DropBox all have physical locations in SoMa—in fact, one block is home to companies worth a total of about 50 billion dollars.

Fast Food for Foodies

171

Because of its high concentration of young employees, SoMa is full of great lunch spots. **Deli Board**, a sandwich shop, specializes in corned beef and pastrami. The menu changes every day. Try the Jay (if you're lucky enough to see it on the menu when you go): three layers of thinly sliced turkey, spicy peppers, provolone and their special sauce [1058 Folsom St.].

At **Darwin Cafe**, the sandwiches are served on a crunchy French bread, like in Paris. There are some surprising flavor combinations, like Nutella and mascarpone or turkey, rhubarb jam, roasted almonds, garlic mayonnaise and Brie; but also classics like ham, Gruyère and Dijon [212 Ritch St.].

For comfort food, I recommend **Citizen's Band** (A), a modern diner with a truly eclectic menu, with mac and cheese, poutine, coleslaw, ramen and farro salad [1198 Folsom St.].

For a quality coffee after your meal, go by **Sightglass Coffee** (B), a two-story café with an industrial look. The coffee is roasted on-site, in full view of the customers. Sightglass serves as a de facto office for a number of young entrepreneurs. On the first floor is Affogato Bar, which serves the famous Italian dessert of a scoop of ice cream drizzled with espresso [270 7th St.].

Gourmet Food in the SoMa

172

Bar Agricole (A) is a restaurant for every occasion. In front of the restaurant, you can eat on the large terrace with a fountain and plenty of greenery—in a Zen atmosphere. Inside, the long bar serves the best cocktails in the country (from $11 to $17). They go great with oysters and appetizers. The Californian cuisine of chef Melissa Reitz is terrific, and the dishes are colorful (citrus salad with green lentils, lime confit and chrysanthemum, etc.). The acrylic curtains that hang from the ceiling, the wooden slats that line the walls, the servers' uniforms and the photos above the bar are all from local artisans [355 11th St.].

The restaurant is right next to **Slim's**, a legendary concert venue where you can hear jazz, folk, blues, R&B, hip-hop and heavy metal. Check out the schedule at slimspresents.com/slims [333 11th St.].

At **AQ**, the menu, decor and servers' apparel all change according to the season. The chef, Mark Liberman, offers a four-course set menu ($82) or a tasting menu ($110). For the latter, the servers show you just a list of about 30 ingredients that the chef uses as inspiration for the menu. The concept is farm-to-table. Simple-seeming dishes reveal their complexity as soon as you take a bite. Almonds in a salad turn out to be rings of almond milk panna cotta. What look like walnuts is actually powder that liquefies when it comes in contact with your tongue [1085 Mission St.].

173

An Empty Lot for Food Trucks

173

One of the largest gatherings of food trucks takes place in an industrial area in SoMa. The **SoMa StrEat Food Park** is an oasis in a food desert. The owner of the spot, Carlos Muela, had to wait two years to get approval from the city to fill an empty lot with food trucks. When he finally did, it was an instant success. From traditional Jewish food to Guatemalan, Mexican and Japanese cuisine, you never know what kind of food you'll find; there are about a dozen trucks that are always in rotation. One food truck specializes in bacon and another offers beer, wine, sangria and mimosas on Sundays. There's a toilet on-site, as well as heat lamps, a free Wi-Fi connection, arcade games, and tables in a converted school bus [428 11th St.].

The Mission

This gentrifying Hispanic neighborhood is home to an explosion of colors and flavors. Murals brighten the urban landscape, and restaurants, bars and cafés number in the dozens. While Valencia Street is packed with trendy shops and restaurants, Mission Street, which runs parallel, has remained authentic. As a bonus, you're sure to find blue skies—this is one of the only neighborhoods that stays fog-free.

The Mission

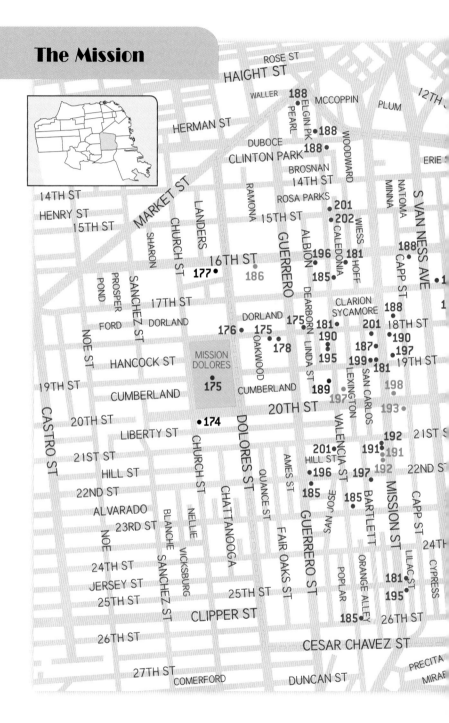

● Sights + photo ops
● Bars + restaurants
● Stores + markets
● Arts + culture
● Activities + walks

10TH ST
JUNIPER
HARRISON ST
9TH ST
BRYANT ST
LANGTON
DORE ST
8TH ST
JORFOLK
BRANNAN
DIVISION

CENTRAL FWY
88
ALAMEDA
DIVISION
BERRY S
CAROLINA
HOOPER
IRWIN ST
HUBBELL

THE MISSION
6TH ST
15TH ST
SAN BRUNO AVE
15TH ST
16TH ST

17TH ST
RHODE ISLAND ST
CAROLINA ST
17TH ST
MARIPOSA ST

TREAT
MARIPOSA ST
UTAH ST
POTRERO AVE
VERMONT ST
SAN BRUNO
18TH ST
MISSOURI ST
CONNECTICUT ST

179●● 179
BRYANT ST
YORK
19TH ST
DE HARO ST
WISCONSIN ST

194● 19TH ST
BAYSHORE FWY
19TH ST
S HEIGHTS
ARKANSAS ST

196●● 203
201

185
KANSAS ST
CAROLINA ST

TREAT AVE
HAMPSHIRE ST
22ND ST
VERMONT
23RD ST
DE HARO ST
CONNECTICUT

5
FLORIDA ST
ALABAMA ST
BRYANT ST
YORK ST
SAN BRUNO

23RD ST
●200
24TH ST
UTAH ST
25TH

183 183
183
183 182
25TH
CAROLINA ST

3 183
184
184
BALMY
25TH ST
26TH ST

184●
LUCKY ST
26TH ST
CESAR CHAVEZ ST

PRECITA AVE
PERALTA AVE
NAPOLEON ST
MULLEN

The Golden Fire Hydrant

174 The terrible earthquake that struck San Francisco in 1906 destroyed almost 80 percent of the city and killed more than 3,000 people. Most of the damage was actually due to fires caused by gas leaks after the earthquake. Making matters worse, many water pipes ruptured, leaving the fire hydrants dry. Firefighters watched helplessly as the city went up in flames. Miraculously, one fire hydrant survived—in the southwest corner of Dolores Park. After battling the fire for more than seven hours, firefighters were able to save the Mission neighborhood from total destruction. Each year, on April 18—the anniversary of the earthquake—the hydrant gets a fresh coat of gold paint from the fire chief and local residents. The event happens at exactly 5:12 a.m.—the moment the earthquake hit. The hydrant is affectionately known as the **Little Giant**. [20th St., at the corner of Church St., outside the park].

Picnic on Hipster Hill

175 Watching the incredible mix of species that populate Dolores Park is a spectacle unto itself. Bongo-players and vegan punks, cyclists and Frisbee tossers, yogis and pot-smokers, Hare Krishnas and hula-hoopers, winos and vendors of cookies, Costco pizza or illicit substances. On weekends, when the weather's nice, around 10,000 people can be found enjoying the expanse of the park. So many of San Francisco's most colorful characters gather here that it almost seems like a miniature Woodstock—in the shade of palm trees. The park's slope has earned the very appropriate name of **Hipster Hill**. In 2016, major renovations were done to the park (to the tune of $20 million); new public toilets [19th St. at the corner of Dolores St.] were installed, among other things. To find provisions for a picnic, head to **Bi-Rite Market** [see Reason #176; 3639 18th St.] or grab a pizza: I recommend **Pizzeria Delfina** [3611 18th St.] or **Farina** [3560 18th St.].

The Grocer

176 "Welcome to my anti-supermarket!" exclaimed Sam Mogannam, owner of **Bi-Rite** grocery store, which has been around since the 1940s. "When a customer walks through the door of my shop, they are treated like a guest in my home."

Stores that sell only local and organic products are an integral part of the neighborhood, and are also a big part of the San Francisco lifestyle. People tend to go shopping several times a week to stock up on fresh produce. The honey comes from rooftop beehives, the vegetables come from his garden in Sonoma County, and the jams are from his mother's kitchen.

The Mogannam family, Palestinian immigrants, bought the business in 1964. Sam worked at his father's grocery store from the age of 6 to 17 after school, and full-time in the summer. He dreamed of becoming a chef, but eventually took over the family business in 1997. He preserved the art deco facade, as well as the original neon lights and light fixtures, but he changed everything that was on the shelves. He also added an open kitchen to prepare takeout food, worthy of the top restaurants, which was unprecedented at the time.

Back then, the area was experiencing some major changes. "Dolores Park was the headquarters for street gangs, all the houses had bars on their windows, and it was not uncommon to hear gunshots." In 1997, a police presence was established in the park, and slowly the tide began to turn.

Today, Sam considers this stretch of 18th Street (between Dolores and Guerrero streets) as the culinary heart of the city, thanks to establishments like Tartine Bakery, the Delfina pizzeria, and his favorite café, Fayes Video & Espresso Bar. Don't leave without tasting his wife's legendary ice cream [3639 18th St.].

The **Bi-Rite Creamery & Bakeshop** counter is about 350 feet (100 meters) west on the same street [3692 18th St.]. The strawberry and balsamic vinegar ice cream (served in spring and summer) is divine, as is Sam's sundae, made with chocolate ice cream, bergamot olive oil, sea salt and whipped cream.

Just next door, at 3674, is **18 Reasons**—a cooking school for struggling families. Founded by Sam, it is a nonprofit organization. "It teaches children to cook with fresh ingredients. For many of them, it's the only time of the week when they eat vegetables. They go home with a bag of food for their families." He sees over 2,500 students each year.

"I want to create a community through food. That is the mission of our grocery store. I'm not doing this for money. I just want to feed people."

The Oldest Church

177 Don't leave the area without taking a look inside **Mission Dolores** (or Mission San Francisco de Asís), just two blocks from the park. The church was built between 1782 and 1791, making it not just the oldest church in San Francisco, but the city's oldest building (that's still intact), period. In the early 2000s, a treasure was discovered hidden behind the huge altar. It was a mural painted by Ohlone Indians when the building was constructed. (Part of this mural has been reproduced on the facade of Mission Community Market, on Bartlett Street [between 21st St. and 22nd St.]). Don José Joaquín Moraga, the Spanish officer who founded both the Mission and the Presidio of San Francisco in 1776, is buried under the altar. The cemetery next to it is believed be a burial site for thousands of Ohlone and Miwok—the indigenous peoples of the region—who helped build the church. The different Mexican, Irish and English names on the tombstones—for example, Luis Antonio Argüello, the first governor of California during Mexican rule—are a reflection of, in part, the fascinating history of San Francisco [3321 16th St.].

The Master Bread-Maker

178 Starting at 4:30 p.m. each day, a line forms in front of Tartine Bakery. Everyone is waiting to get their hands on one of the 250 loaves of sourdough bread prepared by **Chad Robertson**, who is nicknamed the "Jiro of bread" (a reference to the Japanese sushi master). They disappear like hotcakes, in just minutes! I like to go in the afternoon, when the crowd is smaller, to order their legendary grilled cheese.

A visit to San Francisco is not complete until you've tasted the famous baker's creations, and his wife Elisabeth Prueitt's pastries. They met in their early twenties at the Culinary Institute, and have become a power couple in the San Francisco culinary world. Chad, now in his mid-forties, grew up in Texas. While on a trip to Massachusetts, he had a revelation when he discovered the sourdough bread made by noted baker Richard Bourdon (Berkshire Mountain Bakery). It was his first experience with the smell of bread baked in a wood oven. Bourdon became his mentor, and subsequently Chad did an internship in France under another master baker, Patrick Le Port.

When he returned home he opened his first bakery in Tomales Bay (a 90-minute drive north of San Francisco). He spent six years perfecting his art, lost in a hypnotic trance. Chad challenged himself to make a bread that even gluten-intolerant people could digest. To do this, he uses only whole grains milled on-site and a natural

leavener during the fermentation stage, which lasts a few days. He uses a lot of water in his recipe to keep the bread moist, and bakes it in a very hot wood-burning oven. The result is irresistible: a moist, light texture inside with a crispy crust. "A loaf with an old soul!" he calls it. Chad attributes part of his success to where he lives. "The pace of life in San Francisco is slower, so we have time to experiment and really devote ourselves to one thing. In New York, the first priority is to pay the rent! I also believe that San Franciscans appreciate the work of artisans." Chad has chosen to reverse the typical baker's schedule to improve his quality of life. He surfs in the morning and bakes in the afternoon, which is why he starts selling his bread from 5:00 p.m. onward. In the coming years, he plans to open other Tartine stores in San Francisco, Los Angeles, New York and Tokyo. "Tartine is bigger than me now. Now it's up to my teams to carry the torch," he explained during our meeting at Blue Bottle Coffee in the Mission, where many people came up to say hello to him. There's no doubt about it: In San Francisco, he is the foodies' Messiah [600 Guerrero St.].

As I am writing this, Tartine was planning to close its doors temporarily for renovations. The reopening date is yet to be determined. But you can always check out Chad Robertson's other restaurant-bakery. (see Reason #179).

Ceramics and Gourmet Treats

179

Look underneath the cups and plates in any good restaurant in San Francisco: There's a good chance you'll find the inscription "**Heath Ceramics**." If I could afford it, all my dishes would bear that inscription. Influenced by the Bauhaus movement and New Mexico pottery, ceramist Edith Heath (1911-2005) founded her pottery brand in 1947. Seventy years later, her company continues to produce artisanal mid-century modern style dishware. You can watch the works being created at the shop in the Mission. For a free guided tour, book your spot at heathceramics.com/san-francisco [2900 18th St.].

At the same location, there's also an outlet of the popular **Blue Bottle Coffee** chain. And, it's the home of **Tartine Manufactory**, the new artisanal bakery-restaurant by Chad Robertson (owner of Tartine Bakery). The Manufactory is another place where you can watch master craftspersons at work, as its bakers operate a flour mill behind a large window. In this 5,000-square-foot (465-square-meter) space, everything is made by hand: ice cream, jams, pickles, breads, pastries and even pizzas, using long-fermented dough. Never has pizza been this easy to digest.

The Danger Dog Experience

180

Another tradition in the Mission (especially after a night of imbibing) is to eat a **Danger Dog**: a bacon-wrapped hot dog that's made on carts on street corners. Served with grilled onions, jalapeno peppers, ketchup, mustard and mayonnaise, it's San Francisco's version of New York City's Dirty Water Dog...except that it's a lot better. Just follow your nose on Mission Street or Valencia Street [between 16th and 24th St.].

The Quest for the Best Burrito

181 A never-ending debate rages on in San Francisco: Where can you get the best burrito? Everyone has their own personal list; so here's mine: First, **La Taqueria** (A), for its ambiance, and for its friendly owner, Miguel Jara. The burritos here don't have rice. Try the Carnitas (braised pork), his most popular fare. [2889 Mission St.].

If the lineup looks too long, head for **Taqueria Cancún** (B), which is a bit farther north on the same street. The decor is like a Mexican festival, popping with colors. Their specialty is the Burrito Mojado (wet burrito), topped with spicy salsa, guacamole and sour cream [2288 Mission St.].

I also love **Pancho Villa Taqueria** for its enormous burritos, its salsas and its shrimp tacos [3071 16th St.]. **Taqueria El Buen Sabor**, an authentic family taqueria, is the ideal local restaurant. You can eat for a measly $5. The vegetarian burrito, the guacamole and the quesadillas are absolutely delicious [699 Valencia St.].

A Retro Breakfast

182 For brunch, I like to go to **St. Francis Fountain**, an old ice cream parlor that's steeped in nostalgia. It was founded in 1918 by a family of Greek immigrants. The decor hasn't changed since the 1950s, but the menu has been updated for contemporary tastes. Along with traditional diner meals (with impressive portions) and their famous milkshakes, the menu has a number of vegan options, including their famous blueberry pancakes [2801 24th St.].

A Cultural Walk on 24th Street

183 24th Street between Alabama and Folsom streets is my favorite part of the Mission. The street is lined with trees, and there are many independent shops, like the book and stationary store **Press: Works On Paper** [3108 24th St.]; unique art galleries like **Galería de la Raza**, which displays the work of Latin American artists [2857 24th St.]; authentic Mexican bakeries like **La Victoria**, which has been open since 1951 [2937 24th St.]; Cuban restaurants, such as **El Nuevo Frutilandia**, where you really need to try the Mofongo with roast pork [3077 24th St.]; and Scandinavian-style cafés like **Haus** (the terrace out back is a well-kept secret) [3086 24th St.]. You'll find places of all types that blend together on a single street.

Make a stop at **Wise Sons Jewish Delicatessen**, which specializes in traditional Jewish dishes made with fresh local ingredients. Everything is made in-house, from the rye bread to the chocolate babka to the pickles. Try their pastrami sandwich, along with a matzo ball soup. The egg, cheese and avocado sandwich on a bialy roll is perfect for breakfast [3150 24th St.].

Finish your promenade with an ice cream at **Humphry Slocombe**, a small artisanal shop with original flavors like lime and cayenne, bourbon and cornflakes, kumquat and poppy seed, goat cheese and red wine sorbet, and miso and pear. The flavors change every month—you never know what taste sensations you're going to encounter [2790 Harrison St.].

Technicolor Alleys

184

There are some 3,000 outdoor murals in San Francisco, and most of them are concentrated in the Mission. They bring life to garage doors, store facades and school walls. Two alleys, in particular, are especially worth a visit: **Clarion Alley** [between Valencia St. and Mission St.]; and **Balmy Alley** [between 24th St. and 25th St.], which boasts some 40 murals.

Muralist Patricia Rose has lived in the Mission since the 1970s. She's part of the **Precita Eyes Muralists** collective, a nonprofit organization founded in 1977 to encourage the community to create murals. "It's a reunification project," says Rose, who gives guided tours of the murals. You can book a spot on a tour by emailing tours@precitaeyes.org, or just show up [2981 24th St.].

Diego Rivera is believed to have introduced the mural art form to San Francisco in the 1930s. There was a renewal of murals in the 1970s: most of them, painted by women, reflect the reality of immigrants from Nicaragua, El Salvador and Guatemala, who were fleeing violence. "The Mission has always been a gateway for immigrants," explains Rose.

Today, the murals evoke another reality, that of gentrification. Affluent residents are steadily moving into the neighborhood, pushing out the less advantaged. The murals' political messages denounce Silicon Valley and real estate developers. "This is life in San Francisco. One cycle replaces another, and so it's been since the Gold Rush," she adds.

Foodie Neighborhood

185

The Mission is probably the neighborhood with the most restaurants per square mile. There are spots for every taste and every budget. For pizza and pasta, three restaurants lead the pack: **Flour + Water**, for its Italian cuisine with Californian influences [2401 Harrison St.]; **Locanda Osteria**, for its Roman cuisine [557 Valencia St.]; and **Beretta** for its great selection of antipasti and thin-crust pizzas [1199 Valencia St.].

The bistro **Heirloom Cafe** is a favorite for many chefs because of its fresh seasonal cuisine, Mediterranean influences and great wine selection. The owner, Matt Straus, gives customers a warm welcome, like they were visiting his own home. Regulars know to order the hamburger ($12)—it isn't actually on the menu. The thick, juicy burger comes on a homemade English muffin with Époisses cheese, onion jam and arugula [2500 Folsom St.].

For a gourmet meal, **Aster** (A) offers a four-course fixed price menu for $65. The cuisine is Californian with Japanese influences. When I visited, I was thoroughly pleased by seaweed chips garnished with urchins, cold yellow beet soup, potato dumplings and salmon cooked to perfection [1001 Guerrero St.].

At **Al's Place**, veggies are the stars of the menu, and meat is relegated to side dishes. The young chef, Aaron London, is a genius with flavors. He uses every part of the vegetable: stem, peels, pulp and seeds—nothing is wasted. Order the salad with baby lettuce, avocado and pistachio crumble, and the chef's signature dish, black-lime cod served with curry bouillon. Even the fries ($8) get a special treatment. They're pickled in brine for 96 hours (with cabbage leaves to speed up fermentation), then fried in rice bran oil and served with apple barbeque sauce [1499 Valencia St.].

Bar Tartine has been a neighborhood institution since it opened in 2005. The chefs are inspired by French, Japanese, Hungarian and Scandinavian cuisine. They use different fermentation techniques to heighten the flavors of each dish. Take a seat at the bar and let yourself be amazed. A raw vegetable plate will have you falling in love with a simple radish. The beef tartare, served on a thick slice of rye bread and the sprouted mung bean croquettes are my favorites [561 Valencia St.].

Art that Changes Lives

186

Creativity Explored is an art gallery that's totally unique to San Francisco. Founded in 1983 to support artists with intellectual disabilities, the nonprofit organization helps them create, exhibit and sell their works. The founders, artist and educator Florence Ludins-Katz and psychologist Elias Katz, believe that artistic expression can change lives. It's pretty obvious that they're right. I've never seen such a joy-filled and colorful place, or met so many endearing individuals. The large studio behind the small gallery is open to the public. You can meet the 75 artists, who will proudly show you their art; some are incredibly talented. Aged 20 to 83, they were directed to the place by social workers. They paint, draw, knit and make ceramics. All their materials are provided, and they have access to courses given by professional artists. Fifty percent of sales go back to the artists. Some pieces have even ended up in museums. Open Monday to Friday, from 10:00 a.m. to 3 p.m., and until 7 p.m. on Thursdays. The artists leave at around 2 p.m. The gallery is also open on weekends, from noon to 5 p.m. [3245 16th St.].

The Restaurant Within a Restaurant

187

"Eclectic" is the first word that comes to mind to describe the hit restaurant **Mission Chinese Food**. It was founded by star chef Danny Bowien, the bad boy of the San Francisco restaurant scene. Born in South Korea and adopted by an Oklahoma family, Bowien is a self-taught master of Chinese food. He started by focusing on Szechuan cuisine, and later started adding European influences. In 2001, he opened a pop-up restaurant in a dilapidated Chinese restaurant named Lung Shan on Mission Street (the yellow sign is still there). The owner of Lung Shan agreed to share the kitchen. Bowien's dishes became so popular that he ended up taking over the entire space. The bric-a-brac decor has remained the same: There are paper dragons hanging from the ceiling, and Chinese lanterns and old wallpaper that has stood the test of time. The menu is constantly changing, but some dishes are always available. Try the Salt Cod Fried Rice, the Kung Pao Pastrami, the famous Pork Mapo Tofu or the strange—but satisfying—Mapo Burrito. A portion of the profits is donated to charity [2234 Mission St.].

Ramen, Sushi and More

188

"No Ramen, No Life" is the slogan at **Ken Ken Ramen** (A), a small restaurant with numerous red lanterns hanging from the ceiling, and where they take the art of ramen very seriously. The broths are delectable, and there are a number of vegan and vegetarian options. I recommend the Classic Hakata Tonkotsu (pork broth with braised pork, egg, shallots, mushrooms, pickled ginger and garlic oil). A full meal costs just $13 [3378 18th St.].

I like the ambiance, the hip-hop music and the modern Japanese decor at **Orenchi Beyond**. The ramen soups are prepared in view of the customers, like in Tokyo [174 Valencia St.]. Across the street is one of my favorite restaurants, **Burma Love** (B), which serves Burmese cuisine in a modern setting. Take a seat at the bar if the wait is too long. I always order a tea leaf salad, an eggplant curry and a coconut rice [211 Valencia St.].

Sushi purists take note: **Maruya** is the best restaurant in the neighborhood. To do better, you'd pretty much have to fly to Japan. The restaurant follows the Edomae tradition (the fish comes mainly from Tokyo Bay), the decor is Zen, with wood accents, and the chefs work in silence. If your wallet can handle it, order the chef's omakase menu ($150 per person). You can also order à la carte [2931 16th St.]. For a more affordable—and less intimidating—experience, chef Ao prepares fresh, original sushi rolls at the small restaurant **Sushi Zone** [1815 Market St.].

When you enter the inner courtyard of **Izakaya Rintaro**, you feel like you've been transported to Japan. The chef, Sylvan Brackett (born in Kyoto but raised in California), has filled the space with real Japanese antiques. He asked his father, a talented carpenter, to build all the furniture. The result is utterly Zen. Sylvan recreates classic izakaya (a Japanese tavern) dishes using Californian ingredients. Order the yakitori (skewers of meat or vegetables, grilled over charcoal) or the Teba No Karaage, a Japanese version of fried chicken [82 14th St.].

The Pirate's Emporium

189

Valencia Street between 16th and 24th streets has plenty of independent and eclectic shops, but **826 Valencia** really stands out from the crowd. Kids will love the eccentric store, which sells fake beards, pills to prevent scurvy, pirate flags, prosthetic hooks, compasses, magic powder that helps you escape from the belly of a whale and instruments for polishing silver. It's a general store for pirates. Behind a secret door, there's a writing workshop for kids with learning disabilities. Sales from the store are used to finance the free workshops, which are given by local volunteers. So why the pirate store theme? The building lies in a commercial zone; creating a storefront was the imaginative solution of the cofounders, author Dave Eggers and educator Nínive Calegari. Founded in 2002, the organization now has branches throughout the United States. Each city has a different theme. In New York, it's a shop for superheroes; Los Angeles has a supermarket for time travelers; in Ann Arbor, Michigan, it's a warehouse for robots; and Chicago is home to a store for secret agents. The goal is to appeal to children, so that they enter an environment where their imagination can take flight [826 Valencia St.].

Brunch Time

190

If I'm in the mood for a pastoral setting, I go to **Stable Café** (A), located in a stable that once belonged to James D. Phelan, San Francisco mayor from 1897 to 1902. Next to the café is a lovely flower garden with several tables. It's an oasis in the heart of the city. The menu is plain and simple: egg sandwiches, croque madame, huevos rancheros, granola, panini and quinoa salad [2128 Folsom St.].

When I have a hankering for cheese, I give thanks for the existence of **Mission Cheese**. It serves some of the best grilled cheese in the city. I tend to get California Gold (California cheddar, goat cheese, prosciutto and fig preserves), the Raclette (a bowl of roasted potatoes covered with melted cheese and pickles) or the crispy Mac & Cheese [736 Valencia St.].

When I want to get off the beaten path, I'm never disappointed with **Gracias Madre** (B), a vegan Mexican restaurant that even carnivores will love. I order the Quesadillas de Calabaza (roasted sweet potato, caramelized onions, cashew and pumpkinseed "cheese") and a Tropical Green smoothie (mango, pineapple, spinach, coconut milk, ginger and sea salt). The restaurant serves organic and local ingredients, and it's part of the popular Café Gratitude chain from Los Angeles. Tacos and cocktails are just $5 on weekdays from 3 p.m. to 6 p.m. [2211 Mission St.].

Californian Cuisine and Cinema Under the Stars

191

Foreign Cinema is the perfect spot for a romantic evening. The restaurant has an open-air interior garden decorated with strings of lights. Films—usually classics or newer releases—are projected on the back wall. When I was there, images from Wes Anderson's *The Royal Tenenbaums* lit up the courtyard. It's a huge space. A long corridor lined with candles leads to a large modern loft space with a fireplace, mezzanine, bar and heated outdoor patio (where the films are shown). All the various spaces have tables. An art gallery, **Modernism West**, connects to the patio; you can look at the works of art between appetizers and the main course. The menu is a celebration of Californian ingredients. The husband and wife chefs, John Clark and Gayle Pirie, prepare fresh and colorful dishes: lavender-baked goat cheese with vegetables and crostini; brandade (a cod emulsion); tuna ceviche with mango and avocado; beef carpaccio; Santa Barbara smoked salmon; and a wide selection of oysters. The restaurant is also a great brunch destination. It's best to make a reservation [2534 Mission St.].

The Perfect Theater

192

Alamo Drafthouse Cinema is a theater that's in a class of its own. The Alamo took over a 1920s movie house called the New Mission and completely renovated it. The long counters between the rows of seats serve as communal tables. You order directly from your seat, writing your name and choices on a piece of paper. The cinema offers complete bar service and a long list of original cocktails, milkshakes and snacks: truffle and Parmesan butter popcorn, shishito peppers, freshly baked cookies, salads, burgers, ribs, macaroni with aged cheddar, vegan pizzas and more. You can reserve your seat number ahead of time, just like at a show. It's recommended that you get there early to see the shorts before the main film [2550 Mission St.].

Continue your evening at **El Techo**, the only rooftop bar in the neighborhood [2516 Mission St.].

Self-Portrait as a House

193 A gray Victorian home may catch your attention at the corner of Capp and 20th streets. There's a sign for accordion repairs in the window. For more than 30 years, the house served as the residence and studio of David Ireland, the most influential conceptual artist on the West Coast. Today you can visit his former workplace and home and discover the fascinating universe of this artist.

Inside, visitors to **500 Capp Street** will find furniture, writings and many sculptures made out of objects from everyday life. There's a touch of humor in everything you see. The artist hung little messages beside holes in the walls in the staircase. An example: "The Safe Gets Away for the Second Time November 5, 1975."

Over the years, 500 Capp Street became a kind of self-portrait for David Ireland. Reflecting his personal history and embodying his artistic philosophy, it's his biggest work of art. The artist bought the run-down house for $50,000 in 1975. He spent the next two years stripping it down—almost like an archaeologist—scraping off layers of paint and wallpaper, removing moldings, leaving only bare walls, the skeleton of the building.

The dining room on the first floor is as dark as a cave. It's overflowing with objects Ireland brought back from trips to Florida. On the second floor, the yellow walls are covered in a shiny transparent polyurethane finish. At the end of the day, it glows with a wonderful amber hue.

Ireland left the house in 2004 due to his declining health (he died in 2009). The fate of the place was uncertain until 2008, when patron Carlie Wilmans, granddaughter of famous philanthropist Phyllis C. Wattis, bought the home and created the 500 Capp Street Foundation.

"I visited the house for the first time in 2008, just before it went on sale," says Carlie. "It felt like I was setting foot in another world. The house is quite traditional from the outside, but totally contemporary inside. It has miraculously survived both earthquakes and fires. There is a very special aura about this house, and I wanted to save it at all costs."

Ninety-minute guided tours are given on Wednesdays and Saturdays at 11 a.m., 2 p.m. and 4 p.m. There's a night tour on the last Thursday of each month. Book your ticket ($20 for adults) at: 500cappstreet.org/tours.

Rainy Day Bowling

194

Mission Bowling Club is a retro bowling alley with six lanes. But its menu is really what makes it stand out. Its specialty is gourmet comfort food, as well as cocktails, California wines and craft beers. It's the perfect place to spend the day with friends during inclement weather. On the menu are shepherd's pie, vegan burgers, house-made french fries, ribs, and their famous Mission Burger. Book a lane at missionbowlingclub.com [3176 17th St.].

Another interesting destination on a rainy day is the **Mission Cliffs** indoor climbing gym. It's the oldest in San Francisco and one of the largest, with 50-foot (15-meter) walls and 23,000 square feet (2,137 square meters) of climbing terrain waiting to challenge you. A course is offered for newbies, and you can rent equipment on-site. A day pass costs $20 [2295 Harrison St.].

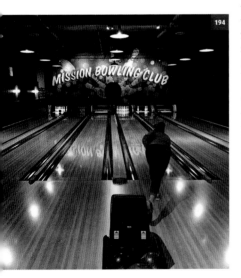

Desirable Desserts

195

Master chef William Werner reinterprets classics of French cuisine at his ultramodern bakery, **Craftsman and Wolves** (A). The menu includes smoked cheddar and hot pepper gougères (pastry puffs with cheese); tahini, passion fruit or hazelnut croissants; double chocolate croissants; Thai coconut green curry ginger scones; hibiscus cake; and egg baked in a savory muffin. The menu changes constantly—there's always a surprise for your eyes and your taste buds [746 Valencia St.].

Attention, chocolate lovers: **Dandelion Chocolate** is worth a visit—even if it's just for the heavenly aroma that envelops this artisanal chocolate maker. Every step of chocolate preparation takes place on-site, in view of the customers—from the roasting of cocoa beans to the wrapping of the delicate finished bars. Take a guided tour of the factory from Wednesday to Saturday at 6:00 p.m. ($5). You get to sample the chocolate at each stage of preparation, and hot chocolate is served at the end [740 Valencia St.].

Mission Pie serves only one thing: homemade pie. All its ingredients—eggs, wheat, fruits, and so on—are from local farms. The pie selection changes daily, and it's seasonal: strawberry and rhubarb in the spring, peach and berry in the summer, pumpkin in the fall, etc. Savor your slice with a latte. They also offer several vegan pies and even savory pies. By employing young people from the neighborhood, the restaurant serves an important social function in the Mission [2901 Mission St.].

195A   197

A Tour of the Bars

196

The Mission is probably the San Francisco neighborhood with the greatest number of bars. It has all types. **Trick Dog** is the most original—and probably the most fun. The bar's theme and its cocktail list change every six months. The menu might be presented as a Pantone color chart, a tourist map of the city, a puppy calendar, a zodiac sign circle or a Chinese restaurant menu that requires deciphering. The last time I went, the menu was a top-secret file, and cocktails had names like Biggie and Tupac, Illuminati, Moon Landing, Elvis Sighting and Area 51 [3010 20th St.].

I'm a regular customer at **Lone Palm**, a candlelit bar where you can drink a martini while sitting comfortably at a table with a white tablecloth. The art-deco-style decor gives it a Miami feel. The little bar is always filled with colorful characters, so fascinating encounters are very possible [3394 22nd St.].

Hideout is a bar "hidden" within another bar. Enter through the door to the bar Dalva, and look for another at the back of the room. It leads to a "secret" bar, less than 500 square feet (45 square meters) in size. They have specialty cocktails with freshly squeezed juices, artisanal syrups and fresh herbs. The decor is eclectic; a famous poster of Farrah Fawcett in a red one-piece bathing suit hangs over the bar [3121 16th St.].

Dance Spots

197

For live music, I like **Revolution Cafe**, a bohemian bar that's popular with local residents. There are concerts every night: classical, pop, world music and jazz (entry is free). On Thursday afternoons, the street is closed to traffic and it becomes a public market [3248 22nd St.].

On Monday nights, I go to Amnesia for live bluegrass. Wednesday evenings are exclusively for jazz. Entry is free [853 Valencia St.]. For dancing, the energy at **Little Baobab** (A) is unbeatable. The Senegalese restaurant transforms into a dance floor at 10 p.m. The tables are pushed back and patrons move to the rhythms of African music, Brazilian music and reggae until two in the morning. Wednesday night is salsa night [3372 19th St.].

San Franciscans pride themselves in choosing organic, local ingredients: duck eggs instead of chicken eggs, amaranth for breakfast instead of boring oatmeal, and ice cream made with buffalo milk instead of cow milk.

The Psychedelic Museum in a Victorian Home

198 From the outside, the white house on 20th Street between Capp and Mission streets looks pretty typical. Inside, however, you'll find a universe beyond all normalcy. It's the **Institute of Illegal Images**—otherwise known as the LSD Museum.

It's also the home of artist Mark McCloud, who has assembled one of the largest collections of psychedelic art in the world. Hundreds of artworks, made with more than 33,000 blotters of LSD, decorate the walls. "The acid on the paper is no longer active because of the effects of time and contact with oxygen," he explained, as I sat on an old sofa in his living room. Above the fireplace is a photo of Albert Hofmann, the Swiss scientist who discovered LSD in 1943. Hofmann died in 2008 at the age of 102. "That's Big Al, the father of LSD," said Mark reverently.

Mark McCloud's mission is to preserve some traces of the history of the drug culture that came to define the 1960s, "so that the youth of today will better understand my generation."

Now in his early 60s, Mark is tall and strong. His long salt-and-pepper hair is combed back; he's missing a tooth and carries two pairs of glasses around his neck. He wears patterned shirts and a velvet jacket that's too big, and his hand is perpetually holding a cigarette. He lights each new one with the butt of the last.

His home is something of a social club for people on the margins of society. The door is always open, and people pass through just to say hi, or to bring him a coffee.

Born in Detroit and raised in Argentina, Mark started taking psychedelic drugs when he was a teen. In 1971, a few days after his 18th birthday, while he was a med student at Santa Clara University in California, he took some particularly strong LSD—called Orange Sunshine—for the first time. It gave him "a feeling of death—and rebirth."

"It completely changed me. After that, I began collecting blotters. That was over 40 years ago. I consider it my duty to tell the story of LSD."

After spending a few years in Paris, he moved to San Francisco in 1971. For a while he lived at Francis Ford Coppola's Zoetrope Studios. He was able to buy the house on 20th Street, thanks to an arts grant from the Reagan administration, in 1983—ironically, right in the middle of the "War on Drugs" era.

Not surprisingly, Mark found himself targeted by the FBI. Agents made seizures at his home and arrested him twice, in 1992 and 2001, charging him with conspiring to distribute LSD. He was acquitted both times. "Never two times without a third! I'm getting ready for them to come back someday!" If you'd like to visit the museum, write to Mark at mark@ blotterbarn.com [2475 Mission St.].

The Supper Club

199

Lazy Bear is different from most restaurants. To dine there, first you buy a ticket on their website, as you would for a concert or a theater performance. You pay for the meal and tip in advance. The idea is that when you finally get there, you'll feel like you've been invited for dinner at someone's home.

Forty people come together to share this gourmet experience that is carefully prepared by the chef, David Barzelay. Guests are first welcomed by a hostess in a checkered shirt; she leads you to the mezzanine, which is decorated like a mid-century modern chalet. There you spend some time chatting with the other guests, drinking punch and enjoying some hors d'oeuvres. Forty-five minutes later, you're escorted to one of two large tables. The meal is about to begin. Seating is assigned—it's another way to encourage new interactions. There's no separation between the kitchen and the dining room, so you can see the cooks at work.

"We will interrupt you many times during the meal," warns David Barzelay ("Lazy Bear" is an anagram of his name). Barzeley will appear and ask that each guest introduce themselves to their neighbor. Voila, the ice is broken for you.

Everything is now in place for the 14-course symphony to begin. The menu changes each week. During my visit, it included English creamy green pea soup, a grilled onion broth, halibut with truffles, rabbit, lamb, and myriad desserts with unexpected flavors. The menu is always presented in a notebook, which comes with a pencil, so that guests can take notes during their meal.

It's a singular experience—but it'll cost you. The meal is $155 to $185 for 14 services. Tickets must be purchased a month in advance at lazybearsf.com [3416 19th St.].

The Secret Gallery

200

Every day, scores of people walk by the little green and yellow building with curtained windows at the end of 24th Street, without suspecting that a secret art gallery lies within. There's only one way to view the **Savernack Street Gallery**: Turn on the light switch beside the door and peer through the peephole. Inside, you'll see a small room, with miniature art that appears life-sized. The gallery was started in 2013 by the artist Carrie Katz, who wanted to make a statement about how hard it is for emerging artists to break through in San Francisco—mainly because of high real estate prices. The space you're looking at is the only one she could afford. The exhibits change each month, and it's open for perusal 24 hours a day [2411 24th St.].

Cafés for Connoisseurs

201

In San Francisco—maybe even more than in Seattle—coffee is not taken lightly. Each San Franciscan is loyal to their own favorite independent chain, and frequents the café religiously. Get ready to do some serious sipping.

Here are my favorite cafés in the Mission. For a great latte, I like **Sightglass Coffee** (A), the nicest café in the city (in my opinion). It has black-and-white-tiled flooring, a long wooden counter, burgundy leather banquettes, big, paned windows that let beams of light stream in, high ceilings, exotic plants plus an aqua-blue facade—the interior design alone is worth the trip. It's the café everyone wishes they had in *their* neighborhood [3014 20th St.]. There's also a bigger location in SoMa, (see Reason #171).

Four Barrel Coffee roasts its beans in-house and serves coffee in lovely ceramic cups. Tip: When the lineup is too long, duck into the alley behind the café. You'll find a tiny service window, and there are milk crates to sit on. Insiders know the score [375 Valencia St.].

Ritual Coffee buys its beans from small coffee producers around the world. They are lightly roasted to bring out their delicate flavors. The Valencia Street location is modern and open, with a pretty cactus garden in the back. Another paradise for laptoppers [1026 Valencia St.].

For a good espresso, I like **Linea Caffe**, a tiny café with big open windows and a few tables on the sidewalk (perfect for people-watching). Their waffles are irresistible [3417 18th St.].

A Bar for Tea Purists

202

Samovar Tea Bar serves excellent chai teas that steep in large copper pots, matcha teas with milk and a number of rare teas. With its steam machines and its sleek white decor, it feels like a scientific laboratory [411 Valencia St.].

The Patron Saint of Counterculture

203

"Welcome to Alcatraz!" exclaimed **Ron Turner**, unlocking the gate to his den, a treasure trove of unusual objects collected over the decades. A life-size statue of Bruce Lee dominates the room. There is also a Wurlitzer jukebox, pinball machines, an old piano, a human brain in a jar, and a few taxidermic animals. The room is at the back of a 16,000-square-foot (1,500-square-meter) warehouse—a mishmash of giant circus posters, stacks of documents and shelves full of books. It's a wonder Ron can find his way around. I'm in the offices of **Last Gasp**, a publishing house in the Mission neighborhood founded by Ron over 45 years ago, that publishes underground comics and graphic novels. Ron Turner, "Baba Ron" to his friends, is a local hero. Physically, he's a cross between Santa Claus and Jerry Garcia. He's worked all sorts of jobs, including dishwasher, railroad brakeman and laboratory assistant. He also studied experimental psychology at the University of California, Berkeley in the 1960s. It was there that he published his first comic, *Slow Death Funnies*, to raise money for the Ecology Department and the first Earth Day in 1970. The department asked him to print 10 copies—but he printed 20,000: "I had to figure out how to sell all those copies on campus and in the shops around town," he explained. Ever resourceful, that's when he came up with the idea of founding his own publishing house. In 1972, he published *It Ain't Me Babe*, the first comic book made entirely by women. Although he now only publishes between 12 to 20 new titles per year, Ron was one of the largest publishers in the underground culture that was part of the protest movement of the 1960s and 1970s. "At the time, we couldn't even find a publisher who would print the word 'fuck.'"

Ron Turner has contributed enormously to supporting and encouraging independent arts and literary culture in San Francisco. Today, in his mid-seventies, and after undergoing two surgeries on his hip, he uses a cane to get around; however, this hasn't kept him from delivering his books to small bookstores and sex shops around the city. Keep your eyes peeled: You might see him driving around town in his blue minivan [777 Florida St.].

Haight-Ashbury, Castro and Noe Valley

The cradle of counterculture since the 1960s, Haight-Ashbury has become a pilgrimage site for those who want to see the remaining traces of hippie culture. The Castro is the epicenter of the gay community, and it has its share of interesting shops and colorful characters. Noe Valley is a calm, quiet neighborhood where the sun always seems to be shining.

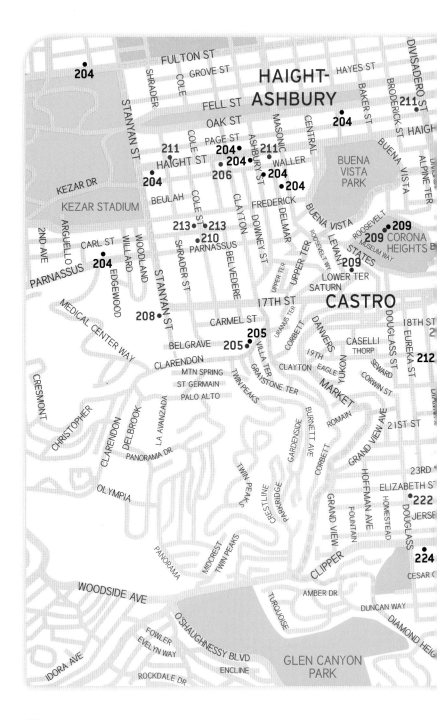

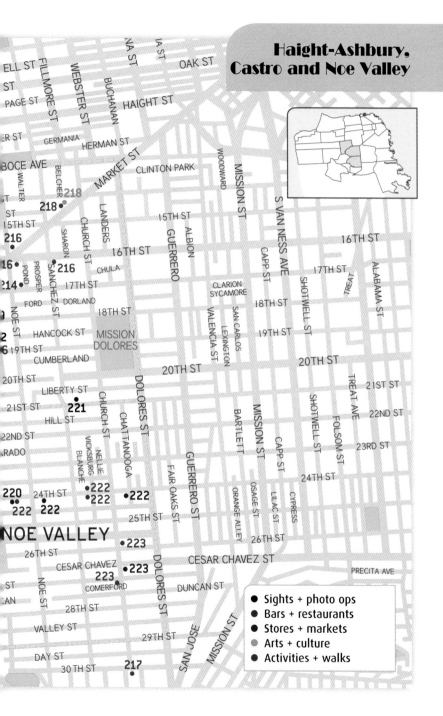

Haight-Ashbury, Castro and Noe Valley

NA ST
IA ST
OAK ST
ELL ST
FILLMORE ST
ST
PAGE ST
WEBSTER ST
BUCHANAN
HAIGHT ST
ER ST
GERMANIA
HERMAN ST
BOCE AVE
BELCHER
MARKET ST
CLINTON PARK
WOODWARD
MISSION ST
WALTER
218
ST
218
LANDERS
15TH ST
ALBION
S VAN NESS AVE
16TH ST
15TH ST
216
SHARON
CHURCH ST
GUERRERO
CAPP ST
ALABAMA ST
16
PROSPER
SANCHEZ ST
216
16TH ST
CHULA
17TH ST
TREAT
214
POND
17TH ST
CLARION
SYCAMORE
SHOTWELL ST
FORD
DORLAND
18TH ST
NOE ST
18TH ST
VALENCIA ST
SAN CARLOS
LEXINGTON
19TH ST
HANCOCK ST
MISSION
DOLORES
2
19TH ST
6
CUMBERLAND
20TH ST
20TH ST
20TH ST
LIBERTY ST
CHURCH ST
DOLORES ST
TREAT AVE
21ST ST
21ST ST
221
BARTLETT
MISSION ST
SHOTWELL ST
22ND ST
HILL ST
CHATTANOOGA
CAPP ST
FOLSOM ST
22ND ST
VICKSBURG
23RD ST
RADO
NELLIE
BLANCHE
GUERRERO ST
24TH ST
220
24TH ST
222
222
222
222
FAIR OAKS ST
OSAGE ST
ORANGE ALLEY
LILAC ST
CYPRESS
222
25TH ST
NOE VALLEY
223
26TH ST
26TH ST
CESAR CHAVEZ
223
CESAR CHAVEZ ST
PRECITA AVE
223
NOE ST
COMERFORD
DUNCAN ST
CAN
28TH ST
● Sights + photo ops
VALLEY ST
29TH ST
SAN JOSE
MISSION ST
● Bars + restaurants
● Stores + markets
DAY ST
● Arts + culture
30TH ST
217
● Activities + walks

A Hippie Pilgrimage

204

Haight-Ashbury was once a bastion of hippie culture. Times have changed, and the neighborhood obviously isn't what it was in the 1960s. Still, traces of the era of the "San Francisco Sound" remain. The area is famous for its colorful Victorian homes—some of these are the actual places that the biggest rock stars and other legends of the counterculture once called home. Why did it happen? In the 1950s, the City of San Francisco made plans to build a highway that would cut through—and destroy—part of the neighborhood. Many residents fled, and the price of real estate dropped drastically. Attracted by the cheap rent, artists and hippies flooded into the neighborhood. The highway never came to be, but the artists stayed. This would change the culture of the city forever.

Jimi Hendrix lived in an apartment above a tobacco store at 1524 Haight Street. In its current state, the building is dilapidated and old curtains blow in the breeze; it makes you think that the bohemian spirit lives on in its current tenants. Not far from there, look for the pink-and-white building [635 Ashbury St.]. **Janis Joplin** lived in one of these apartments at the end of the 1960s. (She also lived in the gray house at 122 Lyon Street.) On Ashbury Street, just south of Waller Street, the home of **Jerry Garcia** and the **Grateful Dead** [710 Ashbury St.] still draws fans. The current owners had to install a small fence to keep visitors from sitting on the steps. The famous group spent time living there, commune style, during 1967's now-mythical Summer of Love. A few minutes away, you can see the house where Sid Vicious lived during the final days of the Sex Pistols [32 Delmar St.]. The opulent home of the rock group **Jefferson Airplane** is just north of Golden Gate Park [2400 Fulton St.]. You'll know it by the ionic columns and its neo-

classical style. The apartment where **Hunter S. Thompson** lived while he was associating with the Hell's Angels is south of the park [318 Parnassus Ave.]. They say you can still see bullet holes: souvenirs of that truly eccentric character and his wild companions.

Be sure to visit **Amoeba Music**, a store in a 24,000-square-foot (2,200-square-meter) former bowling alley. At a time when most record stores are closing, Amoeba is an anachronism: It's as popular as ever. It's the place to go to discover that rare experimental jazz album you've been hoping to find for ages. It also has a collection of more than 30,000 DVDs, and free concerts are held there from time to time [1855 Haight St.].

The Unknown Summit

205 Another place where I like to get a view of the city and take spectacular photos is **Tank Hill Park**. The slope is about 650 feet (200 meters) high. A public bench has been installed, facing the entire city; someone has inscribed *Enjoy San Francisco* on it. You can get there by car: Drive to the end of Belgrave Avenue and climb the last few steps to the top. There was a large drinking-water reservoir there at the end of the 19th century. After the attack on Pearl Harbor in December 1941, authorities planted eucalyptus trees around it to hide it in case of attack by the Japanese. Today the reservoir is gone, but the trees remain.

The Bar from *One Thousand and One Nights*

206 **Zam Zam** (formerly Aub Zam Zam) is a legendary bar in San Francisco. A who's who of famous poets and musicians have spent time within its walls. With its subdued red lighting, Persian-style decor, arched doorways and 1930s jazz music, the sultry vibe is perfect for a romantic date. The mural behind the horseshoe-shaped bar illustrates the tragic love story between a Persian king and an Armenian princess. Opened in 1941, Zam Zam seems to be an establishment that time forgot. The only update seems to be the conversion of a cigarette machine into a jukebox. Take a seat at the bar and order a classic martini (with gin). The former owner, Bruno Mooshei, was known to kick people out of the bar if they ordered vodka martinis. He also insisted that women order first [1633 Haight St.].

The Queen of Drag

207

Of the 40,000 immigrants who arrived by boat in San Francisco in 1849, only 700 were women. The gender ratio was so disproportionate that some men dressed up as women to entertain fellow men in the taverns and saloons. Drag queens have been thriving here since the Gold Rush, and have increased in number due to the empowerment of the LGBT movement in the 1960s. Decked out in lavish wigs, extravagant makeup and high heels, drag queens have become icons in San Francisco. They are involved in politics (José Sarria, the first openly gay candidate for election in the United States, was also a drag queen), as well as in public life (drag queens even read stories to children in libraries).

Heklina, the stage name of Stefan Grygelko, is one of the best-known faces in town. Born in Minneapolis, Stefan was drawn to San Francisco in 1991, when he was 23 years old. "A friend told me that it was a party town, and I needed to get out of my hometown. I fell in love with the city immediately. I felt at home among all the artists and creative people, and in the underground scene and the gay community." Becoming a drag queen was something he sort of fell into. "I knew long ago that I would never work a nine-to-five job. I worked in a bar in the 1990s; I was involved in theater, and I started doing more and more female roles. The transition was natural." His stage name comes from the Hekla volcano in Iceland (his mother is from Iceland).

Stefan has gone through several phases. "At first, you do it for fun, to make a living. After a while, you go through an identity crisis because people always expect to see you in drag, and you don't know who you are. Now, I appreciate all the attention I get when I'm dressed up, as well as the anonymity when I'm just myself."

It's now been over 20 years that he has been dressing in drag—up to five times a week. In 1996, he started the popular Trannyshack club; for 12 years, the weekly show was the most popular one in town. The club has hosted celebrities such as Gwen Stefani, Lady Gaga and Mary Wilson of The Supremes, among others.

Today, Stefan is the owner of the **Oasis** nightclub [298 11th St.], which hosts weekly performances featuring drag queens, drag kings (women dressed up as masculine stereotypes) and faux queens (women dressed up as drag queens). "It doesn't matter to me what's between your legs, it's what you do on stage that interests me!" Heklina explains.

208

The Eucalyptus Forest

208

What I love so much about San Francisco is the easy access to nature. Without even leaving the city, you can climb peaks, go surfing or get lost in a forest of eucalyptus. One of my favorite hikes is the **Interior Greenbelt** trail at **Mount Sutro**. The mist swallows up the treetops on foggy days—some are as high as 200 feet (60 meters). The air is humid and the fragrance of eucalyptus is invigorating. To reach this magical place, climb the wooden staircase wedged between two houses on Stanyan Street, south of 17th Street. Countless people walk by the plain staircase without suspecting that an enchanted forest sits at the top. You'll encounter mountain bikers and a few local residents walking their dogs, but it's really a quiet area.

Urban Hiking

209

From **Corona Heights Park**, you get a panoramic view of downtown San Francisco and Sutro Tower. You can also watch the fog unfurl over the Twin Peaks like a woolly blanket. The terra-cotta-colored hill is completely wild, and it'll make you feel like you're in Arizona. The wind up there is so strong that it gives you a sense of vertigo. Stand on the rocks and imagine you're king or queen of the city. The entrance is at the corner of Museum Way and Roosevelt Way. When you're leaving the park, take Levant Street. Near the end of the street, on the left, you'll see a flower-lined staircase: That's the **Vulcan Stairway**, which will bring you down to Ord Street. Almost all the houses along the stairs are only accessible by foot. I shudder to imagine moving in or out of a home there.

209

A Colorful Brunch

210

After my walk, I go to **Zazie**, a French bistro with a pretty flowered terrace (heated) behind the restaurant. It's a popular spot for brunch—don't let the lineup discourage you. The eggs Benedict dishes are a specialty, and the ones with crab and avocado are absolutely delicious. The Mediterranean roasted vegetable plate and the gingerbread pancakes are also on my list of favorites. The tip is included in the bill [941 Cole St.].

Comfort Food

211

For a substantial and affordable brunch in a diner atmosphere, **Pork Store Cafe** has been a staple since the 1970s. It's especially popular on weekends, and it's a favorite for those who were out late the night before and need a hangover cure. I recommend the Eggs in a Tasty Nest: two eggs on a bed of hash browns with bacon, grilled green peppers, tomatoes, onion and melted cheddar, served with homemade biscuits. It's even better with a Bloody Mary. They also have vegetarian options and excellent pancakes [1451 Haight St.].

I'll go a long way out of my way to enjoy a big, comforting bowl of soup at **Citrus Club**. It's a restaurant with simple decor where you can eat for just $10. Try the Tom-ka Thai Coconut Soup and their freshly made spring rolls with avocado [1790 Haight St.].

If I'm in the mood for pasta with cheese, Neapolitan pizza or antipasti, I set a course to **Ragazza**. Try the Amatriciana (tomatoes, pancetta, calabrese peppers, pecorino and an egg in the middle). They also make the best tiramisu in town [311 Divisadero St.].

210

In the Footsteps of Harvey Milk

212 No other building in San Francisco is more associated with Harvey Milk, his political career and his fight for gay rights than **575 Castro Street**. Milk's store, **Castro Camera**, served as his headquarters during the four electoral campaigns he ran from 1973 to 1977, until he was finally elected as a member of city council. He became the first openly gay elected official in California.

Harvey Milk lived in the apartment just above the store. A mural on the second floor depicts him smiling at a window, wearing a shirt that reads "You gotta give 'em hope!" Today the shop belongs to the **Human Rights Campaign**, the leading defender of LGBT rights in the United States.

Milk's footprints are all over the neighborhood. A school, a recreational center and **Harvey Milk Civil Rights Academy** all bear his name. The open area in front of the subway station at the corner of Castro and Market Street was renamed **Harvey Milk Plaza**. It's the spot where Milk stood on a milk crate and tried desperately to mobilize the gay community. There are several photos of the legendary activist on display there. On November 27, 1978, the night he was assassinated, thousands of residents from the neighborhood and the rest of San Francisco gathered for a candlelight vigil before walking in silence to City Hall.

The huge rainbow flag flying over the plaza was put up in 1997 to commemorate the 20th anniversary of Milk's election victory. The 20 foot by 30 foot (nine by six meters) flag flies 70 feet (21 meters) in the air. It can be seen for miles.

If you want to learn more about San Francisco's LGBT movement, the **GLBT History Museum** tells the story using videos, archival photos and objects—some tragic, like Harvey Milk's bloodied clothes [4127 18th St.].

Since November 2012, it is forbidden to walk totally naked in the streets of San Francisco (except during certain events). But this doesn't prevent some men from walking in the streets of the Castro with a decorative sock covering their genitals! You're not a true San Franciscan unless you've seen a naked guy walking down the street.

The Micro-Neighborhood

213 Lying in the heart of the city and ignored by tourists, **Cole Valley** is a calm, peaceful micro-neighborhood. With its Victorian homes and streets lined with century-old trees, it's an idyllic place for families. There are a few charming businesses on the main drag, Cole Street. **Say Cheese**, a specialty market, makes the best sandwiches for takeout—the one with serrano ham is perfection [856 Cole St.].

Claudio Villani, the friendly Tuscan owner of the wine bar **InoVino**, has assembled a great selection of wines from the Italian Alps. I like to sit at the bar and order a cheese-and-charcuterie platter, and let the sommelier surprise me with a glass. A half-glass of wine is around $5 to $7 [108-B Carl St.].

I'm also a fan of **The Ice Cream Bar** (A), which has milkshakes, sundaes, floats and old-fashioned soft drinks. The art-deco decor is like the interior of a 1930s ocean liner. Everything is made in-house, including the cones [815 Cole St.].

Market Cuisine

214 **Frances**, a small neighborhood bistro with minimalist decor, honors fresh produce. The chef, Melissa Perello, visits the market each day before creating her evening menu. The offering changes each night, but some dishes are staples—like duck confit, ricotta gnocchi, a spicy and sweet kale salad, crispy onions, chickpea fritters, and bacon beignets with maple chive crème fraîche. Finish your meal with their famous "Lumberjack" Cake, with pear, apple, date, coconut and muscovado ice cream. The few tables are highly coveted, so you'll need to make a reservation [3870 17th St.].

213A

Double Bill at the Castro Theatre

215 Seeing a movie at the **Castro Theatre** is a magical experience and a rite of passage. The building has been emblematic of the neighborhood since it was built in 1922, and it's one of the last cinemas from that era that is still running. With its frescoes, large curtain and red velvet armchairs, the room is magnificent. The baroque Spanish Colonial building echoes the architecture of Mission Dolores (see Reason #177).

The Castro screens older repertory films and some newer films, always in a double bill (tickets are $12). A recital takes place before each screening: An organist at the center of the stage plays the score for the 1930s film *San Francisco*, with Clark Gable. It's a great way to keep the crowd entertained while they wait. When the curtain rises, the organ vanishes, the crowd cheers, and the film begins (with no commercials). It's been a tradition for almost 100 years.

The Sing Along events are popular with families and nostalgic twenty- and thirty-somethings. Movies like *The Little Mermaid, Grease, The Sound of Music* and *Frozen* are shown with subtitles. The audience is invited to sing along with every song, to *ooh* and *aah* at each on-screen kiss, to whistle and make a general racket. You can do pretty much anything you can't do in a typical movie theater. Some spectators show up in costume and are invited to parade around on stage. Loot bags are given out, along with accessories related to the film (a crown, a light stick, bubbles or in the case of *The Little Mermaid*, a fake pearl necklace). It's an experience you won't soon forget [429 Castro St.].

Restos in the Castro

216

Anchor Oyster Bar is the place to go if you're looking for seafood. I love the shrimp cocktail, the crab Caesar salad and the clam chowder. Stainless steel tables, a white marble counter and nautical equipment complete the decor at this charming restaurant [579 Castro St.].

When the weather's good, the terrace at **Café Flore** is the best spot to see and be seen. On Sundays, you might run into a few members of the Sisters of Perpetual Indulgence (see Reason #100). The healthy menu has salads, toast with avocado, veggie burgers and a few tasty dishes like biscuits and gravy. Their garlic fries alone are worth the trip [2298 Market St.].

Ike's Place is a sandwich mecca, and it's the most popular sandwich spot in the city. A long line forms in front of the store each day. Everyone wants to get their hands on one of their 80 sandwiches with playful names like Steph Curry One, Super Mario, Tangerine Girl, The Count of Monte Chase-o, Tom Brady, Going Home for Thanksgiving or Jessica Rabbit. I recommend the Menage a Trois. The restaurant has a number of vegan options [3489 16th St.].

For brunch, I like to sit on the terrace behind **Starbelly**. The restaurant serves Californian cuisine, with reinvented comfort-food classics like fried chicken and waffles, and challah French toast topped with caramelized bananas, nuts, maple syrup and mascarpone, with a choice of rosemary sausages or bacon [3583 16th St.].

Eiji, a small Japanese sushi restaurant on the edge of the Castro, is renowned for its tofu, made to order with soy milk. Oboro Tofu is the dish to ask for. It comes to your table in a ceramic pot, which releases a cloud of steam when you lift the lid. The tofu inside is soft and smooth. The dish is served with an assortment of condiments (sesame seeds, daikon, chili paste, chopped green onions, ginger and tamari). The Strawberry Mochi dessert is unforgettable: a ripe strawberry wrapped in layers of sticky rice paste, served cold. It's like having a precious jewel served on a plate [317 Sanchez St.].

218A

Superior Cocktails and Tapas in a Century-Old Building

218 For decor and ambiance, it's hard to beat **Cafe du Nord** (A). The bar is in the basement of a wonderful building from 1907 that was entirely restored a few years ago. The architecture is Amsterdam-esque. It's a great place to sip a cocktail (try the Martini du Nord) and try dishes to share (the nuts with chili and lime leaf are irresistible). At the back of the bar is the **Viking Room**, a "secret" room in which 40 people can sit. There is also a small stage. The menu here is more elaborate (oysters, Caesar salad, lamb shanks and a delicious hamburger). Try the Cioppino, a chowder overflowing with shellfish and fresh fish in a savory tomato broth. The art-deco decor, candle lighting and live jazz make it a great spot for couples. Oysters and champagne are half-price after midnight. On the main floor, the restaurant **Aatxe** serves Basque cuisine, with 1990s hip-hop playing in the background. Take a seat at the bar and order different tapas dishes, like the Spanish fried rice, pickled mussels, the salted cod and cabbage salad, fried artichokes, and garlic shrimp. Indulge in a gin and tonic while you're at it. It's like taking a direct flight to San Sebastián, Spain [2174 Market St.].

The Top Restaurant for Chefs

217 Dining at **La Ciccia** is an experience that you'll remember for a long time. All the chefs I spoke to when I was researching this book named it as their favorite restaurant. La Ciccia is an intimate place with a red brick facade, at the edge of Noe Valley. The owners, Massimiliano and Lorella, will transport you to Sardinia. They prepare classics from their native land, such as octopus stew in a spicy tomato broth and fresh pasta with bottarga (salted mullet roe). Finish your feast with delicious Sardinian cheeses, served with honey and flat bread from the region [291 30th St.].

220

The Store that Sells Everything

219 **Cliff's Variety** is a family business that has been around since 1936. More than just a hardware store, Cliff's sells everything: wigs, stationery, beads, flags, games, costumes, kitchen items and artists' materials. You'll walk out with products you never knew you needed! The owners, Ernie and Martha Asten, were the first people in the neighborhood to hire homosexuals in the 1970s [479 Castro St.].

The Chocolate Social Club

220 In Jack Epstein's specialty shop, **Chocolate Covered**, you'll find more than 800 kinds of chocolates made by 100 companies from 19 countries. Sixty-two-year-old Epstein has been passionate about chocolate for more than 20 years, and also about his neighborhood, Noe Valley. "It's like a small village, right here in the heart of San Francisco. People know each other, *and* there's more sunshine here than in other neighborhoods," he says. Over the years, his shop has become something of a social club for various locals. "Every evening, we watch *Jeopardy* together."

Epstein also has another passion: gift boxes. More than 5,000 of them line the walls of his little shop, most printed with the name of different San Francisco streets. To decorate them, he uses cyanotype, a photographic process that creates a Prussian blue print. The gift boxes cost $18 to $35, and for $10 more you can get one personalized [4069 24th St.].

The Christmas House on Steroids

221 Tom Taylor and Jerry Goldstein have been transforming their home into a giant Christmas village for more than 30 years now. Huge Christmas stockings are hung above the garage door, and they use a crane to place the star on top of their 65-foot (20-meter) fir tree—a tricky business, since the street is very steep. The fake gifts at the foot of the tree are as big as cars, and the tree ornaments are the size of beach balls. The **Tom & Jerry Christmas House** attracts about 30,000 visitors a year, especially on December 24. It's a tradition to get your photo taken with Santa Claus. Tom and Jerry spend over a month decorating their home; they go so far as to add steel beams to the base of the tree so that it can support the weight of decorations. The house stays decorated from December 10 to January 1 [3650 21st St.].

221

A Gourmet Walk down 24th Street

222 24th Street is the main artery of Noe Valley, but it's off the usual tourist circuit. It's a great area for hanging out, discovering new specialty shops and local restaurants. The **Noe Valley Farmers' Market** has stalls that sell fresh produce on Saturday mornings, along with live music and activists seeking signatures for their favorite cause [3861 24th St.]. The street is packed with gourmet shops, like **Noe Valley Bakery** [4073 24th St.], which makes delicious scones, cookies and cupcakes for kids, and **24th Street Cheese Co.**, a San Francisco institution that sells some 300 kinds of local and imported cheeses. You can sample everything [3893 24th St.].

I love the boutique with Breton-style apparel, **Mill Mercantile**. They sell delicate jewelry with pearls, beautiful objects for the home, Aesop beauty products, marinières (those striped seamen's sweaters), leather sandals, ceramic dishware and design magazines

[3751 24th St.]. **The Podolls** (A), a boutique owned by Lauren and Josh Podoll, sells clothing made from natural fibers, silk tunics, comfortable pullovers and a fantastic collection for kids. There's a log cabin in the middle of the store for children to play in while their parents shop [3985 24th St.].

For excellent sushi, I like to go to **Saru**, a small restaurant that serves the freshest fish imaginable. The chef, Billy Kong, even makes his own soy sauce. Try the yellowtail appetizer (the fish is called *hamachi* in Japanese) with truffle oil [3856 24th St.]. **Firefly** is a cozy neighborhood restaurant that offers simple food with no frills. They focus on comfort food, like delicious fried fish and several vegetarian options [4288 24th St.]. You'll find the best pasta in the neighborhood at **Lupa Trattoria**, an authentic restaurant that serves Roman cuisine [4109 24th St.]. For great tapas, go to **Contigo**, a Catalan restaurant that also serves paella on Tuesdays [1320 Castro St.].

Cookbook Paradise

223

Located in a former butcher shop, **Omnivore Books on Food** (A) is a little bookstore that specializes in cuisines from different eras and from around the world. For those who love cooking, it's a dream come true. The owner, Celia Sack, collects old cookbooks, some from as far back as 1850. There are also a number of books on related subjects, ranging from 19th-century farming manuals to books on modern urban agriculture techniques. It's perfect if you're looking for a gift for the person who has everything [3885 Cesar Chavez St.].

One of my favorite spots for brunch is **Chloe's Cafe**, a block north of the bookstore. Order scrambled eggs with avocado and the crepes with bananas and nuts [1399 Church St.]. In the other direction, a block south of the bookstore, **Eric's Restaurant** serves tasty Chinese food. Try the mango beef and the vegetarian egg rolls [1500 Church St.].

224

223A

The Rainbow House

224

When I think of San Francisco, I think of the colors of the rainbow. Designed by graphic designer and civil rights activist Gilbert Baker, the gay pride flag is everywhere in the city. In 1978, the committee behind the pride parade asked Baker—a friend of Harvey Milk—to come up with a new symbol. Baker decided on the colors of the rainbow because he wanted to represent the diversity of the LGBT community. One Noe Valley house proudly and uniquely displays the colors of the flag; it's worth taking a look and snapping a pic. The horizontal wooden slats are painted in violet, blue, green, yellow, orange and red. **The Rainbow House** is on Clipper Street, between Douglass and Diamond streets.

Potrero Hill, Dogpatch, Bayview, Bernal Heights, Glen Park and Diamond Heights

The view of the Financial District from Potrero Hill is magnificent. The industrial buildings of Dogpatch have been taken over by artists and turned into studios; surrounding restaurants have become top destinations. Overlooked by tourists, Bernal Heights is a neighborhood of families and dog owners. It's the place to be if you want to see the real San Francisco lifestyle.

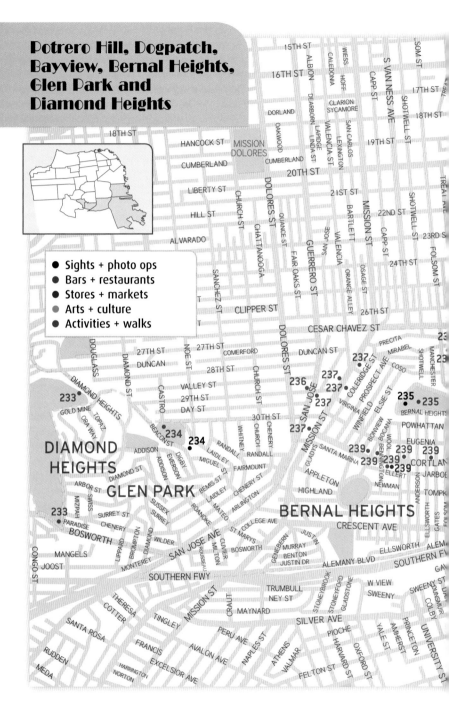

Potrero Hill, Dogpatch, Bayview, Bernal Heights, Glen Park and Diamond Heights

- ● Sights + photo ops
- ● Bars + restaurants
- ● Stores + markets
- ● Arts + culture
- ● Activities + walks

MISSION DOLORES

DIAMOND HEIGHTS

GLEN PARK

BERNAL HEIGHTS

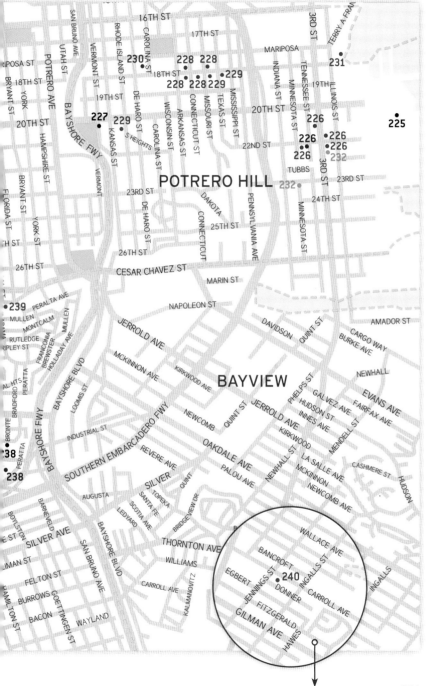

Sketching San Francisco

225 Wendy MacNaughton always has a pen in hand and a sketch pad under her arm. Whether she's in a park, a coffee shop or a subway car, she sketches the people around her and the strange objects she finds on the sidewalk, and notes the snippets of conversation she overhears on the street. While most people walk with their noses buried in their smartphones, Wendy carefully observes and documents the lives of San Franciscans. She knows the city and its people better than anyone.

I discovered her through her book of illustrations, *Meanwhile in San Francisco*, a gem that speaks of the city, its nuances and the characters that call it home. Wendy likes to draw people that society has forgotten: the poor, the marginalized and the elderly...

She agreed to show me around her studio in the Noonan Building, an old wooden structure on Pier 70, in the Dogpatch district, which is one of the oldest shipyards in the United States. The building dates from 1940 and once housed the managers' offices for the Port of San Francisco. It has been converted into artists' studios: ceramists, painters, sculptors and filmmakers now share the space. "When I found this place, I had the feeling of having discovered a secret hideout," explained Wendy, who studied art and has a Master of Social Work.

Her studio is an explosion of color. The radiators are painted fuchsia and walls are covered with sketches, photos and inspirational quotes. Her desk is stacked with sketchbooks and glasses filled with her favorite type of pen: the Micron Pigma 01. A huge safe stands in the middle of the room, a relic of the building's commercial past. It rests on a pedestal, without which it would fall through the floor." I don't know what's in it, but that's part of the charm and mystery of the place."

Through the large windowpanes in her loft, you can see cargo ships gliding slowly to the Port of Oakland, carrying goods from Asia. Also in the distance you can see the great harbor cranes that bear a strange resemblance to the AT-AT walkers from Star Wars (according to legend, they were George Lucas' inspiration). On the left you can see the AT&T ballpark. "When the Giants win, I see the fireworks from my office," she says.

Wendy is aware of how lucky she is: Few artists are able to live well from their art in San Francisco today. She has published a dozen books, and her illustrations appear regularly in *The New York Times*, *The Wall Street Journal* and *Time Magazine*, among others. "All the artists I know have lost their studios," she explains. Wendy is concerned about the fate of her city, which is becoming less and less diverse—a city which has both extreme wealth and extreme poverty. This dichotomy is reflected in her work. She draws the homeless who use the library as a refuge, and the programmers, tourists and business people strolling down 5th Street, while just one block away, on 6th Street, there are only homeless people to be seen. Her work as an artist is also a form of social work, which gives a voice to those who otherwise might not have one.

A Day in Dogpatch

226

A former industrial zone by the waterfront, Dogpatch has become the neighborhood at the cutting edge of cool—the new art district. A number of its warehouses and factories have been converted into artist studios and artisanal workshops. The area was named for the packs of dogs that would gather to feast on meat scraps thrown out by slaughterhouse employees.

I like to have brunch at **Just For You Cafe** (A), a diner with a saloon atmosphere. The aroma of bacon entices potential customers from the sidewalk. This is the spot for eggs, pancakes, French toast, frittatas and huge beignets, as well as for Cajun and Mexican dishes. They also make their own bread [732 22nd St.]. Brunch at **Serpentine** is another must in this neighborhood. Located in a former canning factory, the restaurant has an industrial design, with high ceilings and concrete walls. The menu has market cuisine like buckwheat pancakes and eggs Benedict with crab [2495 3rd St.].

You don't have to go far to try the artisanal ice creams at **Mr. and Mrs. Miscellaneous** (B). They're just across the street. Try the lavender ice cream or the bourbon and caramel, or sample their homemade candy. Their peanut brittle is truly addictive [699 22nd St.].

Next, visit the **Museum of Craft and Design**, one of the only institutions in North America devoted to contemporary practices in craftwork and design. The museum's shop has a variety of original pieces that make perfect gifts [2569 3rd St.].

For lunch, I like to get a table at **Piccino** (C). The modern trattoria is set in a large canary-yellow Victorian home—it's impossible to miss. The menu includes antipasti, appetizers with market vegetables, fresh pasta and pizza. There are a few tables outside and a small coffee shop next door [1001 Minnesota St.].

If you like design, don't miss **Workshop**, located right nearby—it's both a workshop and a boutique. Every two months, a different artist sets up in the studio in the back and works in view of visitors. The pieces they create are reproduced and sold in the shop. Workshop sells clothing, bags, stationery, objects for the home, dishware and so on. The items are avant-garde but functional [833 22nd St.].

When the afternoon is winding down (but before 5 p.m., to avoid the rush), I like to visit **Magnolia Brewing Company** (D), a large industrial space that's rustic and decorated with flowers. The brewery has dozens of beers on tap; it also houses **Smokestack**, one of the best barbecue restaurants in the city. Give your order at the counter and take a seat at one of the large tables. Their brisket is worth its weight in gold; the chef, Dennis Lee, uses superior quality Waygu beef [2505 3rd St.].

Dogpatch Saloon (E), just across the street, has been a local institution since 1912. With the tile floor, wooden walls, vintage photos, gas fireplace and a small stage for live jazz on Sundays, the atmosphere is truly warm. The building was stunningly restored a few years ago. Regulars like to come by with their dogs and quaff a beer while watching sports on TV [2496 3rd St.].

226 E

The Windiest Street

227 Most tourists think that the windiest roadway in San Francisco is Lombard Street. But they clearly don't know about **Vermont Street** in Potrero Hill, near the U.S. 101 highway. With its seven curves and its steep incline, this street definitely takes the prize. The windy part begins at 20th Street and ends lower down on 22nd Street. Descending this serpentine cement path in a car is dizzying. Vermont Street isn't quite as pretty as Lombard Street, but it has the advantage of being much less busy. You can spot the street in several films, including *Magnum Force* with Clint Eastwood (1973) and *Bullitt* with Steve McQueen (1968).

226C

226B

226D

226A

229 A

The Neighborhood on the Side of a Hill

228

Potrero Hill, a residential neighborhood with steep streets, is off the beaten track. It's often swaddled in fog, and things move a little slower there—it's one of my favorite places to get away from the hustle and bustle of the city. The topography offers superb views of the Financial District and San Francisco Bay, and there are some great places to eat. It's no surprise that it's often used as a location for film shoots. My favorite restaurant in the area is **Sunflower**, an unpretentious Vietnamese place. It's quick and cheap, and popular with locals. I order the spring rolls and the curry vegetables with coconut milk and steamed jasmine rice. Delicious [288 Connecticut St.].

Just across the street is **Goat Hill Pizza**. When the restaurant opened in 1975, there were no other businesses in the area. The name was inspired by the goats that grazed in the pastures of Potrero Hill. Toppings are generous and the sourdough crust is just thick enough. They offer all-you-can-eat pizza for $12.95 on Mondays from 4 p.m. to 10 p.m. The servers circulate with slices of pizza fresh out of the oven. There's really no reason not to sample them all [300 Connecticut St.].

Chez Maman, a charming French bistro with a small terrace, is the culinary focal point of the neighborhood. They serve comfort food, like steak frites, a ham and Gruyère crepe, marinated mussels, hachis Parmentier (a French version of shepherd's pie) and croque monsieur with ratatouille. You'll feel like you've been transported to France [1401 18th St.].

Umi, a well-kept local secret, has a wide selection of sushi at an affordable price. The chef uses only sustainable fish [1328 18th St.].

The Architectural Breakfast

229

Lodged in a former architect's studio, **Plow** (A) has one of the best brunches in town. The menu is simple, focusing on traditional American dishes (eggs, bacon, hash browns, ricotta and lemon pancakes). What makes each dish stand out is the quality of the local organic ingredients. If you don't want to spend a long time waiting, I recommend getting there before it opens (7 a.m. on weekdays and 8 a.m. on weekends) [1299 18th St.]. Put your name on the list and go spend the time at **Farley's**, the café on the other side of Texas Street. They have lots of magazines to flip through while you enjoy a hot brew [1315 18th St.].

Right nearby is **Hazel's Kitchen**, which has good sandwiches and salads. You can easily fill up for just $10 [1319 18th St.]. In the same neighborhood, I also like the sandwiches at **Chiotras Grocery**. The cheerful family grocery store has been around for over 100 years. There are a few tables on the sidewalk and a quiet balcony at the back where you can enjoy your meal—a freshly made rosemary garlic turkey sandwich is a good choice [858 Rhode Island St.].

The Gold Rush Brewery

230 As you approach Potrero Hill, your nose will start to notice yeast and caramel aromas wafting forth from a very special brewery. In 1896 two German immigrants founded the now historic **Anchor Brewing Company**. It's one of the last remaining breweries making steam beer. Ice was hard to come by on the west coast of the United States in the 19th century. The brewers found a solution: They put the fermentation tanks on the roof of the brewery, so that the beer would be chilled naturally overnight by the cool air from San Francisco Bay. Large clouds of steam would loom over the building at night—hence the name "steam beer." Guided tours of the brewery are offered on weekdays. They last an hour and a half, and you get to see the impressive production line, the fermentation tanks, the lab where beers are tested and the noisy bottling process. The visit ends with a tasting of six beers. Book a place ($20) at anchorbrewing.com/brewery/tours [1705 Mariposa St.].

Barbecue Among the Boats

231 I like to relax on the patio at **The Ramp** on a sunny Saturday afternoon. Here's my suggestion: Sit at one of their picnic tables with a Bloody Mary in your hand, and watch the ships sail on the bay. In the distance, you can see cargo ships anchoring in the Port of Oakland. Parked in an industrial zone, the restaurant still has the same decor it had when it opened in the 1950s. (You can see it in the Woody Allen film *Blue Jasmine*). When you get there, you feel like you've found an oasis privy only to insiders. The place is frequented by various types: businesspeople, younger folk who are newcomers to the neighborhood, and construction workers and regulars, for whom the bar is a second home.

When hungry, I order the eggs Benedict with crab, the hamburger or the avocado stuffed with shrimp and dill. After brunch on the weekend, the patio transforms into a dance floor under the sun. The Latin rhythms are electric [855 Terry A. Francois Blvd.].

The New Art Gallery Epicenter

232

Due to soaring rent prices—a 40-percent increase between 2010 and 2015—many of the city's artists and gallerists have been pushed out of their spaces. This problem led collectors and philanthropists Andy and Deborah Rappaport to create the Minnesota Street Project. To counteract the exodus of artists, they renovated old industrial buildings in the Dogpatch neighborhood and rented the spaces to the city's art galleries at low prices. Even though buildings have been transformed, their industrial past is still visible. One has studios for 35 artists; another houses 10 contemporary art galleries and a large atrium where artistic events are held. The third building is an art warehouse. The public can visit the gallery building free of charge. As I write, star chef Daniel Patterson is planning to open a bar and a restaurant on the main floor. Stay tuned [1275 Minnesota St.].

The Green Canyon

233

Glen Canyon Park, a green, 24-hectare canyon in the heart of San Francisco, is definitely not a destination for tourists—many San Franciscans don't even know it exists. That's strange, since it's a magical spot to get away from the noise and the hustle and bustle of the city. Along with Lands End (see Reason #12) and the Farallon Islands, it's one of three spots in the city that are still wild. When you visit, you can imagine that you're the one discovering San Francisco's intimidating topography, as explorers did in the 19th century. There are several trails that wind through the park (wear good walking shoes). You might see owls, eagles, coyotes and maybe even some possums. The steep walls of the canyon are a favorite spot for climbing enthusiasts. The entrance to the park is at the corner of Bosworth and Elk streets, near the recreation center. You can also park at the Diamond Heights Shopping Center and walk down into the canyon by taking one of the trails behind the mall.

232 233

234B 234A

A Swing and a Stairway in the Jungle

234 Don't leave San Francisco without swinging from a tree at the top of a hill. There are many swings attached to branches on the city's 44 hills, but my favorite is the one at the top of **Billy Goat Hill Park** (A). Suspended from a tree on the hillside, you feel like you're floating over the city. Get someone to take a photo of you from behind— it'll be a hit on Instagram. The swing is a target for vandals, so it sometimes disappears, but it's always replaced with a new one. The entrance to the park is on Beacon Street. When you go up Beacon toward Miguel Street, you'll see a sign for **Harry Street** (B) on your left: It's a magnificent wooden staircase bordered by lovely homes. The staircase descends through lush vegetation and bright decorations—It's a miniature paradise!

A Breathtaking View

235 The first time I set foot in **Bernal Heights Park** at the top of Bernal Hill, it was the middle of the night. I walked the trails leading to the summit in total darkness, using my cell phone as a flashlight, seriously wondering what I had gotten myself into. But my intrepidness was rewarded: I'll never forget the moment when I reached the top and the city unfolded before me in a million glowing lights. The summit offers a panoramic view of the Mission and Noe Valley, San Francisco Bay, Coit Tower and the downtown skyline. The hill is much less crowded than others in the city, and from the summit you get the feeling that you have it all to yourself. On my last visit, someone had been ambitious enough to transport an upright piano to the top for an impromptu concert. The park's vegetation changes with the seasons: In winter it's green, reminiscent of a Scottish glen, and in summer the dry yellow landscape looks like the Arizona desert.

237B

Fantastic Ice Cream

236

A true institution since the 1950s, **Mitchell's Ice Cream** has to be on your list of stops. The family business specializes in artisanal ice creams with exotic fruits such as guava, avocado, buko (young coconut), pineapple and mango. Try the surprising flavor of Ube (purple yam) or the popular Grasshopper Pie (mint with chocolate chips). Don't forget to take a number when you enter the shop. There's always a huge line in front, even at 11 p.m., so be prepared to wait [688 San Jose Ave.].

The New Culinary Destination

237

The strip of Mission Street between Powers Avenue and Cortland Avenue is full of new restaurants, like **Old Bus Tavern**, a brewery that serves high-end pub food [3193 Mission St.]; the exquisite sushi restaurant **ICHI Sushi + NI Bar** [3282 Mission St.]; **Coco's Ramen**, where you can savor a big bowl of ramen for under $12 [3319 Mission St.]; **Blue Plate**, a restaurant that serves reimagined American comfort food, with a lovely garden in the back [3218 Mission St.]; the eclectic **Emmy's Spaghetti Shack** (A), with their generous portions and super-kitsch decor [3230 Mission St.]; **PizzaHacker** (B), a trendy Neapolitan pizzeria that's also popular with families [3299 Mission St.]; **The Front Porch**, which serves Southern U.S. cuisine in a family atmosphere [65 29th St.]; **Royal Cuckoo**, a bar that plays only pre-1975 music [3202 Mission St.]; and **Cafe St. Jorge** (C), a Portuguese café where you can get delicious grilled sandwiches and toast topped with avocado [3438 Mission St.].

237A 237C

238

In San Francisco, you have to turn your car wheels all the way when parking on a hill: toward the sidewalk when pointing downhill, and toward the street when pointing uphill. If you don't, you're guaranteed a sixty-dollar fine!

The Street of Optical Illusions

238 A small residential street near U.S. 101 on the edge of Bernal Heights, **Bradfort Street** holds the official title of steepest street in the entire city. That makes it the perfect place to take optical illusion photos. The street slopes at 41 percent north of Tompkins Ave. Local residents are known to have very firm calf muscles. Check it out on Sunday so you can also visit the farmers' market and the **Alemany Flea Market**. It doesn't get much tourist traffic, and unknown treasures await you [100 Alemany Blvd., from 8 a.m. to 3 p.m.].

The Village Within the City

239 Bernal Heights, at the top of a steep hill, beats to its own rhythm. Its patchwork of Victorian homes seems to be from another time. It's no surprise that many families have chosen to settle down there. This also seems to be the neighborhood with the most dogs per resident... With its butterfly garden, **Precita Park** is an ideal place to take kids to play. Sitting on the terrace of **Precita Park Café**, at the edge of the park, you're likely to see some of the local fauna [500 Precita Ave.]. At the other end of the grassy field is **Hillside Supper Club**. Set within a Victorian house, the restaurant serves market cuisine. It's a great spot for brunch, and they offer all-you-can-drink-mimosas for $25 [300 Precita Ave.].

The main shopping street, **Cortland Avenue**, looks like a picturesque urban village. It's a great place to observe life in San Francisco. I love the rhubarb pie at **Little Bee Baking** [521 Cortland Ave.]; the macchiato at **Pinhole Coffee** [231 Cortland Ave.]; the secret garden behind the dive bar **Wild Side West** [424 Cortland Ave.]; the religious paraphernalia decorating the bar **Holy Water** [309 Cortland Ave.]; the gorgeous selection of items for the home at **Heartfelt**, a modern-day general store [436 Cortland Ave.]; and the delicious fish and seafood dishes at **Red Hill Station** (A), one of my favorite places in town (they also have a great kids' menu) [803 Cortland Ave.].

239 A

The Street Photographer

241 **Travis Jensen** left Milwaukee at the age of 18 with a one-way bus ticket and $800 in his pocket. Like many young people, he was attracted to the skateboarding culture of San Francisco. "In the 1990s, San Francisco was the mecca of skateboarding, and I wanted to be part of that community. My parents thought I would come back after four weeks, but I was immediately smitten with the city," he told me while rolling a joint near The Embarcadero, his camera bag by his side. His many tattoos reflect his deep love for the city—for example, he has the Ferry Building tattooed on his forearm.

I wanted to meet Travis because I am a fan of his photography. I discovered him on Instagram (@travisjensen), where he shares black-and-white photos of the city's people and landscapes. "I've always found that, despite what everyone thinks, San Francisco is more beautiful in black and white than in color." He reveals a different side of the city, less showy—neighborhoods not frequented by tourists and faces marked by life's tribulations. "My portraits treat people with dignity and respect. I don't want to exploit them. Street photography is an intricate dance."

Travis knows what it is to struggle to survive. His arrival in San Francisco reads like a movie script: Penniless, he found himself in a slum in the Tenderloin (nobody had warned him about the dangers of that area), in a room barely bigger than a prison cell, where the window was nailed shut to prevent theft. The words "You're dead" were engraved on his door.

"One night I was woken up by banging on my door. A girl was screaming at me to let her in. I didn't know if it was a trick, or if she needed help. I was paralyzed. Seconds later, her pimp came and beat her up. The next day I saw her in the elevator, and she was hiding her black eye behind

Smoked Meat in an Industrial Area

240 Located in a district full of warehouses and loading docks, **Smokin' Warehouse Barbecue** looks like a business that might sell exhaust pipes. Don't be fooled: The little restaurant has the best ribs in the city. As you walk through the streets of this Bayview industrial area, you're going to think you're in the wrong place.

Order at the window, and devour your pulled pork combo at the plastic table out front, or in your car. Bring napkins. The chef, Bill Lee, owns the electronics warehouse behind the restaurant. He built the kitchen to cook his special barbecue dishes for his family, friends and employees. Word of mouth spread, and he decided to open to the public in 2010. Lee uses cherry wood to smoke the meat for several hours, then brushes it with a sweet and sour tomato sauce, and serves it with a thick slice of cornbread. Closed on Saturday and Sunday [1465 Carroll Ave.].

her sunglasses. She asked me if I had needles. It was at that moment that I realized how rough San Francisco can be, and how naive I was. I've seen fights, people getting stabbed. One day I saw a TV fly through a window and hit someone on the sidewalk. Friends have fallen into the hell of drugs... It's a miracle I'm not dead or in prison."

A friend of his then gave him a place to stay. "I slept in the hall, on a futon that folded over me like a taco. It took four years before I had my own room in this city."

Twenty years later, Travis is a professional photographer. He has two children, a house and a full-time career. His photos are published in *The San Francisco Chronicle*, *The Los Angeles Times*, *Forbes* and *Esquire*, and he has done campaigns for Adidas and Apple, among others.

Photography was something that came to him naturally. He was writing skateboarding articles for *The San Francisco Chronicle* and didn't like the images that accompanied his articles, so he decided to become a photographer.

This quickly became a passion and his main source of income. "I unwittingly became a street photographer. I see it as a natural extension of skateboarding: I'm still in the streets, feeding on the energy of the city."

Travis particularly likes photographing the streets and residents of Excelsior, a working-class neighborhood on the southern edge of the city. "It's the best kept secret in town. The people have been there forever—they're the workers who run this city: firefighters, paramedics, and the true fans of the Giants and the 49ers. There are no Starbucks or hipster stores. It's the real San Francisco."

He also teaches street photography to the kids in the neighborhood. "The best gift I ever received was when one of them came and told me that five years before he used to hang out on the corner with a gun in his pocket, but now he hangs out on the corner with a camera in his hand."

Twin Peaks, West of Twin Peaks, Inner Sunset and Outer Sunset

Perpetually immersed in fog, the Outer Sunset neighborhood has a mysterious aura. It's a place for long walks at the edge of the continent on Ocean Beach, for surfing and hanging out in the small restaurants and cafés on Judah and Noriega streets. And climbing the two summits of the Twin Peaks rewards you with unforgettable sights.

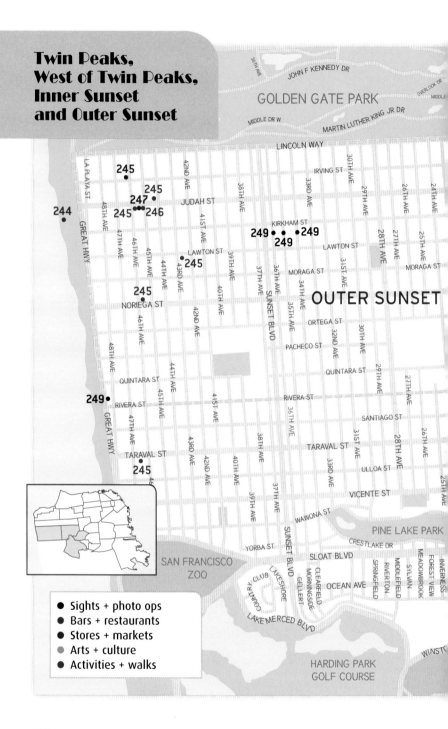

Twin Peaks,
West of Twin Peaks,
Inner Sunset
and Outer Sunset

GOLDEN GATE PARK

JOHN F KENNEDY DR

34TH AVE

OVERLOOK DR

MIDDLE

MIDDLE DR W

MARTIN LUTHER KING JR DR

LINCOLN WAY

IRVING ST

JUDAH ST

KIRKHAM ST

LAWTON ST

MORAGA ST

OUTER SUNSET

NORIEGA ST

ORTEGA ST

PACHECO ST

QUINTARA ST

RIVERA ST

SANTIAGO ST

TARAVAL ST

ULLOA ST

VICENTE ST

WAWONA ST

QUINTARA ST

TARAVAL ST

LA PLAYA ST

GREAT HWY

42ND AVE
48TH AVE
47TH AVE
46TH AVE
45TH AVE
44TH AVE
43RD AVE
41ST AVE
40TH AVE
39TH AVE
38TH AVE
37TH AVE
36TH AVE
35TH AVE
34TH AVE
33RD AVE
31ST AVE
30TH AVE
29TH AVE
28TH AVE
27TH AVE
26TH AVE
25TH AVE
24TH AVE
32ND AVE

SUNSET BLVD

244
245
245
247
245 **246**
249 **249**
249
245
245
245
249
245

PINE LAKE PARK

CRESTLAKE DR

YORBA ST

SLOAT BLVD

OCEAN AVE

SAN FRANCISCO
ZOO

COUNTRY CLUB DR

LAKESHORE

CLEARFIELD
MORNINGSIDE
GELLERT
SPRINGFIELD
RIVERTON
MIDDLEFIELD
SYLVAN
MEADOWBROOK
FOREST VIEW
INVERNESS

LAKE MERCED BLVD

WINSTO

HARDING PARK
GOLF COURSE

- ● Sights + photo ops
- ● Bars + restaurants
- ● Stores + markets
- ● Arts + culture
- ● Activities + walks

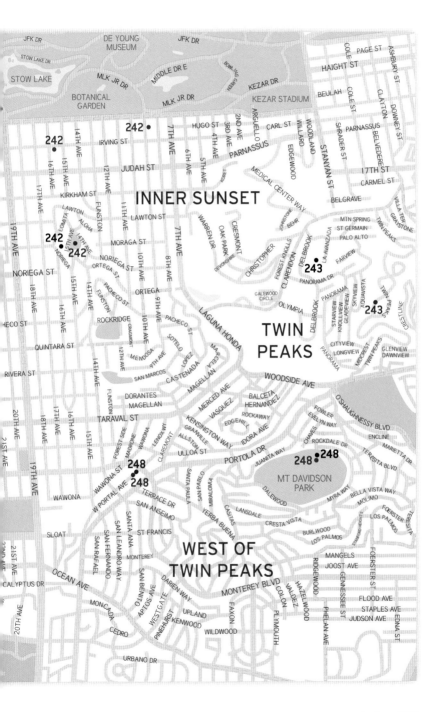

STOW LAKE

DE YOUNG
MUSEUM

JFK DR

JFK DR

STOW LAKE DR

HAIGHT ST

COLE ST

PAGE ST

ASHBURY ST

MLK JR DR

MIDDLE DR E

KEZAR DR

BEULAH

COLE ST

CLAYTON ST

DOWNEY ST

BOTANICAL
GARDEN

MLK JR DR

BOWLING GREEN

KEZAR STADIUM

BELVEDERE

PARNASSUS

SHRADER ST

STANYAN ST

WOODLAND

EDGEWOOD

WILLARD

17TH ST

CARMEL ST

242

242

14TH AVE

IRVING ST

15TH AVE

16TH AVE

17TH AVE

12TH AVE

HUGO ST

7TH AVE

6TH AVE

5TH AVE

4TH AVE

3RD AVE

2ND AVE

ROBERT

ARGUELLO

CARL ST

PARNASSUS

MEDICAL CENTER WAY

BELGRAVE

VILLA TER

GRAYSTONE

JUDAH ST

KIRKHAM ST

LAWTON

ALOHA

FUNSTON

11TH AVE

LAWTON ST

MTN SPRING

ST GERMAIN

TWIN PEAKS

PALO ALTO

INNER SUNSET

JOHNSTONE

BEHR

19TH AVE

LOMITA

14TH AVE

242

242

MORAGA ST

OAK PARK

CRESMONT

WARREN DR

DEVONSHIRE

CHRISTOPHER

FOREST KNOLLS

CLARENDON

DELBROOK

LA AVANZADA

FARVIEW

243

NORIEGA ST

NORIEGA

15TH AVE

14TH AVE

FUNSTON

NORIEGA ST

ORTEGA ST

10TH AVE

8TH AVE

PANORAMA DR

AQUAVISTA

TWIN PEAKS

18TH AVE

161ST AVE

HECO ST

PACHECO ST

ORTEGA

9TH AVE

GALEWOOD
CIRCLE

OLYMPIA

PANORAMA

SKYVIEW

KNOLLVIEW

STARVIEW

GLADEVIEW

243

CRESTLINE

ROCKRIDGE

CRAGMONT

10TH AVE

PACHECO ST

LAGUNA HONDA

**TWIN
PEAKS**

CITYVIEW

LONGVIEW

MIDCREST

TWIN PEAKS

PANORAMA

GLENVIEW

DAWNVIEW

QUINTARA ST

14TH AVE

12TH AVE

MENDOSA

9TH AVE

SOTELO

LOPEZ

MARELA

RIVERA ST

SAN MARCOS

CASTENADA

MAGELLAN

WOODSIDE AVE

O'SHAUGHNESSY BLVD

20TH AVE

21ST AVE

18TH AVE

FUNSTON

DORANTES

MAGELLAN

MERCED AVE

VASQUEZ

BALCETA

HERNANDEZ

ROCKAWAY

FOWLER

EVELYN WAY

ENCLINE

MARIETTA DR

TARAVAL ST

16TH AVE

15TH AVE

FOREST SIDE

MADRONE

WAWONA

LENOX WY

CLAREMONT

KENSINGTON WAY

GRANVILLE

ALLSTON ST

ULLOA ST

EDGEHILL

IDORA AVE

PORTOLA DR

JUANITA WAY

CHVES

ROCKDALE DR

TERSITA BLVD

248

248

19TH AVE

WAWONA

WAWONA ST

W PORTAL AVE

248

248

TERRACE DR

SAN ANSELMO

SANTA PABLO

SANTA PAULA

MIRALOMA

MT DAVIDSON
PARK

DALEWOOD

MYRA WAY

BELLA VISTA WAY

MOLIMO

FOERSTER

TERESITA

SLOAT

SANTA ANA

SAN LEANDRO WAY

SAN RAFAEL

ST FRANCIS

MONTEREY

YERBA BUENA

CASITAS

LANSDALE

CRESTA VISTA

BURLWOOD

LOS PALMOS

STANFORD HEIGHTS

RIDGEWOOD

LOS PALMOS

FOERSTER ST

GENNESSEE ST

21ST AVE

22ND AVE

CALYPTUS DR

OCEAN AVE

MONCADA

SAN FERNANDO WAY

SAN BENITO

APTOS AVE

WESTGATE

PINEHURST

CEDRO

DARIEN WAY

KENWOOD

UPLAND

WILDWOOD

**WEST OF
TWIN PEAKS**

MONTEREY BLVD

COLON

FAXON

PLYMOUTH

WALDEZ

HAZELWOOD

PHELAN AVE

MANGELS

JOOST AVE

FLOOD AVE

STAPLES AVE

JUDSON AVE

EDNA ST

20TH AVE

URBANO DR

242 A

Art Under Your Feet

242

Inspired by the famous Selarón Steps in Rio de Janeiro, the **16th Avenue Tiled Steps** (A), a staircase that leads to the Inner Sunset neighborhood, is extraordinary. The entire length is laid with over 2,000 handmade ceramic tiles and 75,000 fragments of tile. At the base of the steps, the mosaic depicts a seabed; in the middle, the Earth; and in the upper steps, the heavens. Created by two local artists, Aileen Barr and Colette Crutcher, with the help of 300 volunteers, it's a true masterpiece [1700 16th Ave.]. After climbing the 163 steps, you can climb higher by taking another staircase to your right, on 15th Avenue, then another on Noriega Street, which leads to the summit in **Grand View Park**. The park is aptly named: It offers a 360-degree view of the Golden Gate Bridge, with the Pacific Ocean shimmering on the horizon. Later, stop at **Hollow** (B), an adorable little café. Original kitchen accessories and artisanal bath products are sold in the back room [1435 Irving St.]. Or, take a seat on the terrace at **Nopalito**, the best Mexican restaurant in the neighborhood [1224 9th Ave.].

The Beloved Tower

243

"I keep waiting for it to stalk down the hill and attack the Golden Gate Bridge." That's what renowned *San Francisco Chronicle* journalist Herb Caen wrote about **Sutro Tower**. Built between 1971 and 1973, it caused a fair bit of controversy, like the Eiffel Tower and World Trade Center, which were built earlier. Standing almost 1,000 feet (300 meters) tall and painted red and white like a candy cane, it was seen as a monstrosity by most residents. Today, it's an unmistakable symbol of the city, printed on mugs and T-shirts and even tattooed on forearms. Coit Tower and the Golden Gate Bridge are for tourists; Sutro Tower is for San Franciscans. At 1,811 feet (552 meters) above sea level (including the height of Mount Sutro, on which it rests), the transmission tower is the highest point in the city. It looks over San Francisco Bay and even rises higher than the fog patches that regularly blanket the neighborhood. The tower was built because San Francisco's many hills interfered with broadcast reception; it's used by some 15 television and radio stations. My favorite viewpoint for the tower is from Twin Peaks, the hills next to it. Both hills are approximately 922 feet (281 meters) in height, making them the second highest point in San Francisco. Twin Peaks Boulevard is the only road that leads to the ridge.

Sunset at Ocean Beach

244

Having a bonfire at Ocean Beach is a tradition that goes back to the 1970s. On some nights you can see about a dozen fires burning. Friends and strangers gather around the flames—some playing a guitar, some roasting marshmallows, and most drinking beer. The largest beach in San Francisco, Ocean Beach runs along the city's west coast for three miles (five kilometers). I love walking the length of the beach and watching the surfers; you truly feel like you're at the edge of the continent. The beach is submerged in fog from morning until late afternoon, except in September and October, the sunniest months. The fog gives the scenery a mysterious charm. The section south of Lincoln Way is the most popular, since it's close to the cafés and shops on Noriega and Judah streets, the two commercial arteries. At low tide, you can see an interesting sight from Ortega Street: In the sand is the wreck of a ship that grounded in 1878. And, of course, the beach is also the perfect spot to watch the sunset.

245 B

Surf and Coconuts

245

The vibe at Outer Sunset, the area next to Ocean Beach, couldn't be more different from the hectic pace of the city. With the surf shops and bohemian cafés, it's a place that makes you feel like you're on vacation—even though you're just 20 minutes from downtown by car. Surfers like to refuel at **Devil's Teeth Baking Company**, which has a tasty breakfast sandwich (buttermilk biscuit, scrambled eggs, cheddar and bacon) for under $6 [3876 Noriega St.], and at **Andytown Coffee Roasters**, for their strong espresso and fresh scones [3655 Lawton St.]. I go to **Judahlicious** (A) [3906 Judah St.] for acai bowls and healthy smoothies; and I love **Trouble Coffee** for their legendary cinnamon toast. Follow the surfers' example and get the Build Your Own Damn House trio (fresh coconut—with a straw—coffee and toast). Enjoy it on the small terrace outside [4033 Judah St.].

For surfing equipment, clothing, swimsuits, books and movies, **Mollusk Surf Shop** (B) is an institution. With its numerous sculptures and wooden boats, the shop is a fantastic sight [4500 Irving St.]. Surfers usually finish their day at **The Riptide**, a dive bar frequented by interesting characters. With its fireplace and hunting trophies on the walls, it feels like a cottage by the sea [3639 Taraval St.].

245 A

Refuge in a Restaurant

246

In winter and summer alike, the wind blowing in from the Pacific at Outer Sunset can be chilling. **Outerlands** is the kind of place you can't wait to warm up in after a long walk on the beach. The walls of this charming restaurant are covered in beautiful wooden slats. They serve original cocktails, pastries, soups and huge comforting sandwiches on homemade bread. Their crunchy grilled cheese—made on thick slices of sourdough and cooked in a cast iron pan—and their Dutch pancakes are sure bets. You may never want to leave [4001 Judah St.].

The Trendy General Store

247

General Store is easy to love. It's the perfect Northern California shop, blending hippie, vintage, natural and chic. Each item in the store was carefully selected, from the artisanal jewels to the leather sandals, architecture books, ceramics, natural-fiber clothing and organic beauty products. The focus is on quality and uniqueness, so the prices are (understandably) high. There's a secret garden in the back with a large wooden table surrounded by cacti and a little vegetable greenhouse. It's a peaceful haven; you'll want to take a few minutes to enjoy the serenity [4035 Judah St.].

#thatsftree

248 At 928 feet (283 meters) high, **Mount Davidson** is the highest peak in San Francisco. It's also a favorite of the Instagram community. At the top, there's an old tree with long branches that looks like something you'd see in a horror movie. Misty weather only heightens the effect. The tree was uprooted by violent winds some years ago. Visitors like to sit on the branches and have their photo taken with downtown and Sutro Tower in the background; the photos make it seem like you're floating above the city. Tag your pics with the hashtag *#thatsftree* when you post them on Instagram; thousands of Instagrammers have already done the same. West of Mount Davidson is a residential neighborhood called West Portal. The main artery is West Portal Avenue, with small family restaurants, independent shops and saloons—it feels like a Western village. It's a great area to replenish after your walk.

249B

The Rousseau Houses

249 A working class neighborhood with stucco houses, Outer Sunset isn't generally known for its architecture. However, on 34th, 35th and 36th avenues between Kirkham and Lawton streets there's a series of homes with amazing facades, each more outlandish than the last. They resemble dollhouses, Spanish castles and Hansel & Gretel houses. Built in the 1930s by San Franciscan architect Oliver Rousseau, the "**Rousseaus**" (A) are highly coveted real estate. With their unique architecture and indoor gardens, they sell for over a million dollars each. Another house in the neighborhood is pretty spectacular; its façade pays homage to the abstract painter Piet Mondrian. The **Mondrian House** (B) is definitely impressive, and worth a photo [2140 Great Hwy., between Rivera St. and Quintara St.].

248

249A

Oakland and Berkeley

No visit to San Francisco is complete without a trip to the other side of the bay to check out "Brooklyn of the West Coast," Oakland. "Oaktown" is an artistic city with enough galleries and great restaurants to give San Francisco a run for its money. Check out the rich architectural past of the downtown area (heavy on the art-deco style), and explore the up-and-coming Temescal neighborhood. Berkeley is a university town that's bubbling with culture; it's where the Slow Food movement first blossomed in the United States.

1537

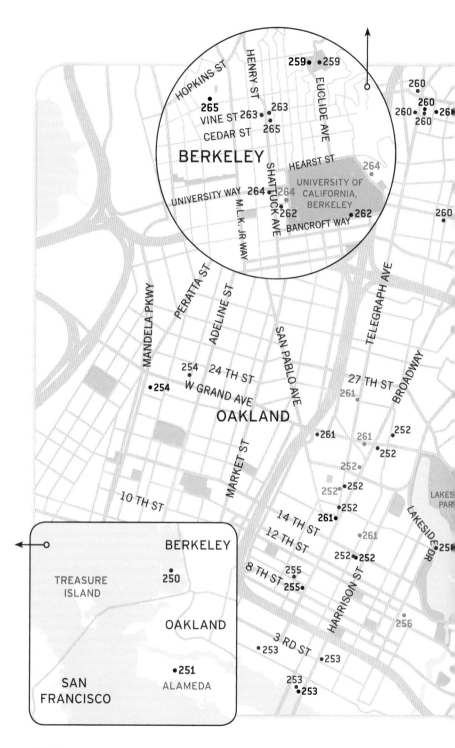

HOPKINS ST

HENRY ST

EUCLIDE AVE

259• •259

260
260
260• ••260
260

265•
VINE ST 263• •263
CEDAR ST 265

BERKELEY

HEARST ST
264

UNIVERSITY WAY 264•

SHATTUCK AVE

UNIVERSITY OF
CALIFORNIA,
BERKELEY

264

M.L.K. JR WAY

•262
BANCROFT WAY

•262

260

MANDELA PKWY

PERATTA ST

ADELINE ST

SAN PABLO AVE

TELEGRAPH AVE

BROADWAY

254•
•254

24 TH ST
W GRAND AVE

OAKLAND

27 TH ST
261•

•261

261•

•252

•252

252•

252•

252•

MARKET ST

252• •252
261•

•261

10 TH ST

LAKES
PAR

LAKESIDE DR

•250

250

BERKELEY

•250

TREASURE
ISLAND

OAKLAND

14 TH ST
12 TH ST

8 TH ST 255•
255•

252••252
HARRISON ST

256

•251
ALAMEDA

3 RD ST
•253

•253

253•
•253

**SAN
FRANCISCO**

Oakland and Berkeley

ST ST

BROADWAY

PLEASANT VALLEY AVE

MORAGA AVE

58

257• •257

257•

DMONT AVE

GRAND AVE

OAKLAND AVE

256•

256• 256
256• •256
256• •256

LAKESHORE BLVD

RAND AVE

PARK BLVD

PARK BLVD

5 TH AVE

E 22 TH ST

E 18 TH ST

14 TH AVE

E 12 TH ST

- ● Sights + photo ops
- ● Bars + restaurants
- ● Stores + markets
- ● Arts + culture
- ● Activities + walks

The Temple of Kitsch

250

For a tropical getaway just 20 minutes from downtown San Francisco, head to Emeryville, just across the Bay Bridge. In the marina lies a restaurant that brings the flavors of Polynesia to the mainland. You'll find tiki sculptures and a cocktail menu the size of an atlas—you may end up loving it ironically (like I do), but you'll definitely love it.

Born in San Francisco, Victor Jules Bergeron studied mixology in Cuba and Hawaii before deciding to return home and open **Trader Vic's** in the 1930s. His first venture was an establishment on San Pablo Avenue called Hinky Dinks, which had Polynesian-inspired food, decor and cocktails. The place became so popular that he decided to rename it after himself. Today, Trader Vic's is a huge chain, with restaurants all over the world. We have Trader Vic's to thank for the Mai Tai cocktail and for popularizing fusion cuisine in the United States.

The original restaurant moved to Emeryville in the 1970s and was entirely restored in 2010. Its popularity has been growing in recent years. The longtime clientele, who are getting on in years, are now mixing with the newcomers: hipsters. The massive restaurant offers a fantastic view of San Francisco Bay—especially at night. Order the Mai Tai Wave to sample three mini-versions of the famous cocktail, and the barbecue ribs and the duck egg rolls [9 Anchor Dr.].

251

The Great Antiques Fair

251

On the first Sunday of every month, a large antique and vintage fair sets up on the airstrip of the formal naval base at Alameda, an island in San Francisco Bay, near Oakland. The rows of kiosks at the **Alameda Point Antiques Faire** stretch as far as the eye can see—it's the biggest antiques fair in Northern California. You can see San Francisco and the Bay Bridge on the horizon. There are about 900 kiosks selling furniture, trinkets, dishware, jewelry and clothes, as well as a few food trucks. Parking is free from 6 a.m. to 3 p.m., but you have to pay to enter. There's a complimentary shuttle to and from the Alameda Ferry and the fair [2700 Saratoga St.].

250 251

252B 252A

A Night Downtown

252 A true hub of art and culture, Oakland is sometimes called the new Brooklyn. Formerly in the shadow of San Francisco, Oakland is now experiencing a renewal. Many artists and young families have fled the high cost of living in San Francisco to build a life on the other side of the bay. I like to admire the downtown art-deco architecture, or see a show at the majestic **Paramount Theatre** (A). Built in 1931, it's a venue for symphonies, ballets and old movies [2025 Broadway]. The **Fox Oakland Theatre** (B), which opened in 1928, has an ornate facade adorned like a Middle Eastern palace. All kinds of music concerts are held there [1807 Telegraph Ave.].

Pleasure is guaranteed with tacos at **Xolo** [1916 Telegraph Ave.], market cuisine at **Plum Bar + Restaurant** [2216 Broadway] and Asian cuisine at **Hawker Fare** [2300 Webster St.]. **Darling's Elixirs**, a speakeasy with white tiles housed in an old pharmacy [1635 Broadway], makes brilliantly prepared cocktails; and **Woods Bar & Brewery** makes craft beer with imaginative flavors. There's a friendly atmosphere on the large terrace with a fire pit; it's a great place to relax [1701 Telegraph Ave.]. **Longitude**, an upscale tiki bar where customers don clothing reminiscent of the Prohibition years, is a definite change of scenery [347 14th St.]. If you want to fit in there, look through the racks at **Over Attired**, a vintage store specializing in pre-1960s items [337 14th St.].

The Historic Port and Home of Jack London

253 If you go to **Jack London Square** in the Port of Oakland, you can visit the log cabin where the famous American author lived during the Klondike Gold Rush. The cabin was discovered in the 1960s, then dismantled and rebuilt in Oakland, London's birthplace. London was one of the first American writers to make a fortune with his craft. He liked to hang out at the dive bar near the hut, **Heinold's First and Last Chance Saloon**, which opened in 1880. London was likely inspired by the saloon and his cabin when he wrote his novels *The Call of the Wild* and *The Sea Wolf*. The bar is lit with oil lamps. Nothing has been updated; the walls are covered in World War II photographs, and dozens of sailors' caps hang from the ceiling. A clock in the corner has read 5:12 ever since April 18, 1906—the day of the terrible San Francisco earthquake. The bar's name means *sailors' last chance for a drink after a long sea voyage or just before they embarked on their next one* [48 Webster St.].

For a good coffee, go to **Blue Bottle Coffee**. It offers a free coffee tasting from 11:30 a.m. to 3 p.m. [300 Webster St.] each Sunday. If you're hungry, try the tapas on the terrace at **Bocanova** [55 Webster St.] or sushi with live jazz in the background at **Yoshi's** [510 Embarcadero West].

254B

Tanya's Soul Food

254

Once violent and maligned, West Oakland is a neighborhood that's transforming quickly (like the rest of the city). Gentrification leaves no stone unturned in the Bay Area. Amid the warehouses in this industrial area, a number of restaurants have been set up in old buildings. **Brown Sugar Kitchen** (A), owned by Tanya Holland, is worth visiting, if only for their signature dish: Buttermilk Fried Chicken & Cornmeal Waffle, served with brown sugar butter and apple cider syrup. Tanya reinvents this American classic using only organic products from nearby farms [2534 Mandela Pkwy.]. Also in West Oakland, go to the sunny courtyard of a former warehouse for Korean specialties at the fusion cuisine restaurant **FuseBox**. The employees wear shirts that say "I bleed kimchi." [2311 Magnolia St.]. Don't miss the huge metal statues, relics of the Burning Man festival in the courtyard of the **American Steel Studios** warehouse (B) [1960 Mandela Pkwy.].

Old Oakland

255

Be sure to visit **Swan's Market**, a food court in a superb 1890s building [538 9th St.]. **Miss Ollie's** (A), a Caribbean restaurant with tropical decor, serves comfort food for a good price. Order the jerk shrimp and the fried plantains [901 Washington St.]. Two nearby shops are worth a visit: **Marion and Rose's Workshop** for stationery and home accessories [461 9th St.], and **Umami Mart** for great Japanese kitchenware [815 Broadway]. Lined with classic Victorian-era homes, the streets of this neighborhood are the prettiest in Oakland.

256A

An Afternoon at Lake Merritt

256

A large nature reserve where you can kayak, picnic and see pelicans, **Lake Merritt** is the center of life in Oakland. At night, the lake glows with a garland of more than 4,000 lights. It doesn't take long to walk the perimeter. I usually start at the south end of the lake so I can see the original exhibitions at the **Oakland Museum of California**. It's been known as the People's Museum since it opened in 1969 [1000 Oak St.].

Then I walk north, on the right side of the lake, to the **Grand Lake Farmers Market**, held every Saturday at the corner of Grand Avenue and Lake Park Avenue. It's the perfect place to sample fresh produce, have some tea, and mingle with local residents. Across the street is **Grand Lake Theatre** (A), which opened in 1926; it's one of my favorite theaters [3200 Grand Ave.]. Then I continue on Grand Avenue, which has some of the best restaurants in the city and some great independent shops. Notables include **La Parisienne**, the little bakery owned by French chef Karim Bedda, who makes almond croissants and flan that are absolutely heavenly [3249 Grand Ave.]; **Alchemy Bottle Shop**, a charming spot where you can find spirits and elixirs, from small producers, that are delicate and unique [3256 Grand Ave.]; **Oak Common**, a shop with thoroughly California-style clothing and accessories [3231 Grand Ave.]; and **Walden Pond Books**, a little gem of a bookstore that's beloved in the neighborhood [3316 Grand Ave.]. The shelves are packed with new and secondhand books. The bookstore is located right beside the popular restaurant **Boot & Shoe Service** with its wood-oven pizzas and California cuisine [3308 Grand Ave.]. The wait can be long, so some customers choose to do a little shopping while they wait for their table. You can also wait at the wine bar **Ordinaire**, just a bit farther up on the same block [3354 Grand Ave.].

Camino is the best restaurant in the neighborhood. Camino transforms a simple salad into a truly unforgettable meal. All the ingredients are cooked in a wood oven, and testify to the chef's incredible mastery of flavors. Tips are not accepted, and guests sit at communal tables [3917 Grand Ave.]. **Penrose** is another spot that uses a wood oven to cook flatbreads with toppings, fish and vegetables. Order the roasted chicken and Brussels sprouts [3311 Grand Ave.]. Be sure to venture into **The Alley** piano bar, a legendary spot where anyone can get on the microphone and sing, accompanied by Rob Dibble on piano [3325 Grand Ave.].

A Picturesque Avenue

257

Piedmont Avenue, between West MacArthur Boulevard and Ridgeway Avenue, is one of my favorite parts of Oakland. With its church, ice cream shop, bookstores, early 20th-century theater (Piedmont Theatre) (A) and its small independent shops, you might start to think you're in Pleasantville. Make a stop at **Neighbor**, a contemporary general store with beautiful objects for the home, chosen carefully by the owner, Dana Olson [4200 Piedmont Ave.]. Dana has two other stores on the same avenue: The jewelry and accessories store **Good Stock** [4198 Piedmont Ave.] and the vintage clothing store **Mercy Vintage** [4188 Piedmont Ave.]. They're both little gems. The avenue has become a haven for hamburger lovers with the arrival of **KronnerBurger** (B), probably the nicest restaurant in Oakland. In a brick building that's shaped a bit like an iron, with a clock tower at one end, it has white marble tables, lovely ceramic light fixtures and leather booths. Their signature burger is served with bone marrow on the side, and they also have a veggie burger [4063 Piedmont Ave.]. At **Ba-Bite**, a small restaurant with Mediterranean food, you'll feel like you're at home (that's what the word means in Hebrew). The Israeli chef, Mica Talmor, makes delicious keftas, kebabs, tagines and falafels, and she dotes on customers like a grandmother. I always get the salad trio for $13 [3905 Piedmont Ave.].

A Breakfast that Takes you Back in Time

258

Sherry, a server at **Mama's Royal Cafe** for 35 years, will probably call you "hon;" it's that type of place. The owner, George Marino, displays a collection of old radio sets, and Sherry shows off her apron collection. You'll find everything from kale from a local farm, to (on the other end of the nutritional spectrum) SPAM. They hold a napkin art contest each year, with a $400 prize for the winner. A plate of eggs, pancakes and bacon will only cost you $10. The decor hasn't changed since the 1970s; the exotic trinkets from its previous incarnation—a Chinese restaurant—are still there. It's the type of place you'd love to have in your own neighborhood [4012 Broadway].

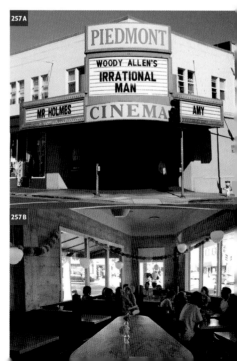

Alleys of Artisans

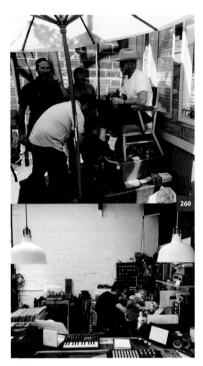

260

Temescal Alley offers much, much more than you'd expect. Independent shops, barbershops, ice cream parlors, flower shops, jewelry stores and cafés can all be found in this dead-end alley off the beaten path in north Oakland. There's a mix of locals and trendy young people, and I love the atmosphere—especially on weekends. If you're looking for unique, delicate jewelry, stop in at **Esqueleto**. At the far end of **Alley 49**, the alley next to Temescal Alley, you'll find a fascinating store called **Book/ Shop**. It sells posters, rare magazines, avant-garde furniture and a selection of books that changes every two weeks. The selection is meticulously curated by the owner, Erik Heywood. Next door is **Doughnut Dolly**. Their fresh donuts are made to order with chocolate or other fillings. The two alleys are off of 49th Street, between Telegraph Avenue and Clarke Street. There are four restaurants in the area that are worth trying. **Juhu Beach Club** offers Indian fusion cuisine that's truly original [5179 Telegraph Ave.]; **Cholita Linda**, with its colorful decor, serves delicious tacos and Cuban sandwiches [4923 Telegraph Ave.]; **Clove & Hoof** is a butcher shop and restaurant that serves great Philly cheesesteaks [4001 Broadway]; and **Hog's Apothecary**, a restaurant in a former Laundromat, offers gourmet hot dogs and has 30 California craft beers on tap [375 40th St.].

The Rose Garden

259

High up in Berkeley, not far from Shattuck Avenue, is a magnificent terraced garden that's designed like an amphitheater. Three thousand roses, in 250 varieties, bloom there annually. The roses are organized by color: red flowers at the top; white, pink and yellow flowers on the lower terraces. **Berkeley Rose Garden** is a public garden that was created in the 1930s. It offers a panoramic view of San Francisco Bay and the Golden Gate Bridge. I like to sit under a trellis and peek at the newlyweds posing for photos. The best time to visit the garden is mid-May [1200 Euclid Ave.].

Friday Street Art

261 I like to visit Oakland on the first Friday of each month for **First Friday**, a celebration of art, music and cuisine. Food trucks and musicians take over Telegraph Avenue between West Grand Avenue and 27th Street, and dozens of art galleries stay open until 9 p.m. To get there, take BART (the train system that serves the Bay Area) from San Francisco, and get off at 19th St/ Oakland station. Find information at oaklandartmurmur.org/firstfriday. **Athen B. Gallery** is a fairly new gallery that represents a number of emerging artists and street artists [1525 Webster St.]. Don't miss the great mural on the wall of **Cathedral Building** (A), a historic building that resembles a wedding cake [1615 Broadway]. The **Great Wall of Oakland** is a 10,000-square-foot (930-square-meter) wall. Art films from around the world are projected onto it, and the parking lot next door transforms into an open-air theater [451 West Grand Ave.]. Then stop at the **Starline Social Club**. It's a combined bar, social club, performance hall and exhibition space. The building is a former saloon from 1893. The decor is minimalist, and they serve small dishes at the bar, as well as excellent cocktails [645 West Grand Ave.].

Historic Baths

262 **Hearst Gymnasium**, a women's gym built in 1925—designed by renowned California architect Julia Morgan—has an interesting feature on its roof: a large marble swimming pool. Students at the University of California, Berkeley, have been taking lifeguarding classes in this very pool since the 1920s. Surrounded by sculpted columns and statues of angels, it's a true architectural treasure. It also offers an incredible view of The Campanile, the university's bell tower and an almost exact replica of the bell tower at St. Mark's Square in Venice. At 307 feet (94 meters) high, it's the third-highest bell tower in the world. The swimming pool is open to the public; buy your $12 day pass at **Pro Shop Café** [2301 Bancroft Way]. The water in the pool is kept at 82°F (28°C), so you can swim all year long. After your swim, head to **Ippuku**, which is near the campus. The Japanese izakaya restaurant has a wide selection of sake, grilled meat and soba noodles [2130 Center St.].

263A 264A 265

Pizza and Jazz on the Sidewalk

263

Any visit to Berkeley should include another mandatory stop: **The Cheese Board Collective** (A), a bakery/cheese shop/pizzeria that opened in the 1970s. Crowds line up for their wood-oven-cooked California pizzas, topped with fresh ingredients and hard-to-find cheeses. They make only one kind of pizza each day. The lineup can be long, but there's always a jazz band playing to entertain customers as they wait [1512 Shattuck Ave.]. The Collective is right across from **Chez Panisse** (see Reason #265) and close to the first **Peet's Coffee & Tea** [2124 Vine St.]. With the high concentration of great restaurants and seasonal organic and GMO-free food stores, the North Berkeley neighborhood has become known as the Gourmet Ghetto. Some of these businesses are responsible for starting the Slow Food movement in the United States; thank them for helping us move on from Velveeta and Folgers. Shattuck Avenue is a top destination for gourmands all over the world. I also like to stop at **Juice Bar Collective**, a small restaurant with freshly squeezed juices and vegetarian dishes for takeout [2114 Vine St.].

Concerts Under the Stars

264

Built on the University of California, Berkeley campus, the **William Randolph Hearst Greek Theatre** (usually known more simply as the Greek Theatre) is an 8,500-seat open-air amphitheater. The architect was inspired by the ancient Greek theater of Epidaurus. President Theodore Roosevelt gave a convocation speech at the theater in 1903. Today, it's a venue for concerts of all kinds, from jazz to electro to rock. You can find the schedule at thegreektheaterberkeley.com. From the highest rows in the stands, you can see all the lights of San Francisco Bay—an utterly magical experience. After the show, I recommend a visit to **Berkeley Art Museum and Pacific Film Archive** (A), right next to the campus. The superb corrugated metal building was designed by the same architects who designed New York's famous High Line Park [2155 Center St.]. After the show, eat at **Comal**, a Mexican Slow Food restaurant with an impeccable cocktail selection. The dish to order is the roasted chicken to share, with the ceviche of the day [2020 Shattuck Ave.].

The Ultimate in Farm-to-Table

265 Eating at **Chez Panisse** in Berkeley is a quasi-religious experience. If you have only one chance to taste what California has to offer, this has to be your destination. The restaurant's founder, Alice Waters, is a pioneer of California cuisine. In 1971, she helped launched what would become the Slow Food and locavore movements in the United States. Most restaurants in the Bay Area eventually adopted this philosophy, sourcing local products and creating menus based on what's available at the markets. A number of chefs in the region worked with Alice before setting out on their own, and still count themselves among her disciples.

Alice Waters fell in love with French culinary tradition when she traveled to France in the 1960s (the name of her restaurant refers to a character from the trilogy of plays by Marcel Pagnol). When she returned home, she started exploring the flavors that had made such a deep impression on her. She turned her focus to local organic produce. It was a huge breakthrough: At the time, frozen and canned food was more or less the norm in the United States.

The restaurant is located close to the University of California, Berkeley, in a lovely wood house. Calming and comfortable, it's reminiscent of a Frank Lloyd Wright building. The dining room on the first floor offers a three- or four-course meal for around $100. Tables can be reserved more than a month in advance.

Personally, I prefer **Chez Panisse Café** on the second floor, where the à la carte menu is more affordable. A wood oven sits in the middle of the room, and there's a counter overflowing with perfectly ripe ingredients. Pro tip: Go before lunch or after 5 p.m., and ask Jonathan (the friendly maître d'), for a table. He should be able to accommodate you. During my last visit, I had a wonderful salad with watercress, fennel, green beans, almonds and figs ($12), followed by couscous and perfectly grilled vegetables, and a bowl of blackberries, blueberries and figs that were sweet and delicious. Everything was served in elegant pottery [1517 Shattuck Ave.].

Alice Waters has made it her personal mission to improve the diet of children. In 1996, she created an edible garden in the yard at Martin Luther King Jr. Middle School, half a mile from the restaurant. Children learn to plant, harvest, wash and cook fruits and vegetables. The **Edible Schoolyard** program went on to spread throughout the United States [1781 Rose St.].

Day Trips

San Franciscans have it pretty good: They're surrounded by some of the most stunning landscapes on Earth. An embarrassment of riches awaits them when they want to escape the commotion of the city. To the north are the wineries of Napa and Sonoma, redwood forests, Mount Tamalpais, black sand beaches and oyster farms. To the south lies a paradise for surfers, a haven for elephant seals, and great local farm produce.

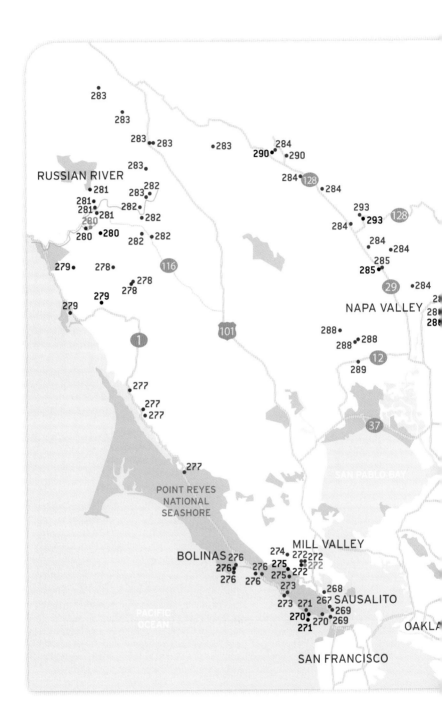

RUSSIAN RIVER

NAPA VALLEY

POINT REYES
NATIONAL
SEASHORE

BOLINAS

MILL VALLEY

SAUSALITO

SAN PABLO BAY

PACIFIC
OCEAN

OAKLA

SAN FRANCISCO

Day Trips

Surf in the Pacific, Just 15 Minutes from Downtown

266

The perfect place to learn the archetypal California sport, surfing, is just a short drive from San Francisco. **Pacifica State Beach** is sheltered from heavy swells and strong wind. That means the waves aren't too intimidating, which is good for beginners. There are several surf schools and shops that rent equipment. One is **Nor Cal Surf Shop**, which offers surfing lessons for $94 a person, or $199 for private lessons [5440 Pacific Coast Hwy., Pacifica].

267A

The Officers' Spa

267

Across the Golden Gate Bridge, among the green hills of the former military base (Fort Baker) in Marin County, lies **Cavallo Point Lodge** (A). This historic hotel's lovely neocolonial houses were once the homes of high-ranking army officers. Rooms are rented at pretty steep prices, but you can also enjoy the facilities by booking a massage or skin treatment at **Healing Arts Center & Spa**. A day pass costs $65 and includes a yoga, Pilates or meditation session, thermal baths and saunas [601 Murray Circle]. Pro tip: After the spa, enjoy a beer at the bar on the second floor of the **Presidio Yacht Club**, at the marina just south of Fort Baker. It's an authentic, unpretentious bar with one of the best views of Golden Gate Bridge [679 Sommerville Rd.].

Bocce and Terraces by the Water

268

Sausalito has a number of good restaurants with a range of prices. If it's a sunny day, stop by **Bar Bocce** (A), a pizzeria with a large terrace by the water and bocce courts [1250 Bridgeway]. The colorful Mexican restaurant **Salsalito Taco Shop** (B) is very family-friendly [1115 Bridgeway]. **Cibo**, a café [1201 Bridgeway], and the gourmet grocery store **Driver's Market** [200 Caledonia St.] both have excellent sandwiches, and the old diner **The Lighthouse Cafe** offers huge breakfasts [1311 Bridgeway]. For seafood, the restaurant **Fish** [350 Harbor Dr.] has no competition. Order the crab sandwich, the tuna poke or the tuna melt. In the evening, head to **Sushi Ran**, one of the best restaurants in the entire Bay Area, headed by the extremely creative chef Taka Toshi [107 Caledonia St.]. I'm also a fan of the food at the French bistro **Le Garage**, housed in a waterfront industrial building. With a glass of rosé in your hand, the view of the sunset is something special [85 Liberty Ship Way].

A Euphoric Bike Trip

269

Riding your bike to Sausalito, over the Golden Gate Bridge, is the most iconic getaway trip in San Francisco. There are different spots to rent a bike at Fisherman's Wharf and North Beach, for about $30 a day (helmet, lock and map included); try **Blazing Saddles** [1095 Columbus Ave.] or **Bay City Bike** [1325 Columbus Ave.].

The trip is about six miles (10 km) from the start of the bridge, so even kids can manage it. Bikes have to use the east sidewalk of the bridge on weekdays and the west sidewalk on weekends. Each side has its advantages. The west side offers a panoramic view of the mouth of San Francisco Bay; the Pacific Ocean stretches into the distance, and you can see ships, fishing boats and the beaches of Marin County. Biking on the east side, the hills and skyscrapers hugging the bay will dazzle you. From your 230-foot (70-meter) high vantage point, it's an exhilarating view.

When you get off the bridge, take Alexander Avenue, on the right, and follow it down to the bay. Continue cycling on Bridgeway along the waterfront until you reach Sausalito. With its colorful hillside houses in the background, you might think you're in the Italian town of Positano.

To get back to San Francisco, take the ferry from downtown Sausalito ($10 to $12, depending on the company). The **Golden Gate Ferry** will bring you to the Ferry Building (see Reason #135); and **Blue & Gold Fleet** will bring you to Pier 41 at Fisherman's Wharf. The ferry rides take about 25 minutes.

Black Sands Beach

270

On the other side of the Golden Gate Bridge, on the hilly peninsula of Marin Headlands (part of the protected Golden Gate National Recreation Area), lies a tranquil black-sand beach. Apart from a few fishermen and the occasional nudist, the stretches of black sand here are practically deserted.

With its view of the city, Black Sands Beach is the perfect spot for a picnic (or a marriage proposal). Take exit 442 after you cross the bridge, then turn left on Alexander Avenue and right on Conzelman Road. Continue for about three miles (5 km), until you reach the parking lot for Upper Fisherman's, on your left. A long stairway (Black Sands Beach Trail) will lead you to the beach paradise. Stop at **Battery Rathbone McIndoe**, half a mile (1 km) farther on Conzelman Road. The 20th-century concrete gun battery is one of the many historic military sites that were built to protect San Francisco Bay from enemy ships. You can climb up on the structure to snap the perfect shot of the Golden Gate Bridge with the city in the background. When you head back, on Field Road, you'll see Nike Missile Site SF-88. The former launch site is a true relic of the Cold War, and it's the only fully restored Nike anti-aircraft missile site in the country. It's open to visitors Thursday to Saturday during the afternoon.

272A

The Picture-Perfect Lighthouse

271

While you're in the Marin Headlands, park at the end of Conzelman Road and follow the path that leads to Point Bonita (the trek is less than half a mile, but very steep in some parts; wear good walking shoes). You'll pass through a tunnel carved out of the rock and cross a suspension bridge, and finally arrive at the **Point Bonita Lighthouse**. The lighthouse, perched on a rock formation, is still operating. It was built in 1855 to guide ships through the treacherous Golden Gate straight. If you're afraid of heights, the visit might give you vertigo. The suspension bridge sways, the waves crash against the cliffs 130 feet (40 meters) below you, and winds can reach 100 miles (160 km) per hour. Seek refuge in the lighthouse; there's a small maritime museum inside, with a guide who can answer all your questions. Visits are free; open Saturdays, Sundays and Mondays from 12:30 p.m. to 3:30 p.m.

On the other side of the Rodeo Lagoon, less than two miles (3 km) from the lighthouse, is the **Marine Mammal Center**, which offers a fun and educational experience for kids. The nonprofit veterinary research facility is also a rehabilitation center for sick or injured marine mammals. Hundreds of seals, elephant seals, sea lions and dolphins are rescued on the California coast each year and cared for at the center before being returned to the ocean. It's open from 10 a.m. to 5 p.m., and entry is free [2000 Bunker Rd.].

271

The Bookstore in the Redwoods

272

Mill Valley is a bucolic little town just 20 minutes north of San Francisco. It's the kind of place that seems like paradise to grow up in. A creek runs through the town, and the city hall occupies a Tudor-style house. Swings hang from multiple trees, and business owners know their customers by name. It's worth the trip just to see the **Mill Valley Public Library** (A). I fell in love with this picturesque spot, which is both rustic and modern. The wooden building has high ceilings and big bay windows that look out on a redwood grove. There are comfortable chairs and wooden furniture made by local artisans, and bouquets of fresh flowers that make you want to stay for hours [375 Throckmorton Ave.].

After a library visit, I like to go to independent stores like **Branded** [118 Throckmorton Ave.]; **Mint** [167 Throckmorton Ave.], which sells women's clothing and accessories; and **Guideboat Company**, which has nautical-style clothing for men and women [129 Miller Ave.]. The best restaurant in town is **Molina**, which serves California cuisine in a lovely house with a big woodstove in the center of the room. The menu changes daily, and the chef uses seasonal ingredients [17 Madrona St.]. For a more casual meal, **Mill Valley Beerworks**, right around the corner, has a great selection of craft beers on tap and small dishes to share [173 Throckmorton Ave.].

272A

270

An English Countryside next to the Pacific

273 Hiding away near the mythical Highway 1 in the Marin Headlands is the **Pelican Inn**. With its seven Tudor-style rooms, whitewashed walls, stained glass windows and period furniture, you'll feel like you've been transported back to 16th-century England. It's a truly romantic place, and a popular honeymoon spot for couples. You don't need to stay at the hotel to enjoy the beauty. The grassy field in front of it is popular with cyclists who want to stop for a beer and fish-and-chips. On weekends, the inn's restaurant serves a traditional English breakfast in the dining room, which is decorated with old photos of British royalty.

To get there, cross the Golden Gate Bridge, take Highway 101 for about 8 ½ miles (14 km) and get off at exit 445 B. Continue on Highway 1 North for about six miles (10 km), then turn left on Pacific Way [10 Pacific Way]. The inn is on the same road that leads to the magical **Muir Beach**, a popular spot for family barbecues and hikes. There's free parking at the end of Pacific Way.

273

THE PELICAN INN

275A

Giant Trees and a Bavarian Chalet

275 Muir Woods (A), a unique old redwood forest just 30 minutes north of San Francisco, is another must-see spot. The forest has coast redwoods, a species with some of the biggest tree specimens in the world. This enchanting 555-acre (224-hectare) area is veined with six miles (10 km) of trails. In Cathedral Grove, some trees are more than 777 years old and measure over 260 feet (80 meters) tall. Try to get there early in the morning (around 8 a.m.) to avoid the crowds; the thick fog at that hour makes the forest feel utterly mysterious. A few hours later, when the first rays of sun start to break through the trees, you'll feel like you're in a dreamworld. Entry is $10 per person, but it's free for those 15 and under [1 Muir Woods Rd.].

From the visitor's center, you're only a 10-minute drive from another incredible destination. In a secluded spot lies **Nature Friends Tourist Club San Francisco**, a magnificent century-old chalet with Bavarian-style carved balconies. It's the perfect place to drink beer in big mugs after a serious walk in Muir Woods. Established in 1912, the private club is part of the Friends of Nature organization, which was founded in Vienna in 1895. Luckily for us non-members, the club opens its doors to the public a few days a year for various festivals that feature costumes, folk music, traditional dances and Bavarian dishes. It's like a Californian Oktoberfest. Check the calendar here: touristclubsf.org/calendar [30 Ridge Ave., at the corner of Panoramic Hwy.].

Mount Tam

274 You can easily combine your Muir Woods excursion with a trip to Mount Tamalpais (which San Franciscans affectionately call "Mount Tam"). At the top, it's the highest point in Marin County (2,576 feet/785 meters), and offers a stunning 25-mile (40 km) panoramic view. To get there from the Tourist Club, take a left and drive down the windy Panoramic Highway for about 3 ½ miles (6 km); go right on Pan Toll Road for over a mile (2 km), then go right on East Ridgecrest Boulevard for three miles (5 km). There's parking just below the eastern ridge of the mountain; from there it's just a few steps to reach Mount Tamalpais' East Peak. The Verna Dunshee is a half-mile trail (1 km) that circles the summit. The views are awesome: You can see Napa Valley, San Francisco and the Farallon Islands jutting out of the Pacific.

A Hidden Hippie Enclave

276 I totally fell in love with **Bolinas**, an hour's drive northwest of San Francisco. Surrounded by water, the town of about 1,600 lives in a bohemian bubble. Here, the surfer is king. Visiting is like being on another planet—even the vegetation is different. Bolinas is geographically isolated, and tectonically as well: Lying on the Pacific Plate, it's moving toward the north, while the rest of the continent, on the North American Plate, is shifting south. Indeed, Bolinas is one of the only communities in the United States situated west of the worrisome San Andreas Fault.

Bolinas' residents want to keep their town out of the spotlight; they even removed the sign on Highway 1 that read "Bolinas 2." Since then, the expression "two miles," has been used in the village in reference to the famous sign. Strangers aren't welcomed with open arms, but Bolinas residents aren't actually hostile. Spending a day in the town does your soul good. Separated from the change and turbulence of the modern world, the town beats at a different rhythm—one of the tides. Dogs walk without a leash, teens drink and smoke on rooftops, and the municipality has neither traffic lights nor a website. The main street, Wharf Road, has a small library, a church, a post office, a community garden, an inn and a few businesses, including a health food store, an art gallery, a retro gas station and a bar that's straight out of a Western movie (**Smiley's Schooner Saloon**) (A). There's also one single restaurant, **Coast Cafe**, which has fantastic blackberry pie. At their Coffee Kiosk, I order a café au lait, breakfast sandwich (the 2-Mile Muffin) or a slice of banana cake, and enjoy them on the steps of the old general store, **Bolinas Super Market** (B). The wall behind the cash in the store is a mosaic of photos of "Bolinas babies." As you sit on the steps, you're likely to spot the town's bearded hippie elder bike guy, *sans* shirt and shoes. Farther on, on Wharf Road, you can see fishermen, a marine biology laboratory and colorful houses on stilts.

On Brighton Avenue, which leads to the beach, you'll see barefoot locals carrying surfboards. You can rent equipment and take surfing lessons at **2 Mile Surf Shop** [22 Brighton Ave.].

When you're heading to Bolinas, stop en route at **Stinson Beach**, a beautiful white-sand beach that's popular with surfers. **Parkside Cafe**, at the edge of the beach, is your destination for brunch [43 Arenal Ave.]. Then continue about 4 ½ miles (7 km) north on Highway 1 until you see Olema-Bolinas Road on your left—it's a road bordered by large trees and dotted with stands where farm produce is for sale. This road will bring you to town.

Oyster Road

277A

277 Tomales Bay, an hour-and-a-half drive from downtown San Francisco, has several oyster farms that are open to the public. Visiting these farms is one of my favorite activities on weekends out of the city. The bay is a sparkling blue, the sun is usually out and the scent of grilled oysters fills the air; it's all guaranteed to give you that vacation feeling. At **Hog Island Oyster Co.**, there are a number of wooden tables by the water and individual charcoal barbeques where you can grill fresh oysters yourself, ordered à la carte. They provide the utensils, condiments and a free lesson (which I greatly appreciated!) on how to open the tricky shellfish without injuring yourself. Remember to book your barbecue in advance (hogislandoysters.com), since it's a very popular spot. You can also show up without a reservation and order oysters prepared for you at **The Boat Oyster Bar**, an oyster-shaped shack. They also serve cold-cut platters [20215 Shoreline Hwy., Marshall].

At **The Marshall Store** (A), oysters are prepared to your taste (lemon and mignonette sauce, BBQ, chorizo, Rockefeller, bacon, grilled with cheese, etc.) and served with big slices of country bread. Sit at a counter by the water and savor your meal with a chilled bottle of white wine or a bowl of rich clam chowder. It's a recipe for total contentment. The place is especially beautiful at sunset [19225 State Route 1, Marshall]. Right next door, **Blue Waters Kayaking** rents boats so you can enjoy a paddle on the peaceful waters of the bay.

Nick's Cove, about four miles (6 km) north of The Marshall Store, is a motel that's been around since the 1930s. It also has a long wharf that stretches out from the shore and a seafood restaurant on the water. Every table offers a fantastic view of the bay, and the bar has an unbelievable decor. Order their Dungeness Crab Mac n' Cheese. You can also stay the night in one of the cottages, all of which are decorated to look like sailors' cabins [23240 California 1]. **Point Reyes Station** is another oyster-lover's paradise; the old railway town has become a top destination for foodies. The popular food stand **Cowgirl Creamery** is another essential stop [80 4th St.], as is **Bovine Bakery**, for their scones [11315 State Route 1].

The Town with a Bohemian Spirit

278A

278 One of the roads leading to **Occidental**, a town of about 1,000 people, is called Bohemian Highway. As soon as you reach the main road, you'll get the picture: Stores sell crystals, herbs and handmade soaps. Occidental probably isn't much different than it was in the hippie era of the 1960s. Surrounded by hills of redwoods, the little village comprises just five blocks of homes. It's about an 80-minute drive from San Francisco, which makes it an ideal destination for a relaxing day trip. There's only one place to stay: **Inn At Occidental**, housed in a charming Victorian house. They serve wine and cheese on the veranda every day at 5 p.m. [3657 Church St.].

Howard Station Cafe (named after the town's old train station) is my favorite breakfast spot in the region. The restaurant, in a Victorian home, serves healthy dishes (poached eggs and quinoa, tofu sandwiches), homemade pastries and delicious omelets and hamburgers. There's a little window on the left side of the house where you can order coffee and smoothies to go. Try the Ohm-Mega 3: almond butter, flax and chia seeds, dates, bananas, blueberries and almond milk [3611 Bohemian Hwy.].

Afterward, head south on Bohemian Highway for three miles (5 km) until you get to Freestone. The magnificent Zen gardens, at the **Osmosis Day Spa Sanctuary** (A), are open to the public. The spa offers a Japanese treatment that's rare in the United States: an enzyme bath. During the treatment, you are submerged in a mixture of finely ground cedar chips, rice bran and enzymes. The natural fermentation that results produces heat and stimulates the metabolism (about $99 per person). Massages and skin-care packages, tea ceremonies and meditation are also offered [209 Bohemian Hwy.].

Stop at **Wild Flour Bread**, the artisanal bakery across the street, for scones and flatbread for the road. Customers are welcome to visit the garden and even to pick their own fruit [140 Bohemian Hwy.]. Get the rest of your provisions at **Freestone Artisan Cheese**, beside the bakery. Be sure to try their fabulous goat cheese [380 Bohemian Hwy.].

When you get back to Occidental at the end of the day, an Italian celebration will await you. The restaurant **Union Hotel** opened in 1879 and has stayed in the same Italian family for five generations. The tables in the dining hall are covered in red-and-white gingham tablecloths, the walls are lined with old photos and the bar next door looks like a Gold Rush saloon. Try the minestrone soup, homemade ravioli, succulent roast chicken and the gigantic pizzas [3731 Main St.]. The **Occidental Bohemian Farmers Market** sets up on the main drag for part of the year. Be sure to try Gerard's Paella; they serve a giant version of the dish, cooked in a six-foot (two-meter) pan. The preparation is a show unto itself ($10 per person).

The World of Alfred Hitchcock

279 Fans of Alfred Hitchcock's *The Birds* should check out **Bodega Bay**, a small fishing village on the Pacific Ocean. A number of scenes from the 1963 horror film were shot there. *The Birds* is based on a novel—set in Britain—by British author Daphne du Maurier; Hitchcock decided, however, to shoot the film in California. He discovered the tiny village about 60 miles (100 km) north of San Francisco while he was shooting *Shadow of a Doubt* in nearby Santa Rosa in 1943. During one of the scenes with attacking birds, the film's characters flee for safety in **Tides Wharf** restaurant. The establishment was later rebuilt, but unfortunately it's no longer recognizable from the original in the film [835 California 1]. Try the fish-and-chips at **Lucas Wharf**, a waterfront restaurant nearby [595 Bay Hill Rd.].

The next stop on your Hitchcock tour should be Bodega, a town five miles (8 km) inland. Remember when the children run out of their school screaming, being chased by birds? The unforgettable scene was shot at the **Potter Schoolhouse** (A) [17110 Bodega Lane]. Today the school is a private home. It's next to **Saint Teresa of Avila**, a Catholic church that appears in the film. The church was also the subject of a famous black-and-white photo by American photographer Ansel Adams [17242 Bodega Hwy.].

From Bodega Bay you can continue north on Highway 1 for three miles (5 km) and turn right on **Coleman Valley Road**; from there it's a scenic 10-mile (16-kilometer) drive to reach Occidental (see Reason #278). High up in the hills, the road offers breathtaking views, and the coastal homes in the distance are the stuff of dreams.

Swimming in Russian River

280 Six miles (10 km) north of Occidental (see Reason #278) on Bohemian Highway, you'll find a small town that greets you with a sign hanging over the main street: "Welcome to Monte Rio, Vacation Wonderland." It's a nostalgic reminder of the era when the railroad was king, which led to a number of resorts being built there. Monte Rio is also where the richest and most powerful people in the world (including almost every U.S. president since Dwight D. Eisenhower) gather every July at a 2,700-acre campground called **Bohemian Grove**. They spend two weeks there sharing their passion for outdoors and theater, drinking and engaging in ultra-secret discussions and mysterious rituals. This club's existence has fueled conspiracy theories ever since it was established in 1872.

Most of its hotels have vanished, but Monte Rio is still a great place for relaxing at a public beach. The **Russian River** has wonderful swimming. Rent an inner tube ($5 an hour) and let the current push you along, or a kayak ($10 an hour). With the old Monte Rio Bridge in the background, the scenery is perfect. The main attraction in town is the **Rio Theater**. Built in the 1950s, it shows classics and indie films. It also serves as a social club, with a café-terrace in the back. The theater was saved from destruction in 2014, when 27 artists from the San Francisco region joined forces to preserve it [20396 Bohemian Hwy.].

A Town that Welcomes All

281

Guerneville is a picturesque and eclectic town in the Sonoma region. The first thing you notice when you get there is the sign that says "A Hate Free Community." The town has been a destination of choice for gay couples since the 1980s, but today it attracts families and hip young people from San Francisco. As a result, some interesting businesses have set up shop on the main street. One of these is **Pat's Restaurant**, a 1940s-style American diner. After 5 p.m. it transforms into **Dick Blomster's Korean Diner** (A), a swank Korean restaurant. The decor stays the same, but the lighting changes to florescent pink. They have creative fusion dishes: The popular fried chicken is served with vanilla coleslaw, the fried rice is made with kimchi and their signature dessert is the fried peanut butter and jam sandwich, served with vanilla ice cream and sprinkled with Pop Rocks (the candy that crackles in your mouth) [16236 Main St.].

Also on the main street, the town's one-time bank has been transformed into a collective space, called the **Guerneville Bank Club**. There's an art gallery in the old safe, historic photos, an accessories shop, the artisanal ice cream shop **Nimble and Finn's**, and the pie stand **Chile Pies Baking Co.** (don't leave without trying the nectarine pie) [16290 Main St.]. For seafood, **Seaside Metal Oyster Bar** is your destination [16222 Main St.]. **Boon Eat +**

Drink has contemporary seasonal food, and serves only wines from the Russian River region. The duck and mac n' cheese are must-tries [16248 Main St.]. The owners also own **Big Bottom Market** [16228 Main St.], the perfect place to stock up with sandwiches, salads and coffee before heading to **Johnson Beach**, the most popular beach on Russian River, at the end of Church Street. After a swim, **El Barrio** is the perfect place for a drink. The bar has a terrace in the back and colorful New Mexican decor [16230 Main St.].

Guerneville is a five-minute drive from **Armstrong Redwoods State Natural Reserve**, which has giant redwoods and a variety of trails (easy, medium and difficult). One of its trees is 1,400 years old; it's been nicknamed Colonel Armstrong, after the lumberjack who decided, in the 1870s, that the area needed to be protected. The tallest tree in the park is over 310 feet (95 meters) high [17000 Armstrong Woods Rd.].

If you want to spend the night in the town, I recommend the boutique hotel **Boon Hotel + Spa**, halfway between the main street and the redwood forest. The 14 rooms are decorated in Scandinavian style. Bikes are available to guests so they can explore the region [14711 Armstrong Woods Rd.].

A Night in the Country

282 For a romantic weekend in wine country, I recommend booking a room at the boutique hotel **Farmhouse Inn** (A) in Forestville. The luxurious bed-and-breakfast is surrounded by vineyards, and the staff is wonderfully attentive. You can taste the region's wines and cheeses by the pool, and indulge in s'mores by a bonfire, relax in the bath bar, enjoy sugar scrubs, have a gourmet breakfast and even get chocolate cookies on your pillow (I was so crazy about these cookies that I discovered, the next morning, that someone had slipped the recipe under my door). The rooms are fairly expensive; you can save half the cost by booking the same day through the Hotel Tonight app (I got a junior suite for half price). The hotel has 25 rooms, a spa and a Michelin-star restaurant—which is a destination in itself. The food is impeccably prepared with ingredients from their garden. The most well-known dish is the Rabbit Three Ways (smoked, grilled and confit). The evening I visited, I had a fantastic cheese, peach and pesto burrata and octopus grilled to perfection. The three-course meal costs $79 [7871 River Rd.].

For a more affordable feast, **Underwood Bar & Bistro** (a 10-minute drive from the hotel) is a well-kept secret. Try their Moroccan lamb sandwich and the smoked trout salad. There's a bocce court in the garden [9113 Graton Rd.]. Right near the hotel, you can rent canoes at **Burke's Canoe Trips** ($65 per canoe). You can easily paddle downstream on Russian River for 10 miles (16 km) all the way to Guerneville, stopping at various points to swim or picnic (it'll take three hours—or four or five if you really take your time). A shuttle will pick you up and take you back to the starting point [8600 River Rd.]. There are great wineries around the hotel, like **Gary Farrell Vineyards & Winery**, which has a superb view of the valley [10701 Westside Rd.]; **Arista Winery**, which makes excellent pinots [7015 Westside Rd.]; and **Iron Horse Vineyards**, where you can try sparkling wines at an outdoor tasting room surrounded by palm trees [9786 Ross Station Rd.]. I also like the wines at **Lynmar Estate** (B); the wooden building resembles a chic hippie house from the 1970s, with a spectacular flower garden [3909 Frei Rd.]. Don't make the mistake of driving past **Mom's Apple Pie**, an institution since the 1980s. Betty's enormous fruit pies are legendary [4550 Gravenstein Hwy. N.].

282A 282B

283A 283B

Epicurean Heaven

283

Healdsburg in Sonoma County (75 minutes north of San Francisco by car) is a top destination for lovers of good food and wine. The region is extremely fertile, and tons of great fresh produce comes from the area around the picturesque town. That makes for an embarrassment of riches for local restaurants. It makes sense that the locavore movement has flourished in Healdsburg. I recommend walking around Healdsburg Plaza in the heart of the city, It's surrounded by small independent shops, wine tasting bars and cafés. **Flying Goat Coffee** is my favorite [324 Center St.]. There are also bistros like **Valette**, which serves rustic California cuisine [344 Center St.], and **Scopa**—their specialties are fresh pasta and pizzas with inventive flavors [109A Plaza St.].

Fill up on cheeses and artisanal breads at **Oakville Grocery** [124 Matheson St.] and stop at **SHED** (A), a huge modern barn that houses a market, a café, a pizzeria, a store with cookbooks and kitchen items and a fermentation bar. Try one of their Shrubs, a fermented drink made from fruit, herbs and vinegar—it's shockingly delicious [25 North St.]. Finish the day at **Chalkboard**, the best restaurant in town [29 North St.]. Order the raw hamachi starter and squid ink gigli. After that, savor a drink at **Barndiva**, another restaurant-bar in a barn. Try the Why Bears Do It cocktail: Meyer lemon vodka, apple juice, bitters and thyme [231 Center St.].

Dry Creek Valley has beautiful landscapes that remind me of Tuscany. My favorite vineyards there are: **Bella Vineyards & Winecaves** (B), where the tasting is held in a cave below the vines [9711 West Dry Creek Rd.]; **Porter Creek Vineyards**, for its relaxed family atmosphere, and for its tasting area, a shed surrounded by dogs and chickens [8735 Westside Rd.]; **Matrix Winery**, for its pinot noir [3291 Westside Rd.]; and **Medlock Ames Winery**, for its sauvignon blanc and its bocce court [3487 Alexander Valley Rd.]. On your way to the area, stop at **Dry Creek General Store**, which opened in 1881. They make good sandwiches and salads, and there's an old-school bar next door [3495 Dry Creek Rd.].

The Wine Kingdom

284

I never get tired of touring the vineyards of Napa. Just an hour from the Golden Gate Bridge, you'll find majestic wineries, incredible estates and luxurious tasting rooms. **Napa Valley** means "land of plenty," because of its fertile soil; but it's also the land of some amazing architecture. It's optimal to book ahead for tastings, and go on weekdays to avoid crowds. I also recommend sharing glasses; you'll save money and be a little less tipsy at the end of the day. There are more than 400 vineyards along Highway 29 and the very scenic Silverado Trail, which is great for cycling. There are options for every taste and budget. Here are my top five wineries that are not to be missed—places I love for the wine as well as the scenery.

1- THE GOTHIC CASTLE

Chateau Montelena Winery (A) was built in 1888 by Alfred Loving Tubbs, who made his fortune in the rope business during the Gold Rush. Located at the foot of Mount Saint Helena, the chateau is surrounded by a lake, a Chinese garden (inherited from the second owners, who emigrated from China), and grape vines as far as the eye can see. This winery was the first to put Napa Valley wines on the map, when their 1973 chardonnay stole the show by beating out top French wines during the historic "Judgment of Paris" in 1976. The competition proved that California has world-class viniculture. The vineyard can be seen in the film *Bottle Shock* (2008). The tasting costs $25 per person; you don't need to make a reservation.

2- THE PERSIAN PALACE

When you see the huge columns, eternal flame and fountains at **Darioush** (B), you'll think you're at the doors of Babylon rather than a California vineyard. The unique architecture is meant to evoke Persepolis, ancient capital of the Persian empire. The owner, Darioush Khaledi, is from Iran. Khaledi arrived in the United States in the 1970s, and made a fortune with a grocery store chain before devoting his energies to winemaking. A tasting of five wines, including their signature cabernet sauvignon, is $40 per person. Reservations are necessary on weekends (darioush.com). The store has beautiful objects and accessories, like beauty products made with rose petals, Maison Michel hats, WANT Les Essentiels bags and Taschen books [4240 Silverado Trail, Napa].

3- THE HEIGHT OF REFINEMENT

Opus One Winery (C) was founded by legendary American winemaker Robert Mondavi and Baron Philippe de Rothschild. The neoclassical-style building (which looks a bit like a spaceship that has landed on a grassy hill) is an attraction in itself—even the road leading to the parking lot is spectacular. For $45, the tasting provides a glass of their current vintage (the portions are generous, so you can share if you like), which you sip on the rooftop terrace with a view of the valley. You'll have to make a reservation for the tasting: opusonewinery. com [7900 St. Helena Hwy., Oakville].

4- THE MEDIEVAL CASTLE

Castello di Amorosa (D) is an authentic replica of a 13th-century Tuscan castle, the only one of its kind in the United States. The 140,000-square-foot (13,000-square-meter) castle has a drawbridge and a 500-year-old fireplace. It houses an enormous two-story hall decorated with Italian art, a dungeon, hidden passages, a torture chamber, a stable, a medieval church and an impressive wine cellar with vaulted ceilings. The owner, Dario Sattui, a fourth-generation winemaker, began building the castle in 1993, after studying medieval castles and Italian wineries. Its specialty is cabernet sauvignon. You can try five wines for $25 a person; no reservation necessary [4045 St. Helena Hwy, Calistoga].

5- JAPANESE ELEGANCE

A visit to **Kenzo Estate**, nestled high up on Mount George on the edge of the Napa Valley, is all about exclusivity. After making an appointment, you go to the security gate and identify yourself on the intercom. Then you take a mile-long (2 km) road through a forest and past a reservoir, until finally the property appears: a luxurious barn with an elegant design. You'll be offered a glass of sauvignon blanc upon arrival. Then you get to visit the caves and have a tasting on the patio, which has a sublime view of the valley. The 3,800-acre (1,500-hectare) area is five times bigger than New York's Central Park. The vineyard belongs to Kenzo Tsujimoto, video game magnate and founder of Capcom. To book a tasting of four wines for $40, go to kenzoestate.com/visit [3200 Monticello Rd., Napa].

Other wineries worth visiting: **Duckhorn Vineyards**, for its sauvignon blanc, merlot and flower gardens [1000 Lodi Lane, St. Helena]; **Robert Sinskey Vineyards**, for its excellent wines and appetizers, vegetable garden and wood-oven pizzas [6320 Silverado Trail, Napa]; **Alpha Omega**, for its modern spaces and poolside tastings [1155 Mee Lane, St. Helena]; and **Cakebread** for its immense cask room [8300 St. Helena Hwy., Rutherford].

Great Food in Napa Valley

285

For lovers of great food, the Napa region is heaven on Earth—particularly the small town of **Yountville**, which has more Michelin stars than any other city in North America. Chef Thomas Keller (three Michelin stars) put the town on the culinary map with his restaurant **The French Laundry**. Opened in 1994, it is considered by many to be the best restaurant in the country—or even the world. You'll need to make a reservation a month in advance (you may have more luck at lunch). The eight-course meal is about $310 per person; service is included, but wine is not. There's also a vegetarian tasting menu. It's not cheap, but it's the experience of a lifetime. [6640 Washington St.].

285 B

If you can't afford to sit and eat at the exceptional restaurant, you can still stroll through the vast vegetable garden across from it. I've never seen anything like it. Keller also owns the excellent French bistro **Bouchon** (A) [6534 Washington St.], which is a little more affordable and has a more casual atmosphere; and **Ad Hoc** (B),

where the famous chef offers his own take on American comfort food. The latter restaurant has a garden with lights; eating there in the summer is lovely. The fried chicken is especially popular [6476 Washington St.]. Other great restaurants in the city: **Ciccio**, an Italian place set up in a former general store (their bucatini and black pepper is fabulous) [6770 Washington St.]; and **Bistro Jeanty**, a friendly French restaurant, where it's essential to try the tomato soup in puff pastry [6510 Washington St.].

285 A

The High-Tech Vineyard

286

The first time I set foot in **Palmaz Vineyards**, I felt like I had wandered onto property belonging to James Bond, or maybe Tony Stark. The president of the winery, Christian Palmaz, showed me around the facilities. The underground complex is 100,000-square-feet (9,300-square-meters). The incredible 18-stories-deep cavern was carved right into the rock of Mount George. Why so deep? Because Palmaz uses gravity to make his wine. At each step of the process, from the de-stemming of the grapes all the way to the bottling, the wine descends a floor-level. No mechanical pumps are used to push the liquid along. Thus the grapes suffer no stress; the tannins, which are responsible for a wine's flavor, are not affected. Rarely have I seen such a perfectionistic approach to a craft. All the water used in the winery is reused—the net consumption is zero.

If you're a wine nerd, or if you simply want to be amazed by how sophisticated their operation is, book a guided tour as soon as possible. I learned a lot about wine during the two-hour visit (the tours are given by members of the Palmaz family), which ended in a tasting of Riesling, chardonnay, muscat, brasa and cabernet sauvignon. You'll also be taken to the end of a platform looking out on a room with 24 stainless steel fermentation tanks—it seems like something from a spaceship. Projected in red and black on the dome above are 24 visual maps. It's a unique computer analysis system that was designed by Christian Palmaz to monitor exactly what's happening in the tanks. Think *Minority Report*, but for wine. Each tank has a probe that measures the sugar, alcohol and fermentation of the liquid. The valuable information allows the winemakers to regulate the temperature of different parts of the tanks with great precision, which results in superior wines.

The data can be sent to an iPhone, iPad or iWatch; in theory, the Palmaz family can make their wines from their sofa. When they bought the winery in the 1990s, it had been lying abandoned since Prohibition. Dr. Julio Palmaz, the patriarch of the family and originally from Buenos Aires, is the inventor of the balloon-stent, a remarkable breakthrough that revolutionized cardiovascular medicine. He sold the patent to Johnson & Johnson; the fortune he made allowed him to finance his growing passion for wine. His wife, daughter and son all work with him; they live on the property, in a house that was built in 1878. In the summer, they hold a huge barbecue, and in autumn it's harvest time. It's an idyllic country life that city folk can only dream of. The vineyard next door belongs to Walt Disney's daughter. The Palmaz family talks about their products like they're liquid gold—and with good reason. At the end of my visit, I signed up for their wine club. Each box that arrives at my home is reason to celebrate. Book your tour by calling 707-226-5587; it's $80 per person [4029 Hagen Rd, about 4 miles (6 km) from Napa].

Japanese Feast in Downtown Napa

287

For an unusual gastronomic experience, book a table at **Kenzo** (the restaurant associated with the vineyard of the same name in Reason #284), an authentic Japanese restaurant in the heart of Napa. With a fixed-price menu of $200 per person, this restaurant is reserved for big occasions. Hiroyuki Kanda, one of the most celebrated chefs in Japan, buys his fish from Tsukiji Market in Tokyo. Kanda, his restaurant in Toyo, has won three Michelin stars for nine consecutive years, so you're in good hands! [1339 Pearl St.]. For a more casual and affordale experience, I recommend **Miminashi**, chef Curtis Di Fede's izakaya. The restaurant with beautiful wood decor specializes in yakitori (small meat skewers). Try their dumplings, ramen soups, rice dishes and their delicious whole roast chicken. Do not leave without tasting their soft, homemade ice cream [821 Coombs St.].

Touring the Wineries, Bohemian Style

288

If Napa Valley is a tiny bit of a snob, Sonoma Valley is its bohemian cousin. The vineyards of Sonoma are more family-oriented, affordable and easy to access. There's no need to book ahead. Some places have free tastings, or free entry if you buy a bottle. My favorite is **Scribe Winery** (A), a charming spot at the end of a path bordered by palm trees. There are picnic tables and garlands of lights in the trees. It's the perfect place to taste "new wave" wines. The young brothers Andrew and Adam Mariani make a skin-fermented chardonnay that you can enjoy sitting on Mexican blankets on the grass outside, while you snack on fruits and nuts from the property. Book a spot by calling 707-939-1858 [2100 Denmark St.]. You'll also be three miles (5 km) from the historic Sonoma Plaza—make a point of going there to eat at **The Girl & The Fig**. The organic restaurant serves Provençal-inspired cuisine. Their selection of cheeses and shoestring fries are legendary [110 West Spain St.].

288 A

The Locavore Diner

289

On the way to Sonoma, stop at **The Fremont Diner**. It's my favorite diner in the country. The small white log cabin on the side of Highway 121 is still happily stuck in the 1950s. There's a rusted-out truck parked in front, and the decor is a hodgepodge of old Coca-Cola boxes and rustic furniture. They serve classic comfort food made with fresh products from nearby farms: dishes include chicken biscuits: a basket of biscuits with homemade jam, a mountain of buttermilk pancakes with vanilla syrup and the pastrami sandwich. There are also some healthy options on the menu. If you're there in the fall, make sure you try the green tomato sandwich [2698 Fremont Dr.].

Geysers and Mudbaths

290

In the north of the Napa Valley is **Calistoga**. The small town is the spa capital of the valley. A strange oasis of geysers and volcanic ash, the area was already an attraction 8,000 years ago. The Wappo Indian tribe, the earliest inhabitants valley's, bathed in the hot springs, which they believed had medicinal properties. Later, during the Gold Rush (and well before the arrival of viticulture), it was a destination for those seeking the fountain of youth. Today, the big draw is the mud bath: the ultimate experience in the area.

The destination of choice is **Indian Springs**, which opened in 1861. The giant pool and steam baths of the oldest spa in California are fed by four thermal geysers. The mineral water they produce blends with pure volcanic ash, creating the famous mixture used in the mud baths. The circuit is about 50 minutes and costs $95. It begins with an immersion from the toes to the neck in a detoxifying mud, followed by a jump into a geyser bath, a steam sauna and a period of relaxation [1712 Lincoln Ave.].

The chic **Solage Calistoga** also offers mud baths and a bath in mineral water from hot springs ($110 per person). The restaurant has an organic farm-to-table menu [755 Silverado Trail N].

Calistoga is also known for its hot-air balloon flights over the vineyards. **Calistoga Balloons** (calistogaballoons. com) offers flights for $239 per person. You may see **Old Faithful Geyser of California** erupting [1458 Lincoln Ave.].

291A 291B

Monster Waves

291

In the **Half Moon Bay** region (A), 45 minutes from downtown San Francisco, you'll find one of the world's most mythical surf spots—and one of the most dangerous. The waves at **Mavericks Beach** can reach up to 60 feet (18 meters), and they break with such ferocity that they can be measured on the Richter scale. Maverick is the name of the German shepherd that accompanied the group of surfers who discovered the spot in the 1960s. The pooch jumped into the waves to join its master, and the owner finally deemed the situation too dangerous and turned back. Jeff Clark was the first to ride the waves, in 1975. He was 17 at the time, and it would be 15 years before others followed in his footsteps. Today the surf star owns **Mavericks Surf Shop**, not far from the beach, where you can rent boards [25 Johnson Pier]. The waves are biggest in the winter, but they're impressive all year round. They form about half a mile (1 km) from the shore, and surfers have to paddle out for 45 minutes to reach them. Today Mavericks is a rite of passage for all big-wave surfers. It takes real bravery to ride these waves. They're bigger than Hawaii's, and the spot is surrounded by cliffs; the reefs rise up dangerously and the water temperature hovers around 59°F (15°C).

Early in the year, the 24 best surfers in the world gather at Mavericks for the Titans of Mavericks competition (titansofmavericks.com). Incidentally, that's where Apple got the name for its 2013 operating system, OS X Mavericks. The beach is at the edge of Pillar Point at Princeton-by-the-Sea. Afterward, head to **Sam's Chowder House** (B) to enjoy a fresh lobster sandwich on the terrace, with a sublime view of the bay [4210 Cabrillo Hwy. N.].

The Town that Loves its Artichokes

292

I came across Pescadero, along the Pacific coast, a little by accident. In the morning, the main street is so calm that you can hear the waves breaking against the cliffs almost two miles (3 km) away. Just over an hour's drive south of San Francisco, the small inland farm community with 600 inhabitants, nestled between green hills and artichoke fields, seems to be frozen in the 19th century. The few businesses seem to be right out of a Western movie. One is **Duarte's Tavern** (A), an institution founded by Frank Duarte in 1894, which has belonged to the same family of Portuguese immigrants for four generations. I love the decor, which has real historical flavor. Their specialty is the artichoke soup, sourced from the garden behind the tavern. People have been known go well out of their way for this sumptuous dish. In the 1930s, Frank's wife Emma started baking pies that quickly became one of their specialties. I recommend the strawberry rhubarb [202 Stage Rd.].

Right across the street you can find the best tacos for miles around at **Mercado & Taqueria De Amigos**. The stand serves great fish tacos with rice and beans for just $8 [1999 Pescadero Creek Rd.]. On the main street, don't miss **Downtown Local**, a nostalgic café that serves Sightglass coffee (see Reasons #171 and #201) and where they play old vinyl LPs [213 Stage Rd.]. Don't leave Pescadero without buying a loaf of artichoke garlic herb bread at **Arcangeli Grocery Co.**—best eaten at the picnic tables beside the grocery store [287 Stage Rd.].

Breakfast in Provence

293

Among the vineyards and olive groves of Napa Valley is a hotel that evokes the south of France. The area's green hills inspired French restaurateur Claude Rouas to recreate the sunny ambiance of a Provençal restaurant in the heart of California's Wine Country.

Auberge du Soleil, which opened in the 1980s, is one of the loveliest spots in the region. For many, staying at the hotel is unaffordable (it's about $1,000 a night during the off-peak season). A good way to enjoy the place on a budget is to visit for breakfast or brunch on the weekend. Ask for a table on the terrace, which has a panoramic view of the neighboring vineyards, the pool and the sculpture garden. The view alone is worth the trip—especially when you savor it with a mimosa. The three-course brunch (about $65) is served from 11:30 to 2:30 on weekends; an à-la-carte breakfast is served daily from 7 a.m. to 11 a.m. (around $25). It's best to make a reservation [180 Rutherford Hill Rd.].

294

The Elephant Seal Reserve

295 One of the biggest elephant seal reserves in the world can be found eight miles (13 km) south of Pigeon Point Lighthouse, at **Año Nuevo State Park**. It's a particularly impressive spectacle from December to March, when thousands of animals gather on the beach to mate and reproduce. Three days after they arrive, the females give birth to the offspring they conceived the previous year. Incredibly, elephant seals can become pregnant about 24 days after they've given birth. Males can measure up to 16 feet (five meters) and weigh 5,000 pounds (2,270 kg). Violent fights erupt in the sand as they struggle to establish domination. You have to walk almost two miles (3 km) to reach the observation platform. Wear good shoes; you'll be walking in the sand for some parts [1 New Years Creek Rd.].

Afterward, stop at **Pie Ranch** (A), a barn that sells farm produce, delicious fruit pies and fresh coffee. I had some memorable chocolate zucchini bread there [2080 Cabrillo Hwy.]. Another stand that's worth a stop on the same route is **Swanton Berry Farm**, where you can pick or buy organic berries and homemade jams [640 Hwy. 1].

Observing the Marine Wildlife

294 The Pacific coast stretching south of San Francisco is enchanting. Pretty much anywhere you choose to stop on Highway 1, you'll see something that you'll never forget. It's no surprise that famous writers like Henry Miller and Jack Kerouac were inspired by the Pacific. For an idyllic view, head to **Pigeon Point Lighthouse** (12 minutes from Pescadero and 75 minutes south of San Francisco). Standing 115 feet (35 meters) tall and perched on a cliff, the white lighthouse has guided ships since 1872. During my last visit, I saw whales and seals on the horizon. The lighthouse building also serves as a youth hostel. A bed with one of the most beautiful views in the world for a ridiculously low price—it's a pretty easy decision [210 Pigeon Point Rd.].

295 A

The Cradle of Silicon Valley

296 In **Palo Alto**, a 45-minute drive south of San Francisco, the locals drive Teslas under the palm trees. All the houses are covered in solar panels, and there are charging stations for electric cars on almost every street corner. The person in front of you in line is probably a multimillionaire investor...or soon to be one. Don't be surprised to spot driverless cars on the roads. Living in San Francisco is a bit like living in the future. This region, which has more than 6,000 start-ups, is experiencing record growth, unlike any since the dot-com bubble of 2000. In 2014, an incredible 58,000 jobs were created in Palo Alto.

There's a very special garage in Palo Alto, with a deep green gate. Bill Hewlett and Dave Packard, two students at Stanford University, founded Hewlett-Packard, Silicon Valley's first company, in 1938. A plaque from the National Register of Historic Places was put up in front of the **HP Garage** in 1989; it's the site where the engineers built their first electronic oscillator. You can take photos of the garage from the sidewalk [369 Addison Ave.]. Continue your technological tour one mile (2 km) farther at a former residence of **Steve Jobs** (A). The magnificent brick building looks like it was plucked from the English countryside. Don't miss the special touch: A number of apple trees are growing in front of the house [2101 Waverley St.].

297 A

A School for the Elite

297 A visit to prestigious **Stanford University** (A) should be a part of any visit to San Francisco. Stanford students played a major role in developing the Internet and have collected about 20 Nobel Prizes. With an annual budget of $5.5 billion, the university was founded by railway magnate, governor and senator of California Leland Stanford and his wife, Jane, in 1891. Students have given the campus the nickname "The Farm," since it was founded on the former site of the Stanford family's farm. The campus is magnificent, with buildings inspired by the colonial style of California's Spanish missions. Don't miss the mosaics at the Memorial Church (where more than 7,500 marriages have been celebrated since 1903), the 20 original Rodin statues, and the view that stretches for miles from the 14th floor of the Hoover Tower. Students give free guided tours from 11 a.m. to 3:15 p.m. every day, starting from the Visitor Center [450 Serra Mall]. In the city, stop by **Evvia**, a friendly Greek restaurant that's open for lunch and dinner. The Greek salad, grilled fish and moussaka are all delicious [420 Emerson St.]. For a coffee and a pastry, go to **Mayfield Bakery & Cafe** [855 El Camino Real].

296 A

Technological Complexes

298 Silicon Valley is the epicenter of the high-tech world; the biggest tech companies on the planet have their headquarters there. Obviously, these headquarters aren't open to the public, but you can still pass by to see the size of the facilities and the frenzy of activity around them. Seeing it in person helps you understand the culture of Silicon Valley. "Silicon Valley is almost a perfect meritocracy. People do not care about your degree," says Nicolas Darveau-Garneau, head of performance marketing at Google. Their impressive complex, the **Googleplex**, is in Mountain View, not far from Palo Alto. "When I hire someone, the key question is would I have a beer with that person? Does he or she have an open mind? Did he or she travel? Qualifications are secondary. One must first be 'Googley.' Most people who have earned millions and even billions of dollars here have never finished their studies. At Google, the performance of everyone, even the cafeteria staff, is evaluated. We must always grow." [1600 Amphitheatre Pkwy].

The employees travel between buildings on the company's multicolored bicycles. From the bike path, you can see the employees' sports fields, east of the complex. Inside the buildings, there are entertainment zones on every floor, including a bowling alley, beach volleyball courts, weightlifting rooms, a pool, a spa and billiard tables. Employees eat for free in one of the many cafeterias or cafés. At the Visitor Center, eight minutes away on foot, you can see some of their inventions, like the Google Maps car. Open on weekdays, from 10 a.m. to 5 p.m. [1911 Landings Dr.].

The **Facebook** complex is located by the water, 15 minutes from the center of Palo Alto [1 Hacker Way]. A giant emoji of a thumbs-up stands at the entrance. Meals are free at Facebook as well. There's also a dentist's office, and on some evenings employees can bring their kids to watch movies on a big screen, with catering provided. At Facebook, employees are urged to choose the department they want to work for.

The **Apple** complex is about 20 minutes from Palo Alto, in Cupertino [1 Infinite Loop]. You can drive around the complex, and fans of the company will find a plethora of unique items in the shop next to the main door, such as T-shirts that proclaim "I visited the mothership" and "I left my heart in Cupertino," and Apple mugs. The second Apple complex, a neo-futuristic building (still under construction as I write these lines) is less than two miles (3 km) from the first complex [19111 Pruneridge Ave.]. It looks a bit like a Star Trek ship that got stuck in the forest.

299A

299 B

McDonald's
on the Moon

299 Near the Googleplex is **NASA's Ames Research Center** (A). It's a remarkable building, and one of the American space agency's main research centers. The scientists working there are involved in various projects, including the search for other forms of life in the universe. The center is open to the public. You can see Hangar One, the vast 350,000-square-foot (32,000-square-meter) structure built in the 1930s to house the U.S. army's airships. You can also see something I truly love: a place called **McMoon's** (B). In 2008, the team at **Lunar Orbiter Image Recovery Project** took over the abandoned McDonald's in the complex. There, researchers are digitizing data tapes from five Lunar Orbiter spacecraft that were launched into space in 1966 and 1967 (hence the building's name). When I visited, I knocked on the door and they showed me around the premises. The menu for hamburgers and Chicken McNuggets above the counter has been replaced by black-and-white photos of the moon, and the kitchen is filled with film strips [take exit 398A from Highway 101, then go right on Moffett Blvd. until you get to Nasa Pkwy.].

The University
to Change the World

300 NASA's Ames Research Center complex is also the headquarters of **Singularity University**. It's one of the most fascinating places I've ever visited. Each summer, about 80 students from 45 countries work intensely to improve the lives of human beings through major advancements in technology. "We form teams, and the goal of each project is to design something that could have a positive impact on the lives of a billion people in the next 10 years," says Kevin Adler, one of the students at the university in the summer of 2015. "It's like a summer camp, but with the smartest brains on the planet!" Artificial intelligence, nanorobotics, information systems, biotechnology, medicine, neuroscience, energy production, space; no field of study is left neglected. The students also delve into questions of ethics, regulation and security. They even have access to the NASA supercomputer, Pleiades, one of the most powerful computers in the world. The university was founded by engineer and physician Peter Diamandis, and futurologist and director of engineering at Google, Raymond Kurzweil. The concept of "technological singularity" designates the moment when artificial intelligence surpasses human capacity. Kurzweil predicts that this shift will happen in 2045. At that time, the distinction between man and machine will be erased; humans will have transcended their biological limits, and old age and disease will be things of the past.

Index

The Index numbers do not refer to page numbers, but to the 300 Reasons to Love San Francisco.

Acknowledgments

Many thanks to the entire team at *Les Éditions de l'Homme*, and to my editor, Elizabeth Paré, for her wise advice. Thank you to Sylvain Trudel, Matthew Brown, Robert Ronald, Louisa Sage and Agnes Saint-Laurent for their incredible rigor and to Josée Amyotte for her enthusiasm.

This guide would not have been possible without the support of my family and my partner, Geoffrey, who introduced me to San Francisco and was the inspiration for this project. Special thanks to Susan and Dennis Mooradian for their hospitality, and to Lelia Wood-Smith for providing me with a place to write.

I would also like to thank the following people for their invaluable help: Sara Mooradian, Jared Byer, Matt and Susie Novak, Daniella Reichstetter and Stowe Beam, Nicolas Darveau-Garneau, Andrew Shapiro, Broke-Ass Stuart, John Slack, Tessa Greenwood and Bronson Johnson, Lisa Nourse, Simi Dube, and Kate and Kristin Wilkinson.